A BRIEF HISTORY OF EARLY OKINAWA BASED ON THE *OMORO SŌSHI*

A BRIEF HISTORY OF EARLY OKINAWA BASED ON THE *OMORO SŌSHI*

Mitsugu Sakihara

Edited by

Stewart Curry

Center for Okinawan Studies
University of Hawaiʻi at Mānoa
Honolulu

Printed in the United States of America

First printing, 2024

Library of Congress Cataloging-in-Publication Data

Names: Sakihara, Mitsugu, author. | Curry, Stewart, editor.
Title: A brief history of early Okinawa based on the Omoro sōshi / Mitsugu Sakihara ; edited by Stewart Curry.
Description: Honolulu : Center for Okinawan Studies, University of Hawai'i at Mānoa, [2024] | Reissue of: A brief history of early Okinawa based on the Omoro Sōshi. Tokyo: Honpo Shoseki Press, 1987. | Includes bibliographical references and indexes.
Identifiers: LCCN 2024000518 | ISBN 9781952460036 (paperback)
Subjects: LCSH: Omoro sōshi. | Okinawa Island (Japan)—History.
Classification: LCC DS895.R97 S23 2024 | DDC 952/.29402—dc23/eng/20240126
LC record available at https://lccn.loc.gov/2024000518

This publication is made possible by the Akamine Endowed Fund.

Published by the Center for Okinawan Studies, University of Hawai'i at Mānoa
1890 East-West Road, Moore Hall 316
Honolulu, HI 96822

Distributed by University of Hawai'i Press
2840 Kolowalu Street
Honolulu, HI 96822

This book is printed on acid-free paper and meets the guidelines for permanence and durability of the Council on Library Resources.

To Masako and Mana
and to the people of Okinawa
and their friends

Contents

Foreword to this Reissue

The publication of Greg Smits's *Maritime Ryukyu: 1050–1650*, which makes extensive use of poems from the *Omoro Sōshi* and makes reference to Mitsugu Sakihara's *Brief History of Early Okinawa Based on the* Omoro Sōshi, encouraged us at the Center for Okinawan Studies to reissue Sakihara's book itself. Taken side-by-side, these two fine books offer us an opportunity not only to explore shifts in methodology in historical research, but also to address the role of authorial voice, and the importance of having space for the indigenous to tell their own story. It should be no surprise that Sakihara reads the poems and songs in the *Omoro Sōshi* much differently than Smits, not just because the field has begun to use these kinds of sources much differently than forty years ago, but because Sakihara is Okinawan—a point that he emphasizes in the Preface to his book (p. xi). It is important, though, to note, that he does not take the stance that, being Okinawan, his voice is therefore privileged, nor is that a point we wish to make here. We do, however, believe it is a voice that should be heard; indeed, it is one of the missions of the Center for Okinawan Studies at University of Hawai'i to make scholarship by Okinawans more readily accessible.

Sakihara starts from what has been seen as the dominant narrative about Okinawa at least since the late nineteenth century—namely, that Okinawa is a "nation" "born from the cohesion and unification of isolated individuals and scattered villages . . ." (p. 1). On the surface, this puts him at odds with Smits, who argues that the process of the formation of a Ryukyu Kingdom spread gradually from the north, involving the *wakō*, often misidentified as "Japanese pirates," but in fact a stateless and rather amorphous group of maritime tribes whose operations ranged from mainland Japan down through Taiwan, the east coast of China, and of course the Ryukyu Islands.

In fact, Sakihara's argument is much subtler than it seems at first glance, and it would be misleading to think of his work and Smits's as diametrically opposed. Like Smits, Sakihara acknowledges the limitations of the "the traditional histories" from the eighteenth century, though he does make use of them in some of his argument. However, he is not uncritical in his use of those sources. He describes their limitations in a way that overlaps, though not completely, with those mentioned by Smits, when he cautions against an ". . . overdependence on and uncritical trust of the official histories which tend to follow a Confucian moralistic bias and which in turn place too much emphasis on the fortunes and vicissitudes of the succeeding dynasties and a series of great heroes, disregarding the life of the common people" (p. 133).

That last clause about disregarding the common people situates Sakihara as a proponent of "bottom up" history, along the lines of Howard Zinn's *A People's History of the United States* (Harper & Row, 1980), an approach that does provide space for indigenous people to speak, and surely Sakihara is aware that his own ancestors must have participated in that history, which in turn contributes to his own sense of identity as "Okinawan." He returns to this focus on "the common people" time and again in this book, and it is especially evident in the *Omoro sōshi* songs he chooses to cite.

Similarly, even though Sakihara uses a discourse still wedded to the modern notion of nation states—something that more recent historians avoid—he recognizes the fluidity of the region, noting "no culture has come into being of itself. . . . The civilizations of China and Japan also had a great impact upon the Ryūkyū Islands" (p. 2). He also argues that a later migration, "most likely from the north" had some impact on early Ryukyu (p. 134), a point that is central to Smits. In fact, Sakihara states "The second period [of Ryukyu's development] extends from the end of the twelfth century—when defeated Japanese sea-going warriors . . . took refuge in the Ryukyu Islands . . ." (p. 135), which is a key assertion of Smits, as well.

Nevertheless, the two scholars overall take very different tacks, and it is instructive to place them in dialog with each other. The first edition of Sakihara's book in 1987 was self-published, with limited distribution. With this reissue, we hope to give it the attention it deserves.

Robert N. Huey
Honolulu, September 7, 2021

Author's Preface

My interest in the ancient history of Okinawa began while I was a student in Oregon in 1951–55 and 1958–60. I was a scholarship student under the GARIOA program (Government Aid and Relief in Occupied Areas). Until my arrival in Oregon, I hadn't the slightest doubt that I was a Japanese. The question never entered my mind. In fact, in 1945, as a member of the high school corps, I fought and was wounded in the defense of Japan in the Battle of Okinawa. However, while in Oregon, I learned that the matter of my nationality was not as clear as I had assumed.

Other Japanese students on campus accepted me as one of them. As far as they were concerned, I happened to be from Okinawa prefecture just as others happened to be from Miyagi or Yamaguchi prefecture. Officially, however, I was not a Japanese. As far as Americans were concerned, I was from Okinawa or Ryūkyū, not Japan. Come to think of it, I didn't have a Japanese passport like other Japanese students. What I had was a certificate of identity issued by the United States Civil Administration of the Ryūkyū Islands. It identified me as a resident of the Ryūkyūs, but nowhere stated that I was a Japanese citizen.

Whenever an American asked me my nationality, I hesitated to reply, thinking "What shall I say, Japanese or Okinawan?" As a foreign student in a small town like Eugene in the fifties, there was no way I could escape the perennial question, "Where are you from?" Having been asked the same question a hundred times, I became less sure of the answer. Some Americans, upon being told that I was a Japanese, would insist, "but aren't you an Okinawan?" "Isn't an Oregonian an American?" I'd reply. It was usually sufficient to stop further questioning. But it didn't stop me from asking myself the same question. The uncertainty of whether I was an Okinawan or a Japanese led to the question "What is an Okinawan, and how is he or she different from a Japanese?" An Okinawan may legally be a Japanese, but is he or she a Japanese in the same sense that a person from Tokyo is a Japanese? Okinawa is said to have been annexed by Japan in 1879. Does that mean Okinawa was not a part of Japan before 1879? Was Okinawa therefore a colonial possession?

In search of the answers, I began to read one book after another on Okinawan history. As one inevitably does, I came across the *Omoro sōshi* "Anthology of the poems of sentiments." Compiled during the sixteenth and seventeenth centuries, it contains over one thousand poems from the villages and islands of twelfth- to early seventeenth-century Okinawa and Amami-Ōshima. These centuries may not be considered ancient with respect to the histories of other countries, but in the history of Ryūkyū, which is a relative latecomer, they constitute the threshold separating the prehistoric era from the historic. During this period, the unorganized, scattered village communities of Ryūkyū gradually united to form a state. The *Omoro sōshi* records the very nascence of Ryūkyū.

As I read the *Omoro sōshi* with the help of works by the pioneer scholars Iha Fuyū and Nakahara Zenchū, I relived the joys and sorrows of the people of those bygone days. I travelled the hills, woods, streams, valleys, and shores where the ancients used to live. I knew how they must have felt in the bright, scorching midday sun in the streets of Shuri and Naha. I knew how alluring the warm blue waters off the shores of Okinawa looked on such summer afternoons. I knew the seas, alive with multitudes of colorful fishes playing among the coral reefs. When the sun set beyond the horizon, painting the skies with flowing, glittering gold, I felt the same awe that the ancients must have felt. Thus, I felt compelled to recreate the Okinawa of the time of the *Omoro sōshi*, when the nameless people living on these islands came to be Okinawans.

I never met Iha Fuyū personally, as he passed away in 1947 before I was even aware of his great work on the *Omoro sōshi.* With Nakahara Zenchū, I was more fortunate. When Professor Nakahara was at the East-West Center as a senior visiting scholar in 1961–62, I had a chance to come to the center to study premodern Ryūkyūan manuscripts and documents under his personal tutelage. When he learned of my interest in the *Omoro sōshi*, he expressed the wish that I would some day introduce this still relatively unknown work to English language readers. Since then, more than two decades have passed, but with the publication of *A Brief History of Early Okinawa Based on the* Omoro Sōshi, I am finally fulfilling the promise I made to Professor Nakahara.

I would like to acknowledge that partial funding for the preparation of this book came from a grant by the Japanese Studies Endowment of the University of Hawai'i (1982). My thanks are also due to the many individuals who have helped me at every turn. Some of them are Dr. Forrest R. Pitts, for encouraging me to study the *Omoro sōshi;* Professor George H. Kerr, for his continuing support and for being instrumental in my coming to Hawai'i; the late Dr. Shunzo Sakamaki and Dr. Robert K. Sakai, for their promoting Okinawan studies at the University of Hawai'i; and lastly Miss Alberta Freidus for her superb editing and numerous constructive comments. Of course I assume sole responsibility for the content of my work.

Finally, I hope that this brief study will help readers to catch a glimpse of life in early Okinawa and that it will stimulate further exploration of this fascinating subject.

Mitsugu Sakihara
Honolulu, Hawai'i, 1987

Note on Japanese and Okinawan Words

Pronunciation presents a vexing problem. In Japanese, a given term in *kanji* (Chinese characters) may be read either in Japanese or Okinawan according to the reader's preference, but for the purposes of this study, it needs to be one or the other. Listing both pronunciations is a possibility, but it is unduly cumbersome and in many cases of doubtful utility.

Consistency seems to call for the Okinawan reading because, after all, this is a book on Okinawan history. From a practical point of view, however, there are problems. First of all, since there has been no standard Okinawan language enforced throughout the Ryūkyūs, and each region, district, and island has its own variation of the language, it is difficult to decide on a single pronunciation. Although Shuri was the capital of the Ryūkyū kingdom, I doubt if the Shuri pronunciation was used in singing an *omoro* of, for example, Amami-Ōshima Island. Secondly, if we are to use the Okinawan pronunciation, shouldn't we be consistent and call this book "A Brief History of Early Uchinaa" instead of "Okinawa"? Even the word *omoro* should be pronounced /umui/ in Okinawan. Was the capital "Shuri" or "Shui" in Okinawan? Is it Ryūkyū or Duuchuu? No one really knows for sure how the *omoro* poets of the fourteenth and fifteenth centuries pronounced these terms. It seems that the original compilers of the *Omoro sōshi* used the so-called traditional orthography rather than transcribing the songs as they heard them.[1] The traditional orthography was in use as late as World War II: *tefu tefu*, for example, was read /chō chō/ in the term for 'butterfly'. Lastly, with the exception of a few epitaph inscriptions in the fourteenth and

1 Though it is true that most traditional accounts subscribe to the "conscious archaization" treatment of *omoro* orthography (details of which are discussed in Chapter 1), recent attention to, among other things, Korean *hangul* transcriptions of fifteenth-century Okinawan in the *Haedong chegukki: eoeum peonyeok* (The Records of Countries to the East of the Sea: a phonetic translation) seems to indicate the subject might warrant reconsideration. There is detailed phonological information in Serafim and Shinzato (*The Language of the Old-Okinawan Omoro Sōshi*, 2020) also.

fifteenth centuries, almost all official documents and records including official histories were written in standard Japanese. Therefore, for the sake of consistency and to avoid the unwieldy alternative listing of both readings, I have decided on the use of the standard Japanese reading for all terms except where noted otherwise.

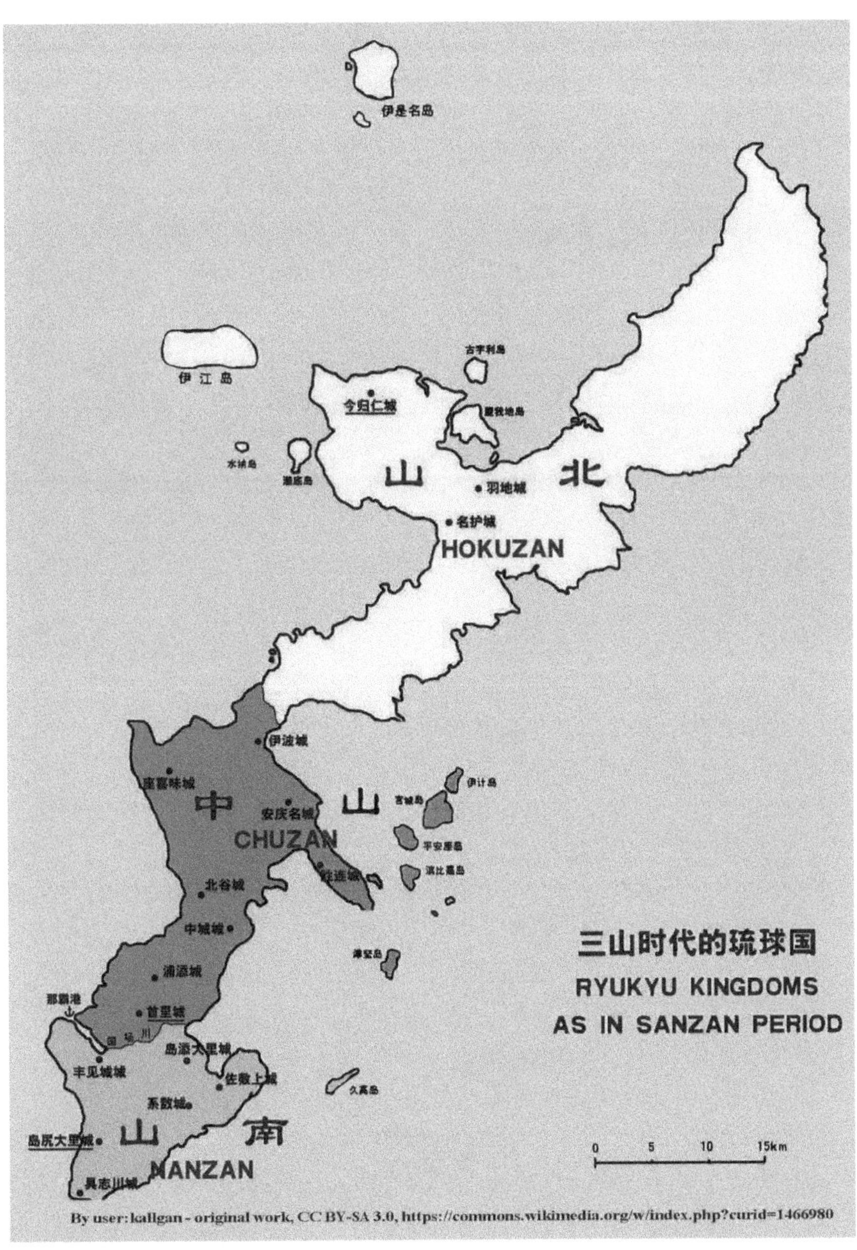

Okinawa, circa fourteenth century

CHAPTER 1

Introduction

For a nation to be formed out of primitive simplicity and ignorance, and for a race to be born from the cohesion and unification of isolated individuals and scattered villages takes a long time; the course of a nation's growth is never simple and direct, but complex and labyrinthine. The human activities carried on within a nation thus born are multifarious, with each locality possessing its own characteristics. In contrast to the days gone by, characterized by relative simplicity, in the modern era of today, there are many diverse elements and opposing forces vying with and contradicting each other. These diverse and heterogeneous functions and characteristics that enter into the formation of the modern world began to emerge in a period of transition when the nation or the race was shaped from the primitive society. Man began more actively manipulating society and nature. In time, the conscious practice of government began to have importance.

This period of transition took place at different times in different societies. In China, it took place roughly from about 1800 BC to about 1700, 1600, or even 1500 BC; that is, from the end of the yet legendary Hsia dynasty to the early Shang dynasty. In Japan, it took place from about AD 500 to 600 or 700, extending over the period of the Soga clan domination, Great Reform of Taika (645), and into the Nara period (710–784). In Okinawa or the Ryūkyū Islands, it took place much later, from about the mid-twelfth century to the thirteenth and fourteenth centuries. It covers approximately the periods of the Shunten (1187–1259) and Eiso (1260–1350) dynasties.

No culture has come into being of itself, not even the great ancient culture of China. The splendid civilization of the Shang seems to have been influenced by the still earlier civilizations of western Asia, most likely through the corridor of Kansu. Japanese culture was in turn stimulated and influenced by that of China. The civilizations of China and Japan also had a great impact upon the Ryūkyū Islands, which were in the process of transition from an ancient village culture to the more advanced culture of a unified kingdom.

In reconstructing the development of the kingdom of Ryūkyū from its humble roots in the scattered self-sufficient villages, I have chosen to make fullest use of the data available in the *Omoro sōshi* as well as in the traditional official records and histories. Since the *Omoro sōshi* was not written as a history or chronicle but is merely a collection of *omoro* poems and chants composed and sung by priestesses and commoners, clearly it alone cannot yield sufficient data for reconstruction. On the other hand, neither the official records nor the chronicles alone can give the entire picture, for these records written either in Japanese or Chinese, the diplomatic languages of the Shuri court, tend to be formal and rigid chronicles of official events, largely ignoring the intimate life of the people. However, with the use of both resources, each complementing the other, I hope for a more accurate and vivid reconstruction of the period of transition under study.

Just what is the *Omoro sōshi?* Why is it important in reconstructing this period of transition in Okinawan history? In answer to the first question, the *Omoro sōshi* is a collection of ancient poems and songs of the villages and islands of Okinawa and Amami, two island groups which constitute the northern half of the Ryūkyū Islands. It comprises 22 volumes written in *hiragana* syllabary with a few simple *kanji.* There are two theories on the etymology of the word *omoro.* The first was advocated by Iha Fuyū.[1] By proving that the word *misezeri (mi*—honorific, *sezeri* 'whisper'; cf. the Japanese word for whisper, *sasayaku),* meaning 'oracle' or 'divine song', synonymous with *omoro,* was older than the word *omoro,* he assumed that the word *omoro* did not originally have the meaning of divine song. He also noted that *omoro-kwenya* (a kind of *omoro* song with the refrain *kwenya* at the end) was written elsewhere as *omori-kwenya,* and that in the *Ryūkyū shintōki* (Records of Shintō in Ryūkyū),[2] the word *shinka* or 'divine song' is written in *katakana* syllabary as *omori.* On the basis of these observations, he says, it is apparent that in older times *omoro* was also called *omori,* and in fact *omori* must have been the older form of *omoro.* And *omori* is *o-mori* (*o-* honorific, *mori* 'woods'[3]) meaning the song that was sung in the woods or at the holy grove, since *omori,* literally, 'woods' and *otake,* literally, 'hill' are only describing the same object from different perspectives. When looked at as a natural object, it is described as *omori,* and when it becomes an object of worship, it is called *otake.*

The second theory was advanced by Miyagi Shinji[4] and Nakahara Zenchū.[5] In contrast with Iha, whose theory was based on the assumption that the *Omoro sōshi* was an accurate representation of the contemporary Ryūkyūan language and should be pronounced as written, Miyagi started out by proving such was not the case. He amassed a wealth of data both from written documents and monument inscriptions, on the basis of which he proved that the writing system used in the *Omoro sōshi* was not phonetic but written in a conventional orthography. It is not a precise recording of the language as spoken but a Japanized rendition of Ryūkyūan in which, for instance, Ryūkyūan *kumu* 'cloud' was represented as Japanese *kumo*. This required the authors and scribes of the *Omoro sōshi* to have a good command of Japanese, which unfortunately they did not. When they recorded the *Omoro sōshi*, they mechanically changed /u/ to /o/ and /i/ to /e/; thus, for instance, *yuki*, the word for snow in both Japanese and Ryūkyūan, appears as *yoki* in the *Omoro sōshi*. Similarly, they seem to have written as *omoro* what actually was pronounced /umuru/, which in turn is derived from *umui*, meaning 'to think' or 'thoughts'. This is caused by overapplication of the rule that in general the /r/ sound in Japanese tends to be dropped in Okinawan so that *ari* 'ant' in Japanese corresponds to *ai* in Okinawan, *mari* 'ball' to *mai*, *tori* 'bird' to *tui*, *mori* 'woods' (see Note 3) to *mui*, etc. When the scribes, lacking sufficient mastery of Japanese, wrote down the word *umui*, they must have automatically changed /u/ to /o/ and 'put back' /r/ (which wasn't there in the beginning), producing the word *omoro*. The fact that even today local priestesses call their divine songs *umui*, not *omoro*, tends to bear this out. This theory of the derivation of the word *omoro* has recently gained wide support among the students of Ryūkyūan culture.[6]

The *omoro* poems incorporate three modes of expression: literature, music, and dance. In fact, the *omoro* poems preceded literature, music, and even dance before these existed as separate arts. *Omoro* poetry is the mother of these arts in the Ryūkyū Islands. As Ryūkyūan society progressed under the influence of the more advanced cultures of Japan and notably China, and the South Seas,[7] a distinctive literature, music, and dance evolved. The intangibles—music and dance—were not recorded and have changed since then, but fortunately the literature was recorded and has come down to us intact.

The earliest poems in the *Omoro sōshi* appear to have been composed in the twelfth century but may be dated earlier. Among the latest are some composed by Shō Nei's queen (1589–1619) in 1610. Thus the *Omoro sōshi* seems to cover five or six centuries, that is, from the twelfth to the seventeenth centuries. But the content, language, and style of the poems definitely belong to an earlier period. Some of the topics are folk legends that were handed down from earliest times. Mentioned in the *Omoro sōshi* are the islands of Amami, Okinawa, Miyako, Yaeyama, and Kume in the Ryūkyū Islands, Kyōto and Kamakura in Japan, China, and Nanban, or the South Seas countries (see Note 7). The total number of poems listed is 1,553 but excluding those that are repeated, the actual number is 1,144. However, the culture of the Ryūkyū Islands has undergone such vast changes over the past four or five centuries that for the average modern Ruÿkyūan, and even for scholars, the *Omoro sōshi* has become an enigmatic and unintelligible legacy. Very few people, in fact, only two, have made major contributions to the study of the *Omoro sōshi.* The first is Iha Fuyū, a pioneer in the field of the linguistic and cultural history of the Ryūkyū Islands and the author of numerous books and publications on various subjects related to the ancient culture of Ryūkyū. The second is Nakahara Zenchū who was a disciple of Iha Fuyū and who succeeded to his position as an authority on the *Omoro sōshi.* After Iha passed away in 1947, and Nakahara in 1964, a number of younger scholars endeavored to follow in their footsteps, but none so far have been able to break completely new ground beyond that accomplished by the lifetime work of the two masters.[8] In spite of laborious and painstaking work, there are still numerous questions which defy comprehensive and definitive treatment of the text in its entirety. I hasten to restate that the present work is intended merely as an introduction to the *Omoro sōshi* in English.

The answer to the second question raised earlier, that of why the *Omoro sōshi* is important in reconstructing the aforementioned period of transition in Ryūkyūan history, lies in the examination of this work as a reflection of the social, cultural, and historical events of its time. That is not to say the *Omoro sōshi* is unimportant for its artistic merit—certainly that is not the case—but its value as a record of the historical and cultural evolution of the Ryūkyū Islands is inestimable. It fleshes out and brings to life the dry bones of the more official annals and chronologies.

The *Omoro sōshi* is often likened to the *Man'yōshū* (Anthology of myriad leaves), and *Norito* (Liturgy) of Japan. The *Man'yōshū*, compiled around AD 789 at the beginning of the Heian period, is Japan's oldest collection of poetry. The *Norito*, compiled between AD 905 and 927, is a collection of ancient Shintō liturgy, prayers, and praise.

Indeed, the *Omoro sōshi* comprises both poetry comparable to that of the *Man'yōshū* and ancient native Shintō liturgies comparable to those of the *Norito.* However, the similarity does not end there. When we trace the historical events in Japan and the Ryūkyū Islands leading up to the appearance of the *Man'yōshū* and the *Norito* on one hand and the *Omoro sōshi* on the other, we are immediately struck by their parallel development.

The *kanji* writing system was first introduced to Japan in AD 538 together with Buddhism from Korea. Sixty-six years later, in 604, the regent, Prince Shotoku, issued the "Seventeen Articles of Constitution," a set of moral principles to guide government officials. In 645, the Reform of Taika was inaugurated to build up a strong centralized government by law and regulation. The *Kojiki* (Records of ancient matters), and the *Nihon shoki* (Chronicles of Japan), formal histories centered around the House of Tenno, were written in 712 and 720 respectively. The *Man'yōshū* followed in around 780. The *Norito* came later, in 905.

In ancient society, once one tribe had succeeded in conquering all other tribes and wished to maintain its position as ruler, military supremacy alone was not enough. The conquerors also had to be able to conquer the other tribes magically. By forcing upon the conquered the worship of their own gods, they could hope to assimilate the heterogeneous tribes into one culture dominated by themselves. Thus, magical power (and later religion or ideologies) was indispensable not only in establishing the basis of the state but also in assimilating the heterogeneous elements in the nation.[9] There is a similar observation in Chinese that the world may be conquered on horseback but must be governed with letters.

The myths and tales contained in both the *Kojiki* and the *Nihon shoki* are obviously not representative of historical fact but rather were more or less constructed and embellished by the scribes or historians of the royal court with the intention of supplying the magical power and logical basis for the position and authority of the ruler, the House of Tenno. The *Man'yōshū* appeared about 780, after the political consolidation of the state, and the *Norito* (or the *Engishiki* [Engi Formulary], of which the *Norito* is a part) was completed still later in 927.

The Japanese *kana* syllabary was introduced in Okinawa in 1187, during the reign of King Shunten. In 1267, a Japanese priest, Zenkan, brought Buddhism to the island for the first time.

In 1404, after a period of internecine warfare among the three rival petty principalities, the Chinese imperial envoy arrived to grant investiture and legitimize the Ryūkyūan dynasty. All Ryūkyū was unified under the leadership of Shō Hashi of the Chūzan Kingdom (Central Mountain Kingdom) in 1422.[10] This dynasty, called the First Shō Dynasty, proved to be short-lived when its seventh king, Shō Toku, was replaced by Shō En, the founder of the Second Shō Dynasty, in 1470. King Shō En, who had earlier served as royal treasurer and mayor of Naha, proved to be a strong and capable ruler who brought prosperity to the kingdom once again. His dynasty continued until 1879, when the Ryūkyūs were formally anned by Japan. Between 1478 and 1526, King Shō Shin centralized the government, requiring the regional lords to reside at Shuri, the capital, under his own watchful eyes. By this important step (which, by the way, preceded by about a hundred years a similar centralization in Japan by the Tokugawa shogunate), King Shō Shin was able to put a stop to the internal wars between the local lords. All the Ryūkyū Islands were now united in peace.[11] The first compilation of the *Omoro sōshi* appeared sixty years later in 1532. The second and third compilations appeared almost one hundred years later in 1613 and 1623.

The pattern was the same in both Japan and Okinawa. First, a system of writing was introduced. Second, a highly developed foreign religion, Buddhism, took root, stimulating the indigenous culture. Third, political unity and peace were secured. Fourth was legitimization by historical writing or by a higher authority. Last was the literature of the *Man'yōshū*, the *Norito*, and the *Omoro sōshi*. In the case of Japan, the *Man'yōshū* appeared about 260 years and the *Norito* about 317 years after the introduction of the *kanji* writing system. In the case of Okinawa, the *Omoro sōshi* appeared 345 years after the *kana* syllabary was introduced. Just as the Nara period (710–784), during which the *Man'yōshū* was compiled, was the first golden age in Japanese history—Japan having fully digested the cultural fare of China and Korea and having made it its own—in Okinawa, the reign of King Shō Shin (1478–1526), during which the *Omoro sōshi* was compiled, was the first golden age in Okinawan history. It was marked by Okinawan mastery of the art of writing and by the assimilation of the more advanced cultures of Japan and China which produced a synthesis of the three cultures which was distinctly Okinawan.

There is yet another important characteristic common to the *Man'yōshū* and the *Omoro sōshi*. That is, unlike earlier or contemporaneous historical documents which, written with obvious political bias, tend to distort history, glorify the royal house, and ignore the common people, the *Man'yōshū* and the *Omoro sōshi* treat of everyday life.

The history of the Ryūkyū Islands is roughly divisible into five periods:[12]

1. Primitive Society	From the pre-agricultural era to about the third or fourth century AD.
2. Village Society	Era of the small agricultural village. From about the third or fourth century to the end of the twelfth century.
3. Warring Period	Era of the petty local lord (*anji*) and of the three warring kingdoms. From the twelfth to the early fifteenth century.
4. Early Kingdom	Independent kingdom of Ryūkyū from 1422 to 1609; eras of the First and Second Shō Dynasties.
5. Late Kingdom	The Second Shō Dynasty as a subvassal of the Shimazu daimyo of Satsuma in Japan from 1609 to 1868.

What we will call the Omoro era spans about six centuries, from the end of the village society, through the era of the local lords, the three warring kingdoms, unification by the First Shō Dynasty, centralization of government and the complete unification of all the Ryūkyū Islands, up to the invasion by Satsuma which resulted in Ryūkyū becoming a semi-autonomous sub-fief of Satsuma while retaining a façade of independence with respect to the outside world.

Concomitantly, Japan—whose history was inextricably linked to that of the Ryūkyū Islands, particularly in the late Omoro era, profoundly influencing the latter—was progressing through the *Insei* or Cloister government, the Kamakura period, warring period, Azuchi period of Oda ascendancy, Momoyama period of Toyotomi, and the formative period of the Tokugawa shogunate. As long as Japan was preoccupied with its own internal wars and affairs and had no energy to expend elsewhere, the tiny kingdom of Ryūkyū was left alone to carry on its peaceful life based on meager agriculture supplemented by lucrative overseas trade. Once Japan was united, however, it turned its attention beyond its borders in a series of overseas adventures such as the invasion of Korea under Toyotomi. Another such expedition, launched against Ryūkyū by the powerful Satsuma clan in 1609, proved fatal to the island kingdom.

CHAPTER 2

Creation Myths

In the old days before a writing system had been devised, stories relating to the origin and history of the ancients were handed down by word of mouth. In time, there appeared a group of professional storytellers who had an extraordinary ability to memorize all the stories that had been handed down to them; stories which, together with accounts of events of their own lifetimes, they handed down in turn to their descendants. Such a professional group, called *kataribe*, was attached to the Japanese imperial court prior to the introduction of Chinese characters to Japan by ca. AD 600. In fact, the *Kojiki* (712), the earliest history of Japan, was recorded by Ō no Yasumaro as related to him by Hieda no Are, an official storyteller. In Okinawa there was no professional group of court storytellers, but this function was in a less conscious and organized manner carried on mainly by the priestesses of the royal court and of the villages. In the early sixteenth century, these stories began to be recorded in writing in the form of the *Omoro sōshi*.

In the process of oral transmission from generation to generation over a long period of time, these myths and legends have undoubtedly undergone some changes. However, as far as the content is concerned,

> in contrast to the modern writer's striving after originality of plot and treatment, the teller of a folktale is proud of his ability to hand on what he has received. He usually desires to impress his readers or hearers with the fact that he is bringing them something that has the stamp of good authority, that the tale was heard from some great storyteller or from some aged person who remembered it from the old days.[1]

There is a strong tendency for the content or plot of a tale to be well-preserved compared with the style or the wording. It follows, then, that in case of a change in content, which is against the general tendency, there ought to be some reason for the change, conscious or unconscious.

Accordingly, by comparing different versions of a tale or myth which purports to tell about a people's past, it may be possible to filter out some facts about the people's prehistory or at least their attitude toward their own past. Perhaps in this sense it is often said that in every legend and myth lies a grain of truth. An analysis of various versions of the creation myth of Ryūkyū may yield that grain of truth and shed light on the mythological era of Ryūkyūan history.

The following creation myth is recorded in the *Omoro sōshi.*

In the Beginning[2]

Tetsu, mukashi, hajimari ya	At first, in the old time, in the beginning
Tedako,[1] ōnushi ya[2]	The Great Sun God
Kiyora ya,[3] teriyoware	Beautifully shone
Mata senomi,[4] hajimari ni	And long, long ago, in the beginning
(Tedako, ōnushi ya)	The Great Sun God
(Kiyora ya, teriyoware)	Beautifully shone
Mata Teda, ichiroku ga[5] Teda hachiroku ga[6]	And the Great Sun God the Grand Sun God
Mata osan,[7] shichemioreba	And looked far down
Mata zayoko,[8] shichemioreba	And bent down, looked down, far away [There was something floating]
Mata Amamikiyo wa,[9] yosewache,[10]	And decreed to Amamikyo
Mata Shinerikiyo wa,[11] yosewache, And	directed Shinerikyo
Mata shimatsukure, tete, wache[12]	And said, let there be islands
Mata kunitsukure, tete, wache	And said, let there be countries [Amamikyo came down from heaven]
Mata kokoraki no,[13] shimashima	And many islands
Mata kokoraki no, kunikuni	And numerous countries [she has made]
Mata shimatsukura, gyamemo[14]	And until the islands were made
Mata kunitsukura, gyamemo	And until the countries were created
Mata Tedaki, ura,[15] girete[16]	And the Sun God grew weary of waiting

Mata Senomi, ura, girete	And the Sun God grew tired of waiting [Let the human seed down]
Mata Amamya,[17] suja[18] nasu-na[19]	And won't you bear the Amamya people
Mata Shinerya suja ya nasu-na	And won't you bear the Shinerya people
Mata syariwa,[20] suja, nashoware	And Holy God, bear the good people

1, 2. *Tedako-ōnushi*	Sun god or goddess. *Ōnushi* is literally 'the great master'. In other parts of the *Omoro sōshi,* the sun is referred to as the great master of the East *(agari no ōnushi). Teda* meaning sun seems to be an alternate form of *teriya* to *tera* or *teda.* In Okinawan, /d/ and /r/ or /l/ are often confused even today.
3. *kiyora*	Literally, 'clean', 'clear', 'pure', etc. In Okinawan, it also means 'beautiful' or 'pretty'.
4. *senomi*	A synonym for *mukashi* but in line 20 used as a synonym for *tedako.* Its meaning is not clear but it may be a contraction of *shinonome* meaning *terushino* or 'shining sun' (*Omoro shinshaku*, 332).
5, 6. *ichiroku, hachiroku*	Here used to mean the Sun god. In most cases, *ichiroku* is used to mean the king. It could be a contraction of *ikiroku* or 'man who would live'. *Hachi* of *hachiroku* is merely opposed to *ichiroku* and has no meaning (*Omoro shinshaku*, 332).
7. *osan*	"To look down far away'. The Sung Chinese word *usan* came to Okinawa through Japan during the Kamakura period. Originally it meant 'to doubt' or 'to suspect', then came to mean 'to see something dimly in the distance' (*Okinawa kō*, 197).
8. *zayoko*	Also spelled *zaryoko,* which comes from *zaroku,* a kind of chair. Its meaning changed further to mean 'to sit on a *zaroku* and look far down'. Also of Ming Chinese origin (*Okinawa kō*, 197).

9. *Amamikyo*	Literally, 'an Amami person'. It is the name of the creation deity of the Ryūkyūs. See the discussion on Amamikyo in the text.
10, 12. *yosewache, wache*	'To command'. *Yose* is a causative form, and *wache* is a term of respect similar to Classical Japanese *tamau*.
11. *Shinerikyo*	'Shineri person'. See the discussion on Amamikyo and Shinerikyo in the text.
13. *kokoraki*	'Many, numerous'.
14. *gyame*	Probably for the Japanese word *kiwame*, meaning 'the furthest limit', which then changed to mean 'as far as', 'until'.
15, 16. *uragirete*	'To wait impatiently or to grow tired of waiting'. *Ura* 'mind or soul', and *kirete* 'to cut off or tear away'. *Ura* of *urayamau* 'to be jealous' etymologically may be the same.
17. *Amamya*	See the discussion on Amamya in the text.
18. *suja ya*	'Sentient beings; living things; the people; the multitude; mankind, the world'.
19. *nasu-na*	*Nasu* means 'to create', 'to give birth'. The verbal ending *-na* has been interpreted by both Iha (*Okinawa kō*, 199) and Nakahara (*Omoro shinshaku*, 333) as a negative ending. Thus the line would mean "do not bear the Amamya man" in spite of its obvious incongruity with the rest of the poem, as Nakahara himself admits. Recently, however, Kamida Soei, citing convincing evidence, solved the problem by redefining the ending *-na* as an interjective particle (*Ryūkyū bungaku josetsu*, 200–201). Agreeing with Kamida, Ikemiya Masaharu advances the argument further. He interprets *-na* to be a particle anticipating agreement, like "would you ..." or "won't you ..." (*Ryūkyū bungaku ron*, 93–109). Here Ikemiya's theory is accepted as most natural and fitting with the rest of the poem.

20. *syariwa*	For lack of a better explanation, Iha tentatively interpreted this to be equivalent to Japanese *sareba* meaning 'then' (*Okinawa kō*, 200). Nakahara disagrees with Iha and says that *syari* is *seari* or *sejiari*, meaning 'one who has spiritual power', namely, a supernatural being (*Omoro shinshaku*, 333). Kamida gives his support to Nakahara (*Ryūkyū bungaku josetsu*, 201). Here Nakahara's interpretation is adopted.

There has been an ongoing controversy among scholars regarding the identity of Amamikyo and Shinerikyo. The term *amamya*, which had the original meaning 'land of the Amami', today refers to antiquity, or the time of *Amamikyo* (var. *Amamiko, Amamiku*), literally, 'Amami person', the ancestral deity of the inhabitants of the Amami and Okinawa islands.

Etymologically, *amami* is derived from *amabe* (*ama* 'fisherman', *be* an occupational group'), fisherfolk who were in the service of the Yamato dynasty of Japan from about the third century AD. Probably the Amabe fishermen who inhabited the western coast of Kyūshū gradually moved southward to the Ryūkyūs. In time, Amamikyo came to be identified as the creation deity of the islanders.[3]

Shinerikyo (Shineriko, Shineriku) means 'Shineri person'. The etymology of *shineri* is unknown, and there appears to be no record of a Shineri people. Nor is there any record of *shinerya*. Observing that Shinerikyo is almost always used in conjunction with Amamikyo, Iha Fuyū hypothesized that Shinerikyo is an echo word for Amamikyo for purposes of parallel construction characteristic of the poems of the *Omoro sōshi;* that Shinerikyo has no identity of its own; and that Amamikyo and Shinerikyo are one.[4] The *Chūzan sekan*, the first official history of Ryūkyū compiled in 1650, is often cited in support of Iha's theory, as it mentions only Amamikyo as the creation deity of Ryūkyū.[5] Other scholars of the *Omoro sōshi*, such as Nakahara Zenchū, Hokama Shuzen, and Torigoe Kensaburō agree in general with Iha's interpretation.

Ōbayashi Tairyō states however:

> [I am] not convinced why these gentlemen identified Amamikyo and Shinerikyo as one. Their reasoning seems to be in reverse inference based on the parallelism which frequently appears in the *Omoro sōshi* wherein the same thing is stated repeatedly in different words, and also on the fact

> that Amamikyo alone is mentioned in the *Chūzan sekan*. However, in the priest Taichū's *Ryūkyū shintōki* [which, written in 1605, predates the *Chūzan sekan* by 45 years], there are two deities, Amamikyo and Shinerikyo. Therefore, it seems best to interpret them as two deities. Since these two deities give birth to humans, it would be natural to assume that they are female and male. Furthermore, even such books as the *Chūzan seifu* [comp. in 1697] and *Kyūyō* [comp. in 1745], which appeared later, differed from the *Chūzan sekan* but agreed with the *Ryūkyū shintōki* in describing Amamikyo and Shinerikyo as two—female and male—deities. Based on these facts, it seems to me that the latter view seems to have been widely and traditionally held in Ryūkyū.[6]

If we are to study this question from the content of the story, it would seem more natural and present no contradiction if Amamikyo and Shinerikyo are interpreted to be two dieties, as they represent the primal pair.

But there are two difficulties with Ōbayashi's theory, according to Araki Moriaki. The first concerns a lack of consideration of the concept of deity at the time of the *Omoro sōshi*. The second concerns the danger of relying upon the *Chūzan seifu* and *Kyūyō*, compiled in the late seventeenth and eighteenth centuries respectively, in determining the concept of deity in the much earlier Omoro period, for a transformation had taken place in the concept of deity between the time of the *Omoro sōshi* and the *Chūzan seifu* and *Kyūyō*. The priest Taichū's interpretation of Amamikyo and Shinerikyo as two deities was no more than a Japanese interpretation as Taichū was a visiting itinerant priest from Japan. Araki therefore advocates identifying Amamikyo and Shinerikyo as one deity with two different names. He believes that the very fact that Amamikyo, namely, Shinerikyo, without distinction of sex, gave birth to humans is one of the unique characteristics of the Ryūkyūan mythology.[7]

It seems to me to be a case of hermaphroditism which characterized sorcerers and *kaminchu* priestesses in ancient Okinawa and in some areas in the South Seas.[8] Any clue as to the gender of the deities is conspicuously absent in the *Omoro sōshi*. The same phenomenon is observed in the creation mythology of Japan. Here genesis begins with *Ame-no-minaka-nushi no kami*, who is followed by four more deities who are described as "single deities who are complete by themselves." It was only with the sixth-generation deities, Izanagi and Izanami, that clearly male and female deities appeared.

Even today hermaphroditism is still found among the most primitive forms of life. It seems rather natural that the earliest deities of Okinawa and Japan were also hermaphrodites, and that they became identified either as male or female only with the progress of time. Probably an almighty deity had to be complete in and of itself, including the reproductive function. In the late seventeenth and eighteenth centuries, however, with exposure to extensive Japanese cultural influence, the Ryūkyūan concept of deity became more rational, providing for both male and female. In the *Konkōkenshū*, the earliest Ryūkyūan language dictionary compiled in 1711, this transition is indicated. In one section, the phrase *amamya kara* is defined as 'from olden times'.

It is immediately followed by another phrase, *shinerya kara*, which is defined simply as 'kaeshi no kotoba'—an echo word with no independent meaning of its own.[9] But in another section, *Amamikyo* and *Shinerikyo* are clearly defined as the female and male deities of Ryūkyūan creation,[10] thus making Shinerikyo an independent entity.

I take the position, therefore, that Shinerikyo was originally an echo word for Amamikyo, but later was given the function of a male to form a pair with Amamikyo. I also hold the question of whether Amamikyo was a deity or a person to be quite irrelevant. A dichotomy in which deities and humans are sharply distinguished appears to be totally alien to the Ryūkyūan people. In the Ryūkyūan mind, there is never a clear distinction between god and human. Throughout Ryūkyūan history, there abound instances wherein human heroes who accomplished great deeds, whether in war or in peace, are treated as objects of worship, as deities. It still holds true today. Even an ordinary soul, with no claim whatsoever to fame, joins the world of *kami* after death. Therefore, it appears to me that Amamikyo is the name not of an individual, but of a tribe which arrived in the Ryūkyūs in the distant past and which became the ruling tribe in Okinawa, and that over the long years since, the name Amamikyo has come to denote the ancestral deity of all Okinawans.

A second version of the creation myth of Ryūkyū, found in the *Kikoe-ōgimi ogishiki* (Rituals of the Chief Priestess)[11] compiled in 1875, is as follows:

> In the beginning, the seven *otake* (holy groves)—Aoi in Kunigami village, Kobao in Nakijin village, Shuri-mori, Seyaha, Ben, Kobao on Kudaka Island, and Amatsuji in Tamagusuku—rose from the sea and became dry shoals.
>
> Amamiku and Shineriku,[12] descending from heaven on the seven holy groves, saw that the waves from the east were crossing over into the west, and that the waves from the west were crossing over into the east. Therefore, they went up to heaven and brought back the fountain palm, pine, miscanthus, pandanus, and hibiscus *(hamabo)*, and Tentaishi (presumably female) had three children. The first was Tensonshi (heavenly

Grandson), the ancestor of the royal dynasty. The second was Konkon (probably a corruption of Kunkun or Kimigimi), the ancestor of Kikoe-ōgimi-ganashi (the chief priestess of the royal family), and the third was Shuku-shuku, ancestor of the local *noro* priestess.

A third version of the creation myth, recorded by the priest Taichū in the *Ryūkyū shintōki* (Records of Shinto in Ryūkyū),[13] is as follows:

> Long ago, in the beginning, when there were as yet no humans, Heaven sent down a pair, male and female. The male was called Shinerikyu, and the female, Amamikyu. They lived with their huts side by side. At this time, the island was yet so small that it was floating on the waves.
>
> Therefore, the *tashika* tree was brought forth and planted to build mountains. Next, *shikyu* grass was planted, and also pandanus, and then the island was formed.
>
> Though there was no consummation of the Yin and Yang between them, because their residences stood side by side, the passing of the wind became instrumental in the pregnancy of the female. Three children were born. The first was the progenitor of the masters of the various places (i.e., the *anji*). The second was the progenitor of the *noro* priestesses. The third was the progenitor of the commoners.

The fourth and most elaborate version of the creation myth is recorded in the *Chūzan sekan*, the first formal history of Ryūkyū, written in 1650 by Shō Jō-ken.[14] It goes as follows:

> In ancient times, in the Heavenly City, there was a goddess whose name was Amamiku. The Heavenly Emperor (Tentei) summoned her and said, "Below is a holy place fit for the gods to live. Regrettably, it has not been made into islands yet. Therefore, I command thee to go down and make islands."
>
> Amamiku respectfully obeyed and went down to look. Though it seemed like a holy place, the waves of the eastern sea were crossing over into the western sea, and the waves of the western sea were crossing over into the eastern sea, and it had not yet been formed into islands.
>
> Ascending to heaven, Amamiku begged for earth, stone, grass, and trees with which to make islands. The Heavenly Emperor consented and gave them to her. Amamiku brought them down and formed a number of islands.
>
> First, she created the Asumori of Hedo, in Kunigami; next, Kanahy-abu of Nakijin; next, Chinenmori, Sayahatake, Yabusatsu Urabaru; next,

> Tamagusuku Amatsuzu; next, Kudaka-Kobaumori; next, Shurimori-Madamamori, and, next, the other holy groves and hills of all the islands and countries.
>
> A few thousand years passed but still there were no humans. Thus it was not possible for the power of the gods to be apparent. Therefore Amamiku again went up to heaven and begged for human seed.
>
> The Heavenly Emperor replied, "As you know, there are many gods in heaven, but none are fit to be sent down." However, since this matter could not be ignored, he finally sent down his own son and daughter.
>
> Though there was no consummation of the Yin and Yang between them, because their residences stood side by side, the passing wind became instrumental in the pregnancy of the female. Finally, three sons and two daughters were born. The eldest son was the progenitor of the masters of the country (kings). His was called the lineage of Tenson-shi (lineage of the Heavenly Grandson). The second son was the progenitor of the local lords (the *anji*). The third son was the progenitor of the commoners. The first daughter was the progenitor of the high priestesses associated with the royal family, called *kikoe-ōgimi*. The second daughter was the progenitor of the priestesses of the local community, called *noro*.

E. B. Tylor, in his book *Primitive Culture*, states, "I am disposed to think … that the mythology of the lower races rests especially on a basis of real and sensible analogy, and that the great expansion of verbal metaphor into myth belongs to more advanced periods of civilization. In a word, I take material myth to be the primary, and verbal myth to be the secondary formation."[15] Hence the early mythology is more apt to reflect actual historical fact than the later mythology, and the mythology grows more complex as the society grows more complex.

In the creation myth in the *Omoro sōshi*, the Sun God directs Amamikyo to go down and inhabit the island. The role of Shinerikyo is not clear. As noted earlier, Iha Fuyū and others including myself, support the hypothesis that Shinerikyo, as it appears in the *Omoro sōshi*, is merely an echo word for Amamikyo; that Shinerikyo does not possess a separate male identity and that Amamikyo and Shinerikyo are one. Scholars are by no means in agreement on this issue, and Ōbayashi, for one, takes a contrary view of the matter, as noted earlier.

The unelaborated stage of society that the myth describes is shown by the absence of the hierarchical classes which are so characteristic of the later legends. Although the presence of certain words such as *osan* or *zayoko*—which are of foreign origin and of later import from Japan, possibly during the Kamakura era—makes it possible to judge its recorder to be an intellectual who had some direct or indirect foreign contact, and thus places the actual time of recording this myth in writing relatively late, the form of the myth seems nonetheless quite old and in fact the earliest of the four versions introduced here.

For ease of comparison, these myths can be diagrammed as follows:[16]

1. *Omoro sōshi*

   Sun God
   Amamikyo (Shinerikyo) → humans

2. *Kikoe-ōgimi-ogishiki*

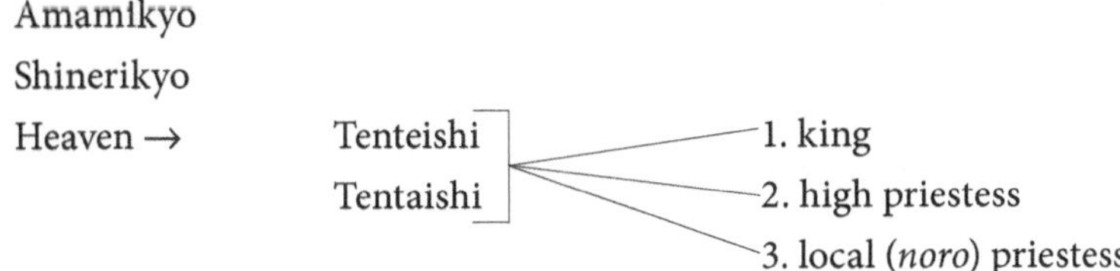

3. *Ryūkyū shintōki*

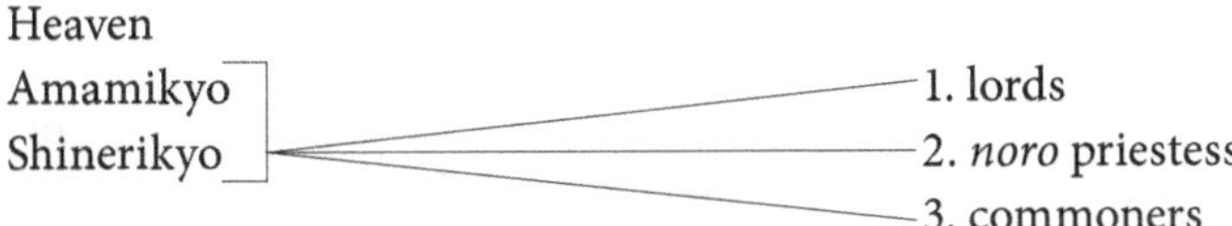

4. *Chūzan sekan*

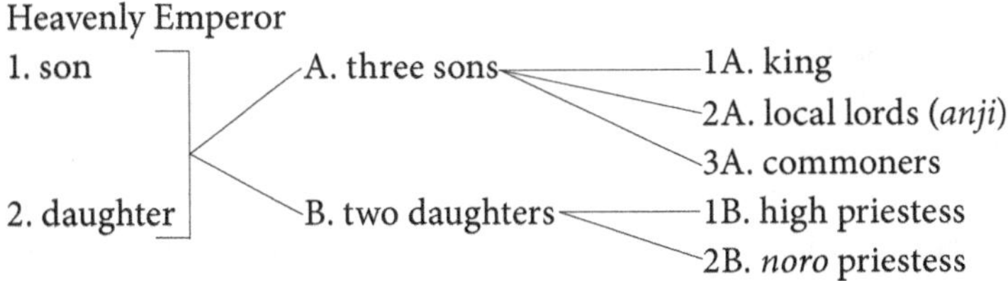

In the myth in the *Kikoe-ōgimi-ogishiki*, Shinerikyo is presented as a male god, creating a more logical female-male pair. However, Amamikyo and Shinerikyo are not the progenitors of the people but are merely intermediaries between an impersonal heaven and the earth. This version of the creation myth creates for

Tenteishi (Son of the Heavenly Emperor) his female counterpart, Tentaishi, who seems to have been made up for the sole purpose of providing a partner for Tenteishi. There is no mention of the ancestor of the common people. This obvious and seemingly deliberate omission and emphasis on religious aspects is clearly indicative of the bias of the author—the high priestess, making this myth less valuable as a historical document than it otherwise might be.

In contrast to the above, the *Ryūkyū shintōki* seems to take a fairly middle of the road view in that it provides for the lords, the priestesses, and the commoners. From the fact that the lords are not further divided into king and local lords and that no distinction is made between high priestess and local priestess, it may be deduced that the form of this myth is probably that of the pre-dynastic era when Okinawa was not yet unified under the king and there were many local lords and as many local priestesses.

When we come to the creation myth in the *Chūzan sekan*, which is only 45 years later than the *Ryūkyū shintōki*, we find a version of the myth which is quite different from that above.

From the following sentences,

1. *Ryūkyū shintōki*	"Though there was no consummation of the Yin and the Yang between them, because their residences stood side by side, the passing wind became instrumental in the pregnancy of the female."
2. *Chūzan sekan*	"Though there was no consummation of the Yin and the Yang between them, because their residences stood side by side, the passing wind became instrumental in the pregnancy of the female god."

it seems quite apparent that Shō Jōken, author of the *Chūzan sekan*, must have had the *Ryūkyū shintōki* as one of his references. He also must have been acquainted with the *Omoro sōshi*. Whereas in the *Ryūkyū shintōki* Amamikyo and Shinerikyo are treated as separate female and male deities, in the *Chūzan sekan*, after the pattern of the *Omoro sōshi*, Amamikyo (called Amamiku in the text) alone is presented. Also, such words as Tentei (Heavenly Emperor) and Tensonshi (lineage of the Heavenly Grandson) are indicative of the author's knowledge of Chinese and are obviously his own innovation.

More importantly, in the *Ryūkyū shintōki*, Amamikyo and Shinerikyo have three children, but in the *Chūzan sekan*, by the request of Amamikyo who created the islands, the Heavenly Emperor sends down his own son and daughter who give birth to three sons and two daughters who are not related to Amamikyo. Moreover, the "masters of the various places" in the *Ryūkyū shintōki*, have become divided into the "master of the country," (i.e., king) and the "local lords" in the *Chūzan sekan*. Also, the "priestesses" of the *Ryūkyū shintōki* have become divided into the "high priestesses" and the "local priestesses."

These variations in the different versions clearly show how changes in the social system influence the form of the folktale. The creation myth found in the *Omoro sōshi* reflects the earliest stage of society: although secular and religious leaders at the village level were accorded a certain power and prestige, stratification was minimal and the social classes were not yet clearly defined. The myth in the *Ryūkyū shintōki* reflects a later stage when numerous petty local lords strove to conquer each other before the strongest among them unified the whole of Okinawa.

The "masters of the various places" mentioned in the *Ryūkyū shintōki* refer to the local lords *(anji)* who, as lords of various small castles, controlled their own lands and people. The *anji* were the only political rulers at this time, and there was no king above them. The *noro* priestesses were selected from among the sisters of the local lords and acted as religious rulers. Therefore, according to the myth in the *Ryūkyū shintōki*, Okinawan society before unification comprised the local lords who ercised political and social sovereignty over their domains, the *noro* priestesses who were associated with the local lords and who ercised religious sovereignty over the same domains, and the commoners or peasants.

Here we find a remarkable instance wherein, in order to uplift and maintain its prestige and to insure the absoluteness, inalienability, and permanency of its sovereignty, the ruling class distinguished its ancestors from those of other classes by showing, on the authority of the creation myth, that it had been from the very beginning genetically and historically different from and superior to other classes.

Whereas the myth in the *Ryūkyū shintōki* seems to belong to the era of preunification, the myth in the *Chūzan sekan* definitely belongs to the later era of the unified, centralized state. At this time, the local lords were brought under the control of the king of Chūzan (king of Ryūkyū). The *noro* priestesses who used to belong to these formerly independent local lords likewise lost their independence and were placed under the control of the high priestess of the royal family. With the supremacy of the king and the high priestess over the local lords and the *noro* priestesses, the "masters of the various places" now had to be divided into two different classes—that of the king and that of the local lords—with each class having a different genesis corresponding to its authority. Similarly, the class of *noro* priestesses, the religious rulers, now had to be divided into high priestesses and local priestesses, also supported by the appropriate geneses. Thus the creation myth in the *Chūzan sekan*, in explaining how Okinawan society under the centralized government of Shuri came to comprise five classes—king, high priestess, local lords, *noro* priestesses, and commoners—reinforced and maintained the prestige of the authorities.

In summation, we have seen how "people" in general in the *Omoro sōshi* became "three children" in the *Ryūkyū shintōki* and "five children" in the *Chūzan sekan*, corresponding to the evolving stratification of Ryūkyūan society, and that the fundamental purpose of the creation myth was to sanctify the ruling class and assure, magically, its ascendancy, thereby maintaining the status quo of the social hierarchy.

Up to this point, I have analyzed and interpreted the meaning of the creation myths in the context of time and history. Now I would like to approach it from another angle, namely, from a geographical perspective.

The last three lines of the creation myth in the *Omoro sōshi* are

Won't you bear the Amamya people
Won't you bear the Shinerya people
Holy God, bear the good people

The term Shinerya, presumably an echo word for Amamya, may be ignored here. However, the interpretation of these lines, supplemented by other data, provides a key to the past of the people of the Ryūkyū Islands. Amamikyo ("Amami person") is said to be the ancestor of the inhabitants of the Ryūkyū Islands, but Amamikyo is also claimed to be the ancestor of the inhabitants of the Amami-Ōshima Islands which lie between Kyūshū and Okinawa. According to an Amami-Ōshima tale, Amamikyo first descended upon Amami-dake hill, located on the boundary between Uken village and Yamato village. Amamikyo governed Amami-Ōshima for a while and left southward.[17]

As noted earlier, there was a group of fisherfolk called *amabe* who lived along the seashores of Japan and who supplied marine products to the Imperial Court as a tax in kind.[18] This group, which made its appearance about AD 275, was spread over a wide region along the coasts of the northern and southern ends of Kyūshū and even along the Ise and Owari coasts of Honshū. It is most likely that *amami* was not the name of an individual but the name of a group or tribe as Katō Sango suggested,[19] and that this group or tribe was one of the *amabe* who moved southward and settled the islands.[20] We know, in fact, that from ancient times, the strait between the Shichitō Islands and the Kuchino-erabu Island near the southern end of Kyūshū has been called Amami-no-watashi, 'Strait of Amami.' Moreover, on Iheya Island (from whence the founders of the two Shō dynasties of Ryūkyū originated) which lies in the northwest of Okinawa—thus in a position to intercept those who came down from Kyūshū—there is a hill called Amami-dake. Furthermore, Iha points out that the frequency of occurrence of the word *amami* in the names of places, gods, and priestesses is greatest in northern Ryūkyū and decreases as one goes southward.[21]

These factors indicate that the early inhabitants of the Ryūkyū Islands migrated from the north. Kanazawa Shōzaburō made an interesting observation from a linguistic viewpoint. In the *Nihon shoki* (Chronicles of Japan, AD 720) southern Korea was called *arihishikara. Arihi* is the archaic written form of the modern word *arp* meaning 'front'.[22] Thus *arihishikara* meant the 'front' of Korea, proving that the ancient Koreans migrated from the north down to and facing the south; therefore, to the ancient Koreans, southern Korea was the 'front' of Korea. Now, the Japanese word for east is *higashi* or *hingashi*, which means to face the sun. And the Japanese word for the west is *nishi*, which is derived from *inishi. Inishi* means the past, indicating the direction from which they came in the past. The ancient Japanese migrated from west to east in the direction of the sun. In Ainu, the word for the east is *moshiripa; moshiri* means 'land', *pa* means 'head'. The west is *moshirigesh. Gesh* means 'buttocks' or 'hips.' Thus, the Ainu word for the west, *moshirigesh*, means the 'rear end' of the land. Therefore it is surmised that the Koreans migrated from north to south, the Japanese from west to east, and the Ainu also from west to east. Now, in Okinawan, *nishi*, whose original meaning is 'the past' (and which in modern Japanese means 'west') means 'north'. Hence, the ancient Okinawans migrated from north to south.[23]

Furthermore, on the question of whether the Okinawans advanced northward from the sea areas to the south or southward from Kyūshū into their islands, Richard Pearson found as follows:

> In the former group [the islands from Okinawa to the north], evidence of early occupation is found at the Yamashita-chō Site in Naha City, which yielded very crude bone tools dated at 31,000 ± 1,000 years BP, and the skeletal remains from the Minatogawa limestone fissure in southern Okinawa, dated at 18,200 BP. Subsequent to these sites there is a long gap, until the first two millenia BC. Sites of this time period show strong affinities with Kyūshū, and it is generally accepted that their inhabitants are the descendants of migrants who came down from Kyūshū through Amami-Ōshima. Fragments of Ichiki Type ceramics,

actually made in southern Kyūshū in the Late Jōmon, have been found in the Urasoe Site north of Naha. Local ceramics appear to have been developed from the Ichiki Type. Evolution of very small populations in isolation seems to have been the case. At the time of the Late Jōmon and Yayoi, when one would expect evidence of new populations if the Ryūkyūs were indeed stepping stones from the south to Japan, the Ryūkyūs were a backwater.[24]

I would like to return for a moment to the last three lines of the Omoro creation myth. In the translation provided earlier, I followed the interpretation by Kamida[25] and Ikemiya,[26] producing the following:

Won't you bear the Amamya people
Won't you bear the Shinerya people
Holy God, bear the good people.

But the traditional interpretation by Iha, and by Nakahara and Hokama with their own minor variations, would have the lines read just the opposite. First, Iha interpreted the lines as follows:

Do not bear the Amamya people
Do not bear the Shinerya people
But bear the people.

He then expanded the meaning of these lines to say that in the modern context it would mean "leave the 'Amamya' and migrate to the distant islands."[27] Nakahara and Hokama added their own interpretation as follows:

Do not bear the Amamya people
Do not bear the Shinerya people
But bear the spiritual people.

Nakahara suggested the possibility that these three lines might refer to a new immigrant group that came later as the conquerors of the aboriginal Amamya people.[28] Hokama expanded this idea to say that the people of the Obotsu lineage who occupied the position of rulers felt the need to clarify their relationship as rulers vis-à-vis the aboriginal peoples of the Nirai lineage and Amamya lineage they ruled.[29] Both suggestions, however, remained only that, as they failed to present further evidence in support of the arrival of a new group of conquerors. At this point, therefore, it seems best to accept the interpretation proposed by

Kamida and Ikemiya as the most natural and reasonable in terms of the context of the creation myth itself.

Turning from Okinawa for the moment, let us examine the creation myths of Japan and China. With respect to the Japanese creation myth, the *Kojiki* (Records of Ancient Matters), compiled in AD 712, tells us the following:

> Hereby, Heavenly God, at the behest of the other gods, commanded the creator pair, Izanagi and Izanami, to build and form the floating chaos below and bestowed them with the "marsh-spear of heaven." The two gods, standing on the floating bridge of heaven, thrust down the marsh-spear of heaven and groped with it in the chaos below. When they pulled it up, the brine from the spear point dropped, coagulated, and formed an island called Onogoro-jima.

Thus we see that the Japanese and Okinawan creation myths are strikingly similar. This similarity becomes even more important when we compare these myths to the creation myth of the neighboring great nation of China, with which they have no semblance of similarity or relationship.

According to the *Shih-pa-shih lüeh*, Outlines of the Eighteen Histories, P'an Ku separated heaven and earth, and formed the sun, the moon, and plants and animals. After P'an Ku, there appeared T'ien Huan (Celestial Emperor) who became sovereign by virtue of wood, rose in the year of the tiger, and governed well by doing nothing. They were twelve brothers, each of whom reigned 18,000 years. Then followed Ti Huang (Terrestrial Emperor) who became sovereign by virtue of fire. They were also twelve brothers, each of whom reigned 18,000 years. Then appeared nine Jen Huang (Human Emperors) who were once more brothers who reigned respectively over nine provinces for about 150 generations for a total of 45,600 years.

In Japanese mythology, wrote Fairservis,

> ... we have a turbulence and movement that most certainly would have been regarded as barbaric by the earth-loving Chinese. One cannot help comparing the Japanese legends of the gods with those of Central Asian peoples. It is here in the Siberian, Mongolian, and Tunguaic versions that we again encounter the storm, wind, and fire gods in all their barbaric splendor. The sun, moon, and stars too have their epic personifications. What is missing is the presence of the sea deities, who play such an important role in the local myths of the Japanese. Except for the sea and water divinities the legends of ancient Japan might well be regarded as another version of the sagas of the nomads of inner Asia.[30]

The Ryūkyū creation myth presented here apparently belongs to the Japanese cultural sphere. It is, however, only one of many myths found throughout the Ryūkyū Islands. There are others whose types and motifs of water and islands are in common with those of the coastal areas of southern China and the South Seas. Just as the Japanese creation myths have elements in common both with areas in the far north of the Asian continent and with the islands in the south, the Ryūkyūan mythology also shows traces and influences from neighboring areas to the north and south.[31]

CHAPTER 3

Life in and about the Village

Building a Village[1]

Ano mori no mori no naeshi,[1]	By the side of that grove,
Shima[2] tachi[3] mo yotashagesa.	Looks auspicious for raising a village.
Kono dake[4] no dake no naeshi,	By the side of this hill,
Kunitachi mo yotashagesa.	Looks auspicious for raising a country.
Itsu haroshi[5] uchikakete,[6]	Hit with the five blade hoe,
Nana haroshi,[7] uchikakete,	Hit with the seven blade hoe,
Itsutsu hoki[8] kirihanchi,[9]	Cut down the five cliffs,
Nanatsu hoki kirihanchi,	Cut down the seven cliffs,
Itsutsu narimono[10] mochiyosete,	Gather together the five drums,
Nanatsu narimono[11] yuisagete.	Bring together the seven drums.

1. *naeshi* — 'Side'.
2. *shima* — 'A village; a community; one's home village; an island'.
3. *tachi* — 'To stand, to raise, to erect'.
4. *dake* — Literally, 'hill, mountain'. In combination with the prefix *o*-, it becomes *otake* or *odake*, meaning 'sacred grove'. Symonymous with *omori.*
5. *itsu haroshi* — *Itsu* 'five', *ha* 'blade', *roshi* 'hoe'.
6. *uchikakete* — 'To throw something over something else', as in throwing a net over an object. Here, of course, it is an exaggerated expression for striking with a five-blade hoe.
7. *nana haroshi* — *Nana* means 'seven', hence, a seven-blade hoe.

8. *itsutsu hoki*	*Itsutsu* 'five', *hoki* 'cliff' or 'bluff'.
9. *kirihanchi*	'To cut off or cut away; to disentangle'.
10. *itsutsu narimono*	Literally, 'five sounding objects', i.e., musical instruments.
11. *nanatsu narimono*	'Seven musical instruments".

This *kwenya umui*,[2] which is sung by the priestess of Okuma village in northern Okinawa, relates the process of the founding of a village in ancient Okinawa. In those days, people generally founded their village on a hilltop or mountainside where there was ample sun and where damage from typhoons and floods was least likely to be inflicted upon them. Downhill, away from the houses, there would be a plain or valley with a stream or spring where the villagers had their rice paddies or fields.

Houses were located on the hilltops and mountainsides for reasons of sanitation and weather. But in the days before there was a strong central authority capable of enforcing the peace, it must also have been for strategic reasons—a village located on a hilltop could defend itself more easily than one located on a plain. However, there was another factor more important in the founding of a village than all of the aforementioned; namely, the sacred grove called *otake* (pronounced /utaki/) or *omori* (pronounced /umui/).[3]

Every village, with the exception of the *yādui* settlements founded in comparatively recent times by upper class gentry-farmers, had an *otake*. The village community originated from this *otake*, and the village organization was formulated with the *otake* as its center—that is, with the belief in the *otake kami* (deity of the holy grove) as its center. All social and ritual activities in the village revolved around the *otake*. The *kami*, however, did not dwell in the *otake*. The *kami*'s permanent residence is conceived to be either *Obotsu-kagura*, located somewhere in heaven, or *Nirai-kanai*, located beyond or under the ocean. On the days of rituals and festivities, the *kami* presented itself at the *otake* to bestow blessings upon the villagers.[4] The village existed by virtue of the relationship between the *kami* of the *otake* and the *makyo* (pronounced /machu/, cognate of *maki* in Japanese)[5] consanguineous group. The *otake kami* protected the village and ensured its welfare and prosperity; thus the *otake* was indispensable to the village.

As mentioned previously, economic and geographic factors including fertility of the soil, availability of water, and so on, were important and had to be considered in founding a village. However, no matter how important these factors may have been, they could not precede or supplant the religious factor. The religious factor was valued at least as much and might even have taken precedence over these other factors.[6]

The *kwenya umui* "Building a Village" clearly illustrates that when a group of people set out to found a village, they looked, first of all, for the proper site for their holy grove. Though the land may have been satisfactory from the standpoint of other factors, if it lacked an auspicious site that could be set up as the *otake*, it might have been reserved for farming, but never for the village proper, that is, for residential purposes. Only after a proper and auspicious site had been selected as the *otake* did the people build their village.

The *otake* was usually located on high land in the village proper. There was almost always a dense thicket or grove of trees and shrubbery, the most distinctive of which were the tall *kuba* (fountain palm) and *māni* (black boxtree), symbols of the holy grove. The *Ryūkyū aoki* (Ryūkyū laurel), *susuki* (*H. sinensis* Anders), and *yamashōga* (wild ginger) were also considered appropriate to the holy grove. In addition to the *otake* which was the physical as well as spiritual center of the village, there were several other sites of worship called *oganjo* (pronounced /uganju/) which, located at the foot of a great tree or rock, roughly encircled the village.

This type of village seems to have represented the earliest form of community organization. It comprised a consanguineous group, or *makyo*.[7] On the highest level, the *makyo* was founded on the relationship between man and the *kami;* thus it can be said that the Okinawan village originated in the *otake*, or holy grove. But on a more finite level, that is, with respect to the relationship of man to man, it could be said that the *makyo* originated with the founding family called *neya* or *nedokoro* (pronounced /niiya/ and /nidukuru/, both meaning 'root house'). The *neya*, as founder of the village, inalienably assumed not only the highest status and honor but also the role of ruler and leader.

However, the *neya*'s political and religious prestige was not solely derived from its having founded the village. Its prestige was derived largely from its relationship with the *kami* of the *otake*. That is to say, the *neya* established the *otake* and thereby gained jurisdiction over its rituals and ceremonies. The *neya* consisted of the *nebito* (pronounced /nichu/, meaning 'root man') and *negami* (pronounced /nigan/, meaning 'root deity'). The head of the neya was the *nebito*, and the *nebito*'s sister was the *negami*. The former had control over political and administrative aspects of the *makyo*, and the latter was in charge of religious and ceremonial aspects. Here we see the earliest form of brother-sister dual sovereignty in Okinawa. Their power was not as strong as that held later by the lord or the king, but they were the rulers of their village community as speakers for the *kami*. For this reason, the *neya* became the center for all the social activities that developed around the *otake*.

In the *makyo* village, there was no aspect of community life, whether economic, political, recreational, or familial, that was not affected by religion to a greater or lesser degree. Membership in the *makyo* and participation in the religious life of the community went hand in hand. The religious and the secular coincided completely. Religious values predominated over and permeated every aspect of life. "Religion is in a position to place its sacred imprint on the value system of the society in a total way," wrote Nottingham, "[and] in the relatively undeveloped state of the other institutions, except the family, religion is likely to provide the principal focus for the integration and cohesion of the society as a whole."[8]

Physically and geographically, the village community developed with the *neya* at the center. It seems certain that a village was founded by one or more families belonging to the same clan.[9] The clan gradually increased in number of households by a process of branching out. The branch households were called *bunke*. At the same time, other clans also moved in to expand the village. As families belonging to other clans moved in, the original *makyo* village lost its characteristic of being composed of one consanguineous group (it seems the word *makyo* meant the consanguineous group as well as a village composed of that group, for the two were one and the same in the beginning) and began to be called by a more recent term, *mura* (related to *mure* 'group, throng, crowd').

Within a *mura*, then, there were two or more consanguineous groups or clans which were called *monchu* (pronounced /munchu/, possibly derived from *mun* 'gate', and *chu* 'person). The *monchu*, which originated as a *makyo*, systematically expanded[10] according to two basic rules. The first governed the location of the *bunke* relative to the *neya*. It specified that the *neya* was to be located closest to and in front of the *otake*. No *bunke* were allowed behind the *neya*, that is, closer to the *otake*. *Bunke* were located to the left or right or in front of the *neya*. The more recent the *bunke* household, the farther it stood from the *otake*. The second rule pertained to the *ya-no-na* (pronounced /yaa-n-naa/), the name of the household. This rule required that all *bunke* households denote, by means of a prefix or suffix to the *ya-no-na*, their relation with, or location in relation to the *neya*. For instance, *miiya* 'new house', *agari-ya* 'eastern house', *agari-jo* 'eastern gate', *iri-imui* 'west *imui*', *matsuni-gwa* 'small *matsune*', *mae-ufuya* 'in front of *ufuya*', and so on.[11]

Thus, in the *makyo* or *mura* village, the religious organization, more than any other institution, played an integral role in overall community activity. The history of the *neya*'s efforts to maintain and secure its prestige and authority is, in fact, central not only to the history of religion in Okinawa, but to the history of the society as well.

It was into this kind of village society that a new wave of immigrants came.

Immigration of the Miruya People[12]

Amamya,[1] miruya,[2] nya[3]	In the age of Amami (gods), Men of Miruya,
Makyo, eradesu, oretare,	Chose this *makyo* and came down,
Momo-sue, tezurare,[4]	And are revered for eternity.
Shinerya,[5] miruya, nya,	In the age of Shinerya (ancients), Men of Miruya,
Futa,[6] eradesu	Chose this *makyo* and came down,
Arakaki no, mya[7] ni	In the garden of Arakaki
Makyo, eradesu	Chose the *makyo* and came down
Oki, ofuji[8] ga, mya ni	In the garden of the forefathers
(makyo, oradesu, oretare)	Chose the *makyo* and came down.

1. *amamya*	In the creation myth, the place where the Okinawan people originated. It also means 'the ancient time'.
2. *miruya*	Usually thought of as a paradise beyond the ocean. Here it is used as a synonym for *amamiya.*
3. *nya*	Equivalent to 'Mr. So and so'. So and so from Miruya.
4. *tesurare*	*Te* 'hand' plus *surare*, passive form of *suru* 'rub'. 'To be worshipped and venerated by rubbing both hands together'.
5. *shinerya*	Synonym of *amamiya.*
6. *futa*	Synonym of *makyo.*
7. *Arakaki no mya*	In the garden of Arakaki. *Arakaki* is a place name, that is, the present day village of Nishime in Gushikawa-son, Kume Island.
8. *oki, ofuji*	*Ofuji* means 'grandfather'. *Oki* ('great') *ofuji* means 'forefathers'.

It seems that the Miruya people from the north were more cultured, and that they were extraordinary in appearance and ability as well—at least in the eyes of the forefathers who were leading a simple life in the *makyo* village. For this reason, the Miruya were received with awe and worshipped as *kami.* Passages like "men of Miruya chose this *makyo* and came down" suggest that the forefathers were proud of the fact that the great Miruya chose to come to their *makyo.* The absence of any disturbance connected with the advent of the new immigrant group, both in the *Omoro sōshi* and in the other historical data, may be construed to indicate that though the number of immigrants may have been large, they did not all come at once, and though they were most likely bearers of a culture more advanced than that of the islanders, they were not essentially different racially or culturally from the islanders. We find all over the Ryūkyū Islands, in the Ōshima group, Okinawa group, Miyako and Yaeyama groups, folktales recording the coming of outsiders, very often Japanese warriors, with very little disturbance. If they had come in great numbers at once, they would have disrupted the life of the islanders, and that would have been noted in some form. That they were almost invariably respected and welcomed seems to indicate they had an advanced culture, but the fact that they formed no homogeneous class or group or left no trace of it if there were such a class or group, seems to mean that their integration was comparatively easy and took place without much conflict, due, perhaps, to their essential affinity to the island people. The last *omoro* described the coming of the Miruya; here is one which describes their appearance:

Man of Miruya Is a Worldly God[13]

Miruya-nya, yonare[1]-kami yareba, Kewaitsu[2]	Because Miruya-man is a worldly god, *Kewaitsu!*
Miruya-nya, yotsuki[3]-kami yareba, (Kewaitsu)	Because Miruya-man is a gifted god, *(Kewaitsu!)*
Miruya-nya, ijiki[4]-kami	Because Miruya-man is a proud god,
Miruya-nya, jakuni[5]-kami	Because Miruya-man is a great land god,
Ichekiriyari,[6]	Proudly,
Kanewakako,[7] sashowache	He wears the *kanewakako* sword,
Ichekiriyari	Gallantly,
Kanemisaki, sashowache	He wears the *kanemisaki* sword,
Kanewakako, himosuzu[8] wa sagete,	On the *kanewakako*, hanging a string of bells,
Kanemisaki, narisuzu[9] wa sagete.	On the *kanemisaki*, hanging ringing bells.

1. *yonare-kami*	This means not only a man well versed in the ways of the world, but more significantly, a man who knows the world that is unknown to ordinary men.
2. *kewaitsu*	Etymology uncertain. Here, it serves as vocal accompaniment—cheers or applause.
3. *yotsuki*	*Yo* plus *tsuki*. *Tsuki* means 'to attach or to be attached'. *Yo* may denote some sort of spiritual power.
4. *ijiki*	'Spirited, gallant proud'.
5. *jakuni*	*Ja* (honorific) plus *kuni* 'country'. Very often, *jakuni* refers to the largest island, Okinawa. Here, however, it seems to refer to some other "bigger and better" country.
6. *ichekiriyari*	Verb form of *ijiki*. See item 4.
7. *kanewakako, kanemisaki*	Types of swords. Exact description unknown.
8. *hamosuzu*	*Himo* 'string' or 'cord' plus *suzu* 'bell'.
9. *narisuzu*	*Nari* 'ringing' plus suzu 'bell'.

Apparently, the main persona or hero of this *omoro* is not a native of Okinawa. Miruya is one of the paired words *miruya-kanaya* (or *nirai-kanai*) which denote the country of eternity or paradise beyond the ocean. The hero is also called *jakuni kami*. *Ja* is an honorific prefix denoting that which is good or beautiful, and kuni means country. It is often used as an epithet for Okinawa Island, the largest of the Ryūkyū Islands. However, here it seems to denote some other, more highly cultured country far beyond the ocean. We are told that the hero has a peculiar type of sword called *kanewakako*. Though we don't know what kind of sword it is, we know there are bells hanging from it, just as bells were hung from the swords and spears of the ancient Japanese warriors. Although this *omoro* does not tell us why and how this Miruya man came to the island, it seems unlikely that he was the victim of a shipwreck, for he is gifted, proud, and spirited. We can almost see him striding confidently through the village, accompanied by the jingling bells which dangle from the hilt of his great fine sword, as all eyes are upon him. Could he have been one of the merchant pirates from Japan that roamed all over the southern seas and China coasts, terrorizing people? Or could he have been a member of a defeated clan in Japan, seeking refuge in one of the islands. Whatever they might have been, those Miruya who decided to settle down found the island society quite receptive. With their knowledge in the civil and military spheres, they were quickly integrated into the upper class. For instance, besides the well-known Tametomo legend and *omoro* that allegedly describe his arrival, there are some historical figures such as the lord of Katsuren, Mochizuki (ca. 1450s) who, judging from his name, was definitely of Japanese descent. This was not at all inconsistent with the contemporary political situation in Japan. That is to say, in Japan, when finally the once powerful Taira clan which had controlled the Imperial Court was thoroughly defeated by the opposing Minamoto clan in 1185, at Dan-no-ura at the western extreme of Honshū, many Taira clansmen, with the Minamoto in pursuit, fled to the numerous islands southward in search of refuge. Indications of the presence of the defeated Taira refugees are seen all over, from Tsushima Island in the north and Yonaguni Island in the south. On many of the islands where they landed, with the exception of Okinawa Island proper, they established themselves as the ruling class. Those who went to Okinawa Island were few in number and did not join the ruling class. This seems to be a strong indication that the fleeing Taira had some knowledge of Minamoto influence on Okinawa (and according to traditional accounts, Shunten, the alleged son of Tametomo, a Minamoto prince, founded the first dynasty in 1187).[14]

With respect to its economy, Okinawa in the Omoro era had already passed the stage of hunting and gathering and was well along in the stage of settled agriculture and (shallow sea) fishing.[15] It is a general maxim that the more primitive the society, the greater the effort required for the acquisition of food. Thus, agriculture, as the single most important source of food, demanded most of the villagers' time and attention. As would be expected in a society such as that of Okinawa in the Omoro era, agriculture was inseparably associated with religion. At each important step in the cultivation of the crops, such as the sowing of seeds and the harvesting of fruits, there was a religious rite either asking for the protection of the *kami* or giving thanks for the crop just harvested. The following *omoro* was sung by the priestesses at the ceremony of *abushi-barai* (pronounced /abushi-baree/, meaning 'clearing away of the rice paddy dikes'), one of the two most important ceremonies related to rice culture, held in the fourth month of the lunar calendar.

Rice Ear Ceremony[16]

Amamikyo[1] ga, uzashi[2] sho	By the mandate of Amamikyo
Kono ōshima, oretare	On this great island descended.
Tomomo,[3] sue	For tens and hundreds of years,
Ogyakamoisu,[4] choware	Let King Shō Shin reign.

Shineryako ga, uzashi sho	By the mandate of Shineryako
Kono tashima,[5] oretare	On this grand island descended.
Hobana, tote, nukiageba	As we offer Thee the rice flowers,
Chirisabi[6] wa, tsukeruna	Let no harm come to the rice.
Hozaki,[7] tote, nukiageba	As we offer Thee the rice ears,
Kosabi[8] mo, tsukeruna	Let no evil come to the rice.

1. *Amamikyo*	Creator goddess of the islands of Ryūkyū.
2. *uzashi*	'To point to, to give a command, edict'. *U* is an honorific, *zashi* or *sashi* 'to point to'.
3. *tomomo*	*To* 'ten' plus *momo* 'hundred'. Same as in the literary or archaic Japanese. *Sue* 'future'.
4. *Ogyakamoisu*	Divine name of King Shō Shin (1478–1526). The divine name was used in addressing the *kami.*
5. *tashima*	Synonym for *ōshima*, meaning 'big island'.
6. *chirisabi*	'Literally, *chiri* means 'dust', and *sabi* 'rust'. However, here it means more than just dust or dirt. It means something dirty and therefore evil that does harm to the growing rice.
7. *hozaki*	Literally, 'ear-point'. *Ina-ho* or *ine-ho* is the word usually used to mean 'rice ear', but here *hozaki* was invented for the sake of alliteration with *hobana* which appears in a previous line.
8. *kosabi*	*Ko* means 'powder', also 'mud powder'. Its meaning here is similar to that of *chirisabi* (see item 6).

The fourth and fifth months of the lunar calendar marked a period called *yamadome* (pronounced /yamadumi/, literally, stopping mountain) or *monoimi* (pronounced /munuimi/, fasting or abstaining), during which all music and singing, cutting of trees and grasses, and going down to the beaches (the latter applicable particularly to women) were prohibited, for it was a time when the rice was most vulnerable, and the people feared disturbing the *kami.*[17] This is corroborated by the account of three shipwrecked Koreans from Cheju Island who were washed up on the shore of Yonaguni Island in 1447. They spent about a year and a half on Yonaguni and on several neighboring islands before they were finally sent back to Korea.[18] On Yonaguni Island they observed:

> In the second month, the rice grows about one foot, and in the fourth month, it is quite ripe. The early ripening rice is harvested in the fourth month, but the late ripening rice is harvested in the fifth month. After it is harvested, it grows again from the old roots left in the paddies. The second growth is even faster and more vigorous than the first. Before the harvest in the seventh or eighth month, the people are circumspect and do not talk loudly. Neither do they howl with their mouths distorted.

Once the rice had been safely harvested, the *yamadome* season ended, and there was great rejoicing.

In the fifth month, all the *noro* and *negami* head priestesses in Shuri assembled at the Royal Castle to offer thanksgiving for the harvest. The king himself participated in this ceremony by singing *omoro* in praise of the *kami.* In the villages, tokens of the first crop were collected and offered to the *otake.* The following *omoro* describes such a festival in the village of Yagi on the shore of Nakagusuku on the Pacific coast of central Okinawa.

Village Festival[20]

Yagi[1] no, Kana-mori[2] ni,	At Kana holy grove, In Yagi Village
Mahitobe[3] no, hyashi[4] utaba	When the villagers beat time,
Kimi[5] mo, nayora[6]	Even the high priestess will dance.
Higa[7] no, Kana-mori ni,	At Kana holy grove, In Higa Village
(Mahitobe no, hyashi utaba,)	(When the villagers beat time,)
(Kimi mo, nayora.)	(Even the high priestess will dance.)

1. *Yagi* — A village name as explained in the text. Yagi often served as a port for trade with Japan through Tokuno Island and Ōshima Island.

2. *Kana-mori* — Name of a holy grove. *Kana* is derived from *kanashi* 'to love'. *Kana* is often used in Okinawan and in archaic Japanese as an affix denoting affection. Though *mori* is used as a synonym for *take* or *otake*, there is a distinction—*mori* refers to a grove, but not necessarily a holy grove, whereas *otake* specifically refers to a grove which is a place of worship, a holy grove.

3. *mahitobe*	*Ma* 'true' plus *hito* 'person' plus *be* 'category' or 'group'. In ancient Japan, *be* meant a professional consanguineous group such as *imibe* or *kataribe*. Here, *mahitobe* means freemen, that is, the villagers in general.
4. *hyashi*	'Marking time, beating time by clapping hands'. Cognate to Japanese *hyoshi*.
5. *kami*	'Priestesses'.
6. *nayora*	'To turn or bend (one's body)', as in dancing.
7. *Higa*	Place name derived from *higashi* 'east'.

The *omoro* above is self-explanatory. In front of the holy grove, the villagers are gathered together, clapping their hands in time as they sing. In the center, perhaps, priestesses are dancing, turning, and bending as if in ecstasy. An air of gaiety is everywhere as the sounds of singing and clapping reecho in the woods and hills around. The following *omoro* tells us the kind of dance performed on the occasion of such a harvest festival.

Dancing Priestess[21]

Goeku,[1] ayamiya[2] ni	In the fair garden of Goeku
Kogane, ge[3] wa uete,	Are planted golden trees.
Kogane, ge ga shita	Under the golden trees,
Kimi no, aji[4] no	How beautifully our revered priestess
Shinoguri,[5] yowaru,[6] kiyora[7] ya	Dances the dance of Shinugu!
Goeku, kusemiya[8]	In the wondrous garden of Goeku
(Kogane, ge wa uete,)	(Are planted golden trees.)
(Kogane, ge ga shita)	(Under the golden trees,)
(Kimi no, aji no)	(How beautifully our revered priestess)
(Shinoguri, yowaru, kiyora ya.)	(Dances the dance of Shinugu!)

1. *Goeku*	Place name of a village in central Okinawa.
2. *ayamiya*	*Aya* plus *miya*. *Aya* by itself means 'figure' or 'design'; as a prefix it denotes beauty of design or figure or simply beauty. *Miya* refers to an open ground in front of the *otake*. It is also called *kami no miya*.

3. *kogane-ge*	*Kogane* is 'gold', and *ge*, 'tree'. Pronounced /kuganigi/. This is another name for the *kunenbo* tree (*citrus nobilis* Lour, king orange). The comma appears between *kogane* and *ge* rather than between *koganege* and *wa* because in the *omoro*, punctuation is placed not at the logical stop but at the musical stop where the singer stops or pauses.
4. *kimi no aji*	*Aji*, usually translated as 'lord (of the small local domain)', became a rank in the court. In later times, queens and princesses were also given this rank. Here it is used as a simple honorific.
5. *shinoguri*	'To dance (the dance called *shinugu*)'. See text, below, on the *shinugu* dance.
6. *yowaru*	Polite form of 'to act' or 'to do'.
7. *kiyora ya*	*Kiyora* 'clean', 'pure', 'beautiful' plus *ya*, an exclamation. Thus, *kiyora ya* means 'how beautiful!'
8. *kusemiya*	*Kuse* + *miya*. *Kuse* is a cognate of literary Japanese *kusushi*, and means 'strange, miraculous, or wonderful'. For *miya*, please see item 2 above.

The dance of *shinugu* that the priestess dances (more likely "priestesses," for generally, *shinugu* is a group dance, but we cannot be certain because the Okinawan language, like Japanese and Chinese, lacks plurals) in the *omoro* above is often written in Chinese characters as *hōnenmatsuri odori*, which means 'rich harvest festival dance'.[22] And that is what it has been for at least the last two or three hundred years. The *shinugu* dance is one of a series of dances called *usudeku*, and it is danced entirely by females at the festival dance in the sixth and eighth lunar months. However, it is believed that *shinugu* dance was once a magical dance symbolic of sexual intercourse performed for the purpose of accelerating the propagation and growth of rice and other grains. Because of its sexual symbolism, it was banned about 200 years ago by the ruling class, which embraced Confucian morality.[23] Iha states that in the early form of the *shinugu* dance, performed at a secluded spot prohibited to men, a number of women led by the priestess danced totally nude, signifying before the *kami* their purity.[24]

In still another *omoro*, which follows below, the sight of a divine parade (the occasion is not known) is vividly described. It is an auspicious day, and the sun is bright in the sky over the village. The hot summer sun is almost unbearable, but the big trees around and within the village create a cool dark shade. The rice paddies and fields are strangely quiet and almost deserted today, but within the village, the air is full of activity. The divine parade approaches; everyone is jovial and cheerful, and even the usually solemn priestess at the head of the parade steps high in good spirits. Dancers in costume and merrymakers in funny masks and disguises lead the parade. At the intersections, they often stop and burst out singing and dancing to the music. Then they form the parade again and go on to the *otake*. All those who line the route are laughing and talking, and they all seem happy and satisfied.

Divine Parade[25]

Seyaru,[1] kuniosoi[2]-gya	Virtuous Priestess Kuniosoi
Oesato-mori, orewache	Descended upon the grove of Uesato,
Momoto, agari,	And rose even for a hundred times,
Fumiagate, choware,	Step high, prevail!
Keuaru,[3] kuniosoi-gya	Spiritual Priestess Kuniosoi
(Oesato-more, orewache)	(Descended upon the grove of Uesato,)
(Momoto, agari,)	(And rose even for a hundred times,)
(Fumiagate, choware,)	(Step high, prevail!)
Kyo no, yokaru hi[4] ni	Today, the day of good omen,
Kyo no, kyakyaro hi[5] ni	Today, the day of brilliance,
Naoryo[6] wa, sadakete[7]	With the dancers guiding,
Amaeyo[8] wa, sadakete.	With the merrymakers leading.

1. *seyaru* — *Se* + *aru*. *Aru* means 'to be, to exist, or to have'. *Se*, pronounced /shii/, is a kind of magical power which dwells in an animate or inanimate object and gives it supernatural or divine power.
2. *Kuniosoi* — Name of the priestess. *Kuni* + *osoi*, literally, 'the ruler of the country'.
3. *keuaru* — *Ke-aru*, cognate of Japanese *ki*, is an ethereal substance like air. Here it is a synonym of *se* (see item 1 above).
4. *yokaru hi* — *Yokaru* 'luck', 'good' + *hi* 'day'.

5. *kyakyaro hi* — *Kyakyaro* + *hi. Hi* is obviously 'day'. But could *kyakyaro* be a form related to Japanese *kagero*, meaning 'heat haze', 'vibrating heat', or the 'shimmer of the air' which is characteristic of the hot Okinawan summer?

6. *naoryo* — Derived from *nayori*, literally, 'to twist'. Here it means one who twists the body in dance, i.e., a dancer.

7. *sadake* — 'To lead, to guide, to head a parade'.

8. *amaeyo* — Derived from *amae* 'to rejoice' or 'to coax'. It may correspond semantically to modern Okinawan *amaeyaa*, in which the suffix *-yaa* serves the same function as the English suffi*r;* that is, it forms a noun from a verb wherein the noun denotes the performer of the action of the verb from which it is derived, e.g., 'worker, singer'.

Fishing was very important to the primitive, primarily agricultural village economy in Omoro era Okinawa, especially for the numerous coastal communities. With the exception of large oceangoing vessels given to the kingdom by China[26] and owned by the king, most boats owned at the village level were dugout canoes, some large enough to carry ten to twenty persons.[27] Fishing technology was not yet highly developed and most fishing was restricted to nearby fishing grounds. Fishing nets were still very scarce and most fishing was done with handlines.

At this stage, villagers could not afford to depend solely on fishing for their livelihood. Apart from the matter of technology, the fish moved seasonally to certain fishing grounds, a matter beyond the control of the villagers. And even if they made a large catch, people didn't know how to preserve it. Therefore, coastal villages depended half on agriculture and half on fishing. When the season came around and the weather was good, they put out the boats to catch fish. During the off season or when the weather was bad, the men stayed home and tilled the farms and paddies.

To the people of the Omoro era, the ocean was more than a source of food. It was also a source of great mystery. For beyond the ocean lay the paradise of *Nirai-kanai*[28] from which all food originated.[29] It was from beyond the horizon that strange and powerful men came, and all treasure and knowledge brought. In fact, it was from beyond the ocean that the Great Master of the East (*Agari no ōnushi*, the Sun God) had come. Therefore, it was natural for the people to kneel in early morning worship of the sunrise over the eastern sea.

Worship of the Sunrise[30]

Agarui[1] no, ōnushi ga	Great Master of the East,
Maekachi,[2] ayosorote,[3]	Let us all be of one mind before you.
Yagumetete,[4] shirarere.[5]	And say, "How revered! How revered!"
Teda ga ana[6] no, ōnushi	Great Master of the Orient,
(Maekachi, ayosorote,)	(Let us all be of one mind before you.)
(Yagumetete, shirarere.)	(And say, "How august! How august!")

1. *agarui* Derived from *agari* 'to rise', hence, the east, where the sun rises.

2. *maekachi* The original is *maekara*, but Nakahara believes this to be a miscopy of *maekachi* and has made a correction. Mae means 'front or before', and *kachi* points to a direction.

3. *ayosorote* *Ayo* + *sorote. Ayo* means 'liver', where man's mind or soul was thought to dwell; thus, it also came to be used as a synonym of mind or soul. *Sorote* means 'to be in order, to be uniform'.

4. *yagumetete* *Yagume* 'to revere', 'to worship' plus *tete* 'having said so' or 'saying so'.

5. *shirarere* *Shirare* plus a repetition of the ending for emphasis. *Shirare* means 'to be known, to say (to a superior)'.

6. *teda ga ana* *Teda* 'sun' + *ana* 'hole' connected by *ga*. It was thought that the sun came up through a hole in the sky over the horizon.

The following *omoro*, which also sings of the sunrise, does not seem to possess as deep a religious sentiment as the preceding one. It merely praises the sunrise as a beautiful sight.

In Praise of the Sunrise[31]

Chiten[1] toyomu,[2] ōnushi	Great Master reechoing in heaven and earth.
Chura[3] no, hana no,	What a sight!
Sai, wataru,[5] mimon.[6]	A bright flower just bloomed all over!
Tenchi[7] toyomu, ōnushi	Great Master resounding in heaven and earth
(Chura no, hana no,)	(What a sight!)
(Sai, wataru, mimon.)	(A bright flower just bloomed all over!)

1. *chiten*	*Chi* 'earth' + *ten* 'heaven'. The usual word order in such a pairing is *tenchi*—heaven and earth—as in line 4, but here it is reversed, perhaps merely as a poetic device.
2. *toyomu*	'To resound, to reecho, to ring'.
3. *chura*	Elsewhere written as *kiyora*, meaning 'clean, beautifu'l, here the native pronounciation is copied as it is, which is unusual in the *Omoro sōshi.*
4. *sai*	*Sai* is *saki* 'to bloom' with the *k* dropped.
5. *wataru*	The sun's beam shining radiantly at once all over heaven and earth like a giant flower.
6. *mimon*	*Mi* 'to see' + *mon* or *mono* '[an] object', therefore, a matter to see, a sight, a spectacular sight. What is seen is usually some sort of activity rather than a still object.
7. *tenchi*	Reverse of *chiten* (see item 1, above).

A boat or ship was the only means of transportation over the vast, mysterious ocean that surrounded the Ryūkyū Islands. It is little wonder that great importance was attached to the building and launching of a boat, an endeavor which also became the subject of religious ritual. In the following *omoro,* we will see the priestess's role in these matters.

On Okinawa Island, the largest in the Ryūkyū archipelago, there was a plentiful supply of timber for shipbuilding, especially from the mountainous hills of northern Okinawa. But even on Okinawa Island, good timber was reserved for the use of the king in building oceangoing vessels. Most villages had to depend on local supplies. On some islands where big timbers were not available, people depended upon driftwood and timber that the currents and monsoon winds or, just as often, violent typhoons carried to their shores. The following *omoro* comes from Kumejima Island where the timber was unsuitable for building large boats.

Prayer for Driftwood[32]

Kikoe, Senokimi ga	May the heart's desire
Omoi no, ogimo,[1]	Of the renowned Senokimi
Tōche,[2] mioyase,	Be realized.
Toyomu, Senokimi ya	May the heart's desire

(Omoi no, ogimo,)	(Of the famed Senokimi)
(Tōche, mioyase.)	(Be fulfilled.)
Makochi,[3] kazu,[4] fukemu	When the straight east wind blows,
Oechi,[5] kazu, fukemu	When the good tailwind blows,
Arakaki no, makyo[6] ni	To the *makyo* of Arakaki
Toirosuki,[7] yorache.[8]	May ten *hiro* long cedar timber drift.

1. *ogimo* — O (honorific) + *hiro* or *kimo* 'liver (thought to be the dwelling place of the mind, soul, or spirit).
2. *tōche* — 'To let something pass'.
3. *makochi* — *Ma-* + *kochi*. *Ma-* is a prefix meaning 'true', 'straight', 'good'. *Kochi*, the same as in archaic Japanese, means 'east wind'.
4. *kazu* — 'Wind'.
5. *oechi* — 'Tailwind'.
6. *makyo* — Ancient consanguineous village.
7. *toirosuki* — *To* + *(h)iro* + *suki*. *To* means 'ten'. *Hiro*, which drops the h in combination, is a measurement of length equal to the outstretched arms of an adult man. *Sugi* is the Japanese cedar *Cryptomeria japonica* D. Don.
8. *yorache* — *Yorache*, derived from Japanese *yoru, yorasu*, means 'to let something come near or drift'.

The following *omoro*, composed on the occasion of a launching ceremony, describes important steps in the course of shipbuilding. The first four lines call upon the captain to sail the *Ukikiyora* (Floating Beauty). The fifth line begins a description of the shipbuilding process. First, the priestess (whose name was Koeshino, and who was a younger sister, and thus the sister goddess of Tarako, the captain) prayed to the deity of the Higatake, a sacred grove, perhaps for permission to cut down the trees there as well as for assistance and protection in building the *Ukikiyora*. The villagers then climbed the Ohagaguchi ascent, selected good shiny timber, and chopped it down. Next, they tied ropes around it and pulled it down to the dockyard where the boat was built. Now that the boat has been built, it will be launched today. After the launch, it will go to the port of Naha where it will be welcomed and blessed by the king.

The Launching Ceremony[33]

Goku[1] no, makoroku[2] yo	Good man of the House of Goku,
Ukikiyora,[3] haryase,[4]	Run the *Floating Beauty.*
Tarako,[5] kainadekoro[6]	Beloved Tarako,
(Ukikiyora, haryase.)	(Run the *Floating Beauty.)*
Koeshino[7] wa takabete[8]	Priestess Koeshino prayed,
Onarikami,[9] takabete	The sister goddess prayed,
Hikatake[10] ni, nobote,	Climbed the Higatake (holy grove),
Ohogakuchi[11] nobote,	Climbed the Ohogaguchi ascent,
Yokaru, ke wa erade[12]	Picked the good timber,
Kyakyaru ke wa,[13] erade	Chose the shining timber,
Mototsukena,[14] natsukete[15]	Tied ropes around the root,
Yamatsukena,[16] natsukete.	Tied lines around the end.
Surakara no,[17] hayaoune[18]	Fast boat from the dockyard,
Suekara no,[19] hayaoune	Fast boat from the shipyard,
Nahadomari,[20] haryaeha[21]	When she runs to the port of Naha,
Oyadomari,[22] haryaeha	When she runs to the Great Port,
Momo oune no,[23] funasaki,[24]	She'll be the head of a hundred boats,
Yaso[25] oune no, funasaki.	She'll be the head of eighty boats

1. *Goku*	A household name still said to exist at Uegusuku, Nakazato-son, Kumejima Island.
2. *makoroku*	*Ma-*, prefix meaning 'true', 'good' + *koroku. Koro* means 'man'. *Makoroku* or *makoroko* is a common noun. The *makoroku* is the center of secular activities in the village and is the same person as the root man or *nebito (nehito)*, brother of the root *kami*, or *negami.* The pair were also called *wonari* (younger sister) and *ekeri* (elder brother).
3. *ukikiyora*	*Uki* 'to float' + *kiyora* 'beautiful'.
4. *haryase*	'To let run, to sail'. Japanese *hashirase.*
5. *Tarako*	Man's name. He is the captain referred to as *makoroku* in line 1.

6. *kainadekoro*	*Kainade* 'to pat' + *koro* 'man', thus, a man loved by everyone.
7. *Koeshino*	Name of the priestess of Uegusuku Village, Kumejima. She is known to have sailed to many islands.
8. *takabete*	*Takabe* means 'to praise (the gods), to pray (to the gods)'. The words of prayer are called *otakabegoto. Takabe* might have originally meant 'to heighten', 'to ennoble', 'to enhance', and hence, to praise the god.
9. *onarikami*	Since the Priestess Koeshino is the sister of Taraki, she is called *onarikami* 'sister goddess'. This also indicates that Tarako is either the head of the *neya* root house or his eldest son.
10. *Hikatake*	Name of the holy grove of the village. *Hika* is derived from *higashi* 'east'.
11. *Ohogakuchi*	*Kuchi* is mouth, or ascent or route when applied to a mountain. The meaning of *ohoga* is not known.
12. *kewaerade*	If the comma were logically placed, the line would read /yokaru-ke-wa, erade/. *Yokaru* means 'good'. *Ke* = *ki*, 'tree'. *Erade* is a conjugated form of *erabu*, 'to choose'.
13. *kyakyaru ke wa*	*Kyakyaru* 'shining' + *ke* 'tree'. For derivation of *kyakyaru*, see Divine Parade, note 5, earlier in this chapter.
14. *mototsukena*	*Moto* 'origin', 'root' + *tsuke* 'to attach', 'to fasten' + na *(nawa)* 'rope', 'cord', 'line'. Thus, the rope tied around the timber.
15. *natsukete*	*Na* 'rope' + *tsukete* 'having fastened or tied'. *Na* is not really needed here, but is merely repeated for emphasis.
16. *yamatsukena*	*Yama* 'mountain' + *tsuke* 'fasten' + *na* 'rope'. It is not clear whether this means a rope tied to a certain part of a timber called *yama* or whether the rope is simply called *yamatsukena* because it is used in the hills.
17. *surakarano*	*Sura* 'dockyard' + *karano* 'from'.

18. *hayaoune*	*Haya* 'fast' + honorific *o* + *fune* 'ship', 'boat'. (The *f* of *fune* is dropped.) Fast boat, ship.
19. *sue*	Meaning unknown, but used here as a parallel for *sura* 'dockyard'.
20. *Nahadomari*	*Naha* is the name of a town. *Tomari* means to stop, hence, a port or harbor. It is often incorporated into place names.
21. *haryaeha*	In the *Omoro sōshi*, there is a tendency to leave out the sonant signs where they should occur. In this case, *haryaeha* could be read as *haryaeba*, related to Japanese *hashireba* which means '[if or] when it runs'.
22. *oyadomari*	*Oya* is parent, hence used as a prefix meaning great.
23. *momo oune no*	*Momo* 'hundred' + *no* 'of + *oune* 'ship(s)'. For *oune*, see item 18, above.
24. *funasaki*	*Funa (fune)* 'ship' + *saki* 'top' or 'front' Thus, at the head of or in front of.
25. *yaso*	Eighty.

The following *omoro* pertains to another boat launching ceremony. It describes, instead of the boat building process, proud and tender concern for the completed ship which has just been launched from the shipyard. It also mentions preparations for a feast or celebration—many wine jars, an offering to the *kami*, have been set out in the yard.

The Launching Ceremony[34]

Tomari, Micherikyo[1]	Mizerikyo of Tomari port,
Soyora soyora,[2] haryase.	May it sail smoothly and calmly.
Yaware,[3] Micherikyo	Mizerikyo of Yawari port,
(Soyora soyora, haryase)	(May it sail slowly and gently.)
Tomari, ayamya ni[4]	In the fair yard of Tomari
Yaware, ayamya ni	In the fair yard of Yawari
Hyaku kame wa,[5] suete	Hundred wine jars set down,
Yaso kame wa, suete	Eighty wine jars set down,

Kami, hokoru,[6] soyakeko[7]	May God be pleased with the boat,
Taka,[8] hokoru, soyakeko	May the Most High be proud of the boat,
Kami hokote kara	Now that God is pleased,
Taka hokote kara	Now that the Most High is proud,
Mikazuki no,[9] mitsuyani[10]	As the new moon grows,
Yokazuki no,[11] mitsuyani.	As the quarter moon grows, [May it sail smoothly.]

1. *Micherikyo* Divine name of a priestess, used in addressing the gods. *Micherikyo* is *Mizerikyo* without the sonant added. *Mizeri* is *misezeri* which means 'divine message, oracle', and *kyo*, as in the case of *Amamikyo*, means 'person'. *Micherikyo* or *Mizerikyo* means, literally, one who reveals a divine message.

2. *soyora* 'Gently, calmly, softly, or slowly, without abrupt motion'. Similar to Japanese *soyo-kaze* 'gentle wind', 'breeze'.

3. *yaware* Related to Japanese *yawara*, meaning soft, tender, subdued, etc. Here it is used to parallel *Tomari*, with the meaning pacific (calm) port.

4. *ayamya ni* *Aya + mya + ni. Ayamya* means 'a fair garden or yard'; *aya* means 'figure, design'; hence, 'beautiful design'. *Mya* is cognate to Japanese *niwa* 'garden', 'yard'. *Ni* is the particle, 'at' or 'in'.

5. *hyaku kame* *Hyaku* 'hundred* + *kame* 'jar', 'wine jar'.

6. *hokoru* 'To be proud of, to felicitate, to celebrate'.

7. *soyakeko* Another name for the boat, etymology unknown.

8. *Taka* 'High', used in parallel with *kami.*

9. *mikazuki* 'Third day moon', i.e., new or crescent moon, since the new moon appears on about the third day each month in the lunar calendar.

10. *mitsuyani* *Mitsu* 'to become full', 'to fill', 'to grow' + *yani*, corruption of Japanese *yoni* 'like' 'as'.

11. *yokazuki* 'Fourth day moon'.

The next *omoro* comes from Tokashiki village in the Kerama Islands. When spring comes around and the wheat is in blossom, and the current at the mouth of the river builds up, it is again time for the villagers to send out the boat of the *negami* (the root *kami)* of the village to catch turtles and dugongs. With the *nebito* (the root man) as captain, they sail from Tsukuchi harbor through mountainous waves to the fishing grounds. Sailing here and there in search of a catch, they meet a ship from the neighboring village of Ama. If their leader asks you if you have caught any turtles, if you have caught any dugongs, says the poem, tell him you haven't caught anything, tell him you don't know anything.

Besides describing the first fishing of the spring season, this *omoro* tells us the following. First, although the boat is communal property and not the private property of the *negami*, it is the *negami*'s boat in the sense that she is the spiritual leader of the village. Second, the spiritual and religious authority of the *negami* as the representative owner of the boat is confirmed and endorsed in actual practice by the captaincy of her brother who is the *nebito*, the secular authority. This is a good instance of the sovereignty practiced by the brother-sister pair at the village level. Third, the last conversation with the leader of the neighboring village seems to reveal a taboo which stemmed not from mere jealousy but from the belief that a village's source of supply is a secret given it by its own *kami* and that it must be guarded from outsiders. Fourth, and last, the expressed object of this fishing—to catch turtles and dugongs—suggests that this fishing trip was made to catch turtles and dugongs which would be delivered to the king as tax in kind. The turtle has always been a symbol of longevity, and the dugong, as the subject of many mermaid tales, was regarded as the source of the elixir of life indispensable in the royal cuisine. In those days, the dugong was protected from random capture by the belief that anyone who caught it would be cursed for seven generations; its capture was sanctioned only when it was to be presented to the king. It was an important item of tax in kind, especially from the Yaeyama Islands. Naturally, there were religious rituals related to dugong hunting. Keeping a hunting ground secret was more than practically desirable; in fact, its disclosure must have become taboo.[35]

The First Fishing in the Spring[36]

Moriaikimi[1]	Priestess of the village,
Kiminisha ga,[2] isōko[3]	Priestess's boat,
Nami tsuriyose,[4] tsuriawache.	Plows through the crests of waves.
Tokashiki no, makoroku	True man of Tokashiki

Makoroku wa, neshari.[5]	Captains the boat.
Tsukuchi no,[6] shiyu no[7]	When the current of Tsukuchi
Ibuchi,[8] agatekureba	Swells up higher,
Aramukya ga[9]	When the new wheat,
Oromukya ga hobana[10]	Sparse wheat blossoms out,
Ichi no, tomo'osoi ga[11]	If the first oarman,
Amano, monomonosha[12]	Head of the Ama asks,
Kame toteru[13]	Have you caught turtles?
Zan toteruteyaha[14]	Have you caught dugongs?
Torantete[15]	Tell him, "I haven't caught anything."
Shirantete, shirarere.[16]	Tell him, "I don't know anything."

1. *moriaikimi* — *Moriai* 'to form a group' + *kima* 'priestess'.
2. *kiminisha* — *Kimi* + *nisha*, an honorific prefix.
3. *isoko* — 'Boat'. Derived from archaic Japanese *itsukomione* 'soldier's boat'.
4. *nami tsuriyose* — *Nami* 'wave' + *tsuriyose* 'lift up together' or 'raise up together'. *Tsuriawache* has a similar meaning. It describes the sight of the waves mounting up and breaking abruptly as the boat plows through them.
5. *neshari* — *Ne* 'root' + *shari* or *shiari* 'to do'. Thus, to be the root of, to act as root, to be principal of, or to be the leader of.
6. *tsukuchi* — *Tsu* 'harbor', 'port' + *kuchi* 'mouth'.
7. *shiyu* — Related to Japanese *shio* 'tide', 'current'.
8. *ibuche* — Verb derived from *ibuki* 'breath', therefore, 'to breathe'. It describes the sight of the rhythmic foaming and rising of the tide.
9. *aramukya* — *Ara* 'new' + *mukya*, corruption of *mugi* 'wheat'.
10. *oromukya ga hobana* — *Oro* 'sparse' + *mukya* 'wheat' + *ga* 'of' + *ho* 'ear' + *hana* 'blossom'. In about February in the lunar calendar, new wheat blossoms out sparsely here and there.

11. *tomo'osoi*	*Tomo* 'stern' + *osoi* 'one who pushes'.
12. *monomonosha*	Meaning unknown. However, Nakahara states that it may be a miscopy of *monoinisha*. *Monoinisha* consists of *mono* 'thing' or 'matter', *i* 'to speak', and *nasha* 'mister', hence, the speaker, the leader.
13. *kame toteru*	*Kame* 'turtle' + *toteru*, related to *toru* 'to catch' and *totta* 'caught'.
14. *zan*	'Dugong, manatee', also called *zan no io*, literally, 'fish of *zan*'.
15. *torantete*	'... saying not to have caught anything'.
16. *shirarere*	*Shirare* means 'to be known, to let be known'. An honorific expression for 'to tell'.

Let us now consider the following account of a communal fishing event from early in the twentieth century:

> In the sea around Okinawa, depending upon the season, there are always various schools of fish and marine mammals migrating from one spot to another. When a big school of fish comes near the shore, the fish are so thick that they even change the color of the sea. One of the most famous is the school of porpoises that comes almost every year to Nago Bay.
>
> For instance, on Tonaki Island, every year when the season begins, the villagers are on the alert for the coming of the fish. Early one morning, the loud beating of a drum is suddenly heard from the top of a hill overlooking the beach. It is the village chief's signal that a school of fish is approaching. In a few minutes, all of the people in the village, young and old, men and women, are out on the beach. All the available boats are put out with nets and spears. Some boats quickly row away to the distance. Some are held in reserve near the inlet. Everyone on shore is waiting and watching tensely with excitement and expectation.
>
> The village chief on top of the hill has a big branch of black boxtree in his hand. As the school of fish moves, he jumps up and down, waving the branch of black boxtree in every direction to signal the boats for strategic movements. He looks as if he is dancing—jumping up and down, waving both hands, and shouting and yelling commands.
>
> When the boats have encircled the school of fish and have gradually chased them toward the nets and shallow water near the beach, the young men impatiently jump into the water and frantically do everything they

can—hitting the water, waving the ropes—to chase the fish into the nets. When all the fish are in the nets, they are so dense that one can't even see the water. Now everyone with a basket scoops the fish into the boats. In a few minutes, the boats are full of fish. Everyone in the water and on the beach is shouting with joy.

In the meanwhile, on the beach, children gather small rocks and pebbles and make piles of them in several places, and they make a fire over them so that the pebbles get red hot. The women make pits in the sand and line the bottoms with leaves of the *nbashi* [*Alocasis macrorhiza* S. Chott] or other leaves making them like big shallow pans.

The fish are washed in brine, placed in the pits, and covered with leaves. The red hot pebbles are shovelled over them. Hot steam shoots off into the air, and a delicious aroma wafts over the entire beach. The people sit on straw mats which are spread around the pits. Wine is passed around among the adults. Children squeeze in among the grownups. The cooked fish are distributed, and a big feast is on. Tongues become light, and the children are gay and jump about. When enough wine has gone around, songs are sung and dances are danced. The entire beach is full of happy people. When everyone has eaten and drunk his fill, and has sung and danced and is now getting tired—it is already late afternoon approaching dark. By three and fours, they go home with leftovers in their hands.[37]

The preceding is a rather liberal translation of a description of a scene on Tonaki Island at the beginning of the 1900s. Are these customs—communal fishing, communal cooking, and communal feasting—not reminiscent of the ancient life? Food has a deep relationship to spiritual life, and the idea that spiritual union among men can be obtained by eating the same food together exists even today. Indeed, the purpose of communal eating and drinking was to strengthen group unity and solidarity.

The following *omoro*, though brief, conveys the spirit of a communal fishing party:

The Village Goes to the Shore[38]

Komaka[1] no, mio[2] ni, ore, mimon	Down the channel of Komaka, what a sight!
Kudaka[3] no, mio ni, (ore, mimon)	Down the channel of Kudaka, (what a sight!)
Zan, ami, musibi, oroche	Cast the dugong nets,

Kame, ami, musubi, oroche	Cast the turtle nets.
Zan, hyaku, komete,	Round up a hundred dugongs,
Kame, hyaku, komete,	Round up a hundred turtles,
Zan, hyaku, toriyari,	To catch a hundred dugongs,
Kame, hyaku, toriyari,	To catch a hundred turtles,
Oki, namasu,[4] seseto[5]	The inner weir fishermen,
Hetanamasu, seseto	The outer weir fishermen,
Tekaji[6] erade, nosete,	And the captain chosen and aboard,
Oki[7] haitate[8] no, isoite,	Boats are hurrying to the off,
Hise[9] haitate no, isoite.	Boats are hastening to the reef.

1. *Komaka*	Name of an island near Kudaka Island.
2. *mio*	'Water route, fairway, channel'.
3. *Kudaka*	Name of an island.
4, 5. *okinamasu, hetanamasu*	Nakahara Zenchū and Shimabukuro Genshichi proposed two different interpretations of these terms. It is difficult to reject either one; therefore, while I have adopted Shimabukuro's interpretation in the translation above (further discussed in the text below), I present Nakahara's interpretation as follows: In examining *okinamasu seseto* and *hetanamasu seseto*, he leaves out *oki ... seseto* and *heta ... seseto as* unknown, but emphasizes *namasu*, which means fish salad, hence, 'to make mincemeat of something'. The translation of the lines would then be something like /To make Oki-namasu fish salad/ /To make Heta-namasu fish salad/. Though the result is not too incongruous, Nakahara leaves too much out of these sentences.
6. *tekaji*	*Te* 'hand' + *kaji* 'rudder' or 'helm'.
7. *oki*	'The offing, the open sea'.

8. *haitate*	Literally, to run, rush, or dash. Here it refers to the boat.
9. *hise*	'Shore reef'.

As previously noted, fish were thought to be a *yorimono* ('that which comes drifting') from the paradise called *Nirai-kanai* beyond the ocean; that is, the people believed the fish to be a gift sent to them by the great *kami* of *Nirai-kanai.* This being the case, they did not actively go out in pursuit of a catch. Instead, they prayed to the *kami* and patiently waited for the *kami* to send a gift. Due to such a passive attitude, most of their fishing was done by means of various stationary weirs. Most usual was the kind called *nagaki* (literally, fish fence; weir), some of which still exist around the smaller islands. In his book *Karimata*, W. W. Burd describes one which he saw off the coast of Karimata village, Miyako Island:

> There are nine of these weirs off the northeastern coast, and six between the arms ending the peninsula. The weirs consist of decomposed coral rocks, built into walls which are nowhere over two feet high. Starting in water a few inches deep at low tide they form "Vs" with the end of the "V" in water about a foot deep at very low tide. At the end of the "V" there is an opening into a sort of club shaped trough called *bufuga*, which is about twenty feet long and four feet wide at the middle. It is from this that the fish are taken, three or four days a month at the lowest tides, being netted out with small nets laid on the bottom. The weirs are said to be very old and are the property of families who are the descendants of those who originally constructed them. Only those families have the right to fish in the traps at the ends of the weirs.[39]

The weirs were built in pairs; one of the pair for low tide and the other for high tide. One pair of weirs, called *noro-gaki*, was reserved for the use of the *noro* priestess as the source of her supply of fish as well as the ritual site for the sea *kami.* The villagers were divided into small groups, each assigned to a specific weir. The group assigned to the inner weir was called in Okinawan *uchinamasushiji* (in the traditional *omoro* transcription, *okinamasusese*, which is roughly translated as 'inner weir tribe'), and the other, assigned to the outer weir, was called *hetanamasushiji* (in the *omoro* transcription, *hetanamasusese*, 'outer weir tribe').[40]

As long as the villagers believed that fish were a gift from the *kami*, the priestess, as intermediary between man and *kami*, was highly respected. She performed her duties not only in praying to the *kami* for an abundant catch but also in finding ideal locations for the construction of weirs. From experience, she found that fish tended to congregate in the dark water in the shadow of a headland woods (where there are trees near the water, plankton thrive) and that the weirs had to be built where the tide lines of both low and high tide would lead the fish into the weirs.[41]

There are some boat *omoro* which merely describe priestesses sailing somewhere. They do not seem to be connected with any religious rituals. Two examples are shown here.

Sailing of the Priestess Akeshino[42]

Akeshino[1] no, kaminisha	Princess Akeshino has,
Yarekae,[2] yayano[3]	*Yareke*, beautiful
Yahou,[4] aorache[5]	Flying jib up, flapping
Nayokasa[6] no, noronisha	Priestess Nayokasa has,
(Yarekae, yayano.)	(*Yareke*, beautiful)
(Yahou, aorache)	(Flying jib up, flapping.)
Asadore,[7] yodore,	In the morning calm, in the evening calm,
Itakyora,[8] tanakyora	On the Itakyora, on the Tanakyora,
Funako,[9] erade, tekaji, erade	Sailors are chosen, coxswains are chosen,
Akeshino wa, sedo,[10] shichosu.[11]	What a good captain Akeshino is!
Nayokasa wa, tetori[12] chosu.	What a good coxswain Nayokasa is!
Sodekyora wa, yutori[13] chosu.	What a good bailer Sodekyora is!
Kazenote[14] ya, hofukuro[15] ni, shinae[16]	Sails are supple in the wind,
Naminote ya, funahara ni shine.[17]	Bottoms are pliant against the waves.

1. *Akeshino*	Name of a priestess of Nakijin in northern Okinawa. She is very well known and appears in many *omoro.*
2. *yarekae*	A refrain.
3,4. *yayano yahou*	*Yaya* 'beautiful' + *yahou* (= *yaho*) 'flying jib'.
5. *aorache*	Derived from *aori* 'flapping', 'blast', 'gust'.
6. *Nayokasa*	Name of another priestess.

7. *asadore, yodore*	*Asa* is 'morning', *yo*, 'evening'. *Dore* or *tore* is 'calm, lull'.
8. *itakyora*	*Ita* 'board' + *kyora* 'beautiful', an appellation used as a synonym for the boat. *Tanakyora* is a synonym of *Itakyora.*
9. *funako*	'Sailor, seaman'.
10. *sedo*	Variation of *sendo* 'seaman', 'sailor', 'master of a junk'.
11. *shichosu*	Variation of *shi-jozu, shi* 'do', *jozu* 'good at', 'skillful at'.
12. *tetori*	*Te* 'hand' + *tori* 'take up', 'hold', or 'handle'. Refers, perhaps, to the handling of the rudder.
13. *yutori*	*Yu* 'bilge'. *Yutori* 'bailer'.
14. *kazenote*	*Kaze* 'wind' + *no* 'of' + *te*. Currents of wind.
15. *hofukuro*	*Ho* 'sail' + *fukuro* 'sack'. Describes the way the sail is catching the full wind.
16. *shinae*	Derived from *shinau* 'bend', 'be pliant' 'be flexible', 'be supple'.
17. *funahara ni shine*	*Funahara* 'ship's bottom' + *ni* 'at' + *shine*, which Nakahara says is a miscopy of *shinae.*

The *omoro* above describes the peaceful sight of the three priestesses, Akeshino, Nayokasa, and Sodekyora, at the helm of the beautiful, billowing-sailed ship.

Sailing of Priestess Akeshino[43]

Akeshino no kaminisha ga	Priestess Akeshino sails
Nanja,[1] kogane,[2] yorache.[3]	The rolling *Nanja-kogane.*
Hariyoru, kiyora ya.	How beautiful!
Nayokasa no, noronisha	Priestess Nayokasa sails
Nanja, kogane, yorache.	The rolling *Nanja-kogane.*
Hariyoru, kiyora ya.	How beautiful!
Asadore[4] ga, shoreba.[5]	In the morning calm.

1, 2. *nanja-kogane*	*Nanja* is related to *nanryo, nanrya*, a Japanese silver coin. From this, it came to mean 'silver'. *Kogane* is 'gold'. Here it is the name of the ship, the *Nanja-kogane*.
3. *yorache*	Derived from *yure* 'rock', 'pitch', 'roll'.
4. *asadore*	'Morning calm'. However, as it does not seem to make sense to say a ship rolling or pitching in the calm, it must mean that the ship is rolling slowly and gently.
5. *shoreba*	The -ba form of the verb 'to do', meaning in context either 'because it is' or 'because it does'.

The following *omoro* deals once again with agriculture. After the crops have been harvested and the *kami* have been properly thanked, crops must be stored in the granaries. The next *omoro* relates in simple verses that a forest of granaries is being built in Hanagusuku, Gushichan-son, southern Okinawa. The granary (in Japanese, *takakura*, or 'high storehouse') is constructed with special features for the storing of rice and other grains. Ordinarily it is hexagonal, but sometimes it is square, octagonal, nonagonal, or even a polygon of sixteen pillars. The pillars are either round or square, and the floor is usually about five or six feet off the ground. The walls, made either of wooden boards or bamboo matting, often tilt outward. The roof is thatched and shaped like a cone. Entry is made by means of a ladder. This type of granary is most frequently seen throughout the Ryūkyū Islands and the Izu Islands south of Tokyō. It is also found in Shizuoka, Japan, and in Formosa.[44]

Building Granaries[45]

Kikoe, Hanagusuku,[1]	In the famed Hanagusuku,
Momo kura,[2] hikitsureru[3]	Granary building,
Okura,[4] gerae.[5]	Hundreds of granaries.
Toyomu, Hanagusuku,	In the renowned Hanagusuku,
(Momo kura, hikitsureru)	(Granary building,)
(Okura, gerae.)	(Hundreds of granaries.)

1. *Hanagusuku*	Name of a village in southern Okinawa. The name means 'flowery castle'.
2. *momo kura*	*Momo* 'hundred' + *kura* 'storehouse'.

3. *hikitsureru*	'To take (someone or something in company), to lead (a company)', possibly a reference to the communal effort required to build structures such as granaries (though this is not reflected in the translation).
4. *okura*	*O*, honorific prefix + *kura* 'storehouse'.
5. *gerae*	'To build'.

On the occasion of building granaries or of filling them up, there seems to have been a festival or ritual of some kind. The following *omoro* comes from Chatan village in central Okinawa. In front of the impressive forest of overflowing granaries, the renowned priestess Kimitoyomi is beating a drum in a magnificent fashion. The lesser priestesses follow in unison, enhancing the sacred and solemn atmosphere of the ceremony as the sound of the drums vibrates and echoes in the neighboring hills and woods.

Drumming Priestesses[46]

Kikoe, Kimitoyomi	Renowned Kimitoyomi,
Setaka,[1] Kimi, toyomi.	Noble-spirited Kimitoyomi.
Uchiche,[2] mimon, Kimi.[3]	What majestic drumming Famed Kimitoyomi!
Kitatan no, mya[4] ni	In the garden of Kitatan,
Aganasa[5] no, mya ni	In the garden of our lord,
Tamayose[6] ga, mae ni,[7]	Where the spirit abounds,
Yoritachi[8] ga, mae ni,	Where the granaries stand together,
Momokuchi[9] no, tsuzumi[10]	Hundred drums,
Yasokuchi no, nariyobu.[11]	Eighty drums thundering the air.

1. *setaka*	*Se* is 'spirit or power (that attaches itself to someone or something)', making that person or object sacred and holy. All priestesses are said to possess it. *Taka* means 'high, noble'.
2. *uchiche*	'To beat, to strike'.
3. *kimi*	Refers to *Kimitoyomi*.
4. *mya*	Also *nya*, 'garden' or 'yard'.

5. *aganasa*	*A* 'I' or 'we', as in archaic Japanese. *Aga* is 'my' or 'our'. *Nasa* is derived from *nasu* 'to make', 'to give birth to', and it means one who gives birth and brings up offspring, i.e., parent. Here it is an appellation of the lord.
6. *tamayose*	*Tama* 'spirit', 'soul', as in *tamashii. Yose* is to draw together.
7. *mae ni*	*Mae* 'front' + *ni* 'at', hence, 'in front of'.
8. *yoritachi*	*Yori* 'to come together' + *tachi* 'to stand'. Here *tachi* refers to the numerous pillars of granaries standing.
9. *momokuchi*	*Momo* 'hundred' + *kuchi* 'piece'. *Momokuchi* means 'hundred pieces of'.
10. *tsuzumi*	'Drum'.
11. *nariyobu*	*Nari* 'to sound', 'to peal', etc., + *yobu* 'to call', 'to echo'.

In Okinawa, the Hokuzan (Northern Mountain) kingdom was defeated by King Shō Hashi of the Chūzan (Central Mountain) kingdom in 1416. The Nanzan (Southern Mountain) kingdom followed the fate of Hokuzan in 1422, completing the unification of Okinawa under the hegemony of Chūzan, the capital of which was located at Shuri. Hence, in the latter part of the *omoro* period, Okinawa enjoyed many decades of peace. In those years, without the frequent interruptions and damage of internal wars, and with all the energy and wealth that could now be directed toward peaceful occupations, the tiny kingdom of Ryūkyū began to prosper as never before. The period approximately coincident with the reign of King Shō Shin (1477–1526) was the first golden age of Okinawan history. Although the signs of prosperity were mainly manifested in the two towns—the castle town of Shuri and the trade port of Naha, which are discussed in more detail below—the general prosperity of the kingdom did not leave the rural areas unaffected.

Two formal histories, *Chūzan sekan* (Mirror of the world of the Central Mountain Kingdom, written by Shō Jo-ken in 1650) and *Chūzan seifu* (Genealogy of the Central Mountain Kingdom, written by Sai Taku in 1701), record the achievements of the two founders of the royal dynasties, King Satto (reigned 1350–1394, founder of the Satto dynasty) and King Shō Hashi (reigned 1422–1439, founder of the First Shō Dynasty) before they became kings. The two rulers gained popularity and power by distributing to farmers agricultural implements made with iron that they purchased from Japanese and other foreign trade ships that frequented the coast of Okinawa.[47] On the islands of Miyako and Yaeyama there are tales, probably older than those above, of how the introduction of iron farm implements eliminated the hitherto frequent famines and instead brought rich harvests. Two brothers and their servants made a long and difficult journey overseas to Satsuma (now Kagoshima, Japan) to purchase iron with which implements were made.[48] The stories above are endorsed by the following information recorded in the official Chinese document, *Tai-ming hui-ten.*[49] In 1372, in one of the earliest trades with Ming China, Chinese envoy Yang Tsai came to Okinawa to purchase horses and sulphur, paying for them with bolts of fine silk and brocade which often served as a medium of international trade in those days. He soon discovered that the Okinawans desired pottery, ceramics, and iron goods much more than fine silks. The next Chinese envoy, Li Hao, brought 70,000 pieces of pottery and 1,000 pieces of iron goods in 1374.

All of this indicates the significance of the change from wooden or stone farming implements to iron implements in the fourteenth and fifteenth centuries (although iron implements might have been known and used earlier than the fourteenth century). For the farmers who had had to struggle with ineffective wooden or stone hoes in tilling the hard red clay found in many parts of Okinawa, the iron hoes and spades must have brought a near revolutionary improvement. It is small wonder that King Satto or anyone else who brought such implements to the farmers was idolized and worshipped.

The following *omoro* eulogizes King Satto, called here Janamoi 'the beloved of Jana,' who ascended the throne not by the ercise of military power but by the peaceful, unanimous recommendation of the assembly of government officials in Shuri who were disgusted with the misgovernment of his predecessor, King Seii (reigned 1337–1349) or rather his mother, the queen dowager, who intervened in the affairs of government.[50]

The lines in this *omoro* "The Treasure House door that / All the lords were weary of waiting / Lord Janamoi has opened," seem to refer to the fact that he was responsible not only for inmporting valuable iron for improved agricultural implements but also for beginning the tributary relationship with China in 1372. This relationship was to last for the next five centuries to the very end of the kingdom and continued to yield significant influence upon the political, economic, and cultural history of the Ryūkyū Islands. King Satto did indeed open the door of the Treasure House.

In Praise of King Satto[51]

Janamoi[1] ya, ta[2] ga, nacharu,[3] kwa[4] ga,	Janamoi, who has borne him?
Koga,[5] kyorasa,	What a beautiful son,
Koga, mibosha,[6] aruyona.[7]	So worthy to your eyes.

Momochara[8] no, agute, ocharu,[9] kochaguchi[10]	The impenetrable treasure houses of the hundred lords—
Janamoi-shu,[11] aketare.	Lord Janamoi has opened.
Janamoi ga, Jana-Uebaru,[12] nobote	Janamoi ascends Jana-Uebaru,
Keyagetaru,[13] tsuyo[14] wa,	And the dew that he kicks up—
Tsuyo kara do, kabasha,[15] aru.	From the dew, indeed, there is a lovely fragrance.

1. *Janamoi*	Name of the lord of Urasoe who later became King Satto in 1350.
2. *ta*	'Who'.
3. *nacharu*	Past tense of *nasu* 'to give birth to'.
4. *kwa*	'Child'.
5. *koga*	Roughly, 'such as', or 'such a … ', leading an exclamatory sentence.
6. *mibosha*	*Mi-* 'look [upon], gaze [at]' + *bosha*, a derived form of the desiderative suffix meaning 'want to'.
7. *aruyona*	*Aru* 'to be', 'to have' + *yona*, exclamatory ending.
8. *momochara*	*Momo* 'a hundred' + *chara*, an old term for lord.
9. *agute, ocharu*	*agute* 'to be unable to …, impossible (to …)'; *ocharu* an ending that references an ongoing state. The term *agute* appears as *arate* 'have washed' in some versions, but it is suggested that *akute* or *agute* is the correct term in this line. *Kōhon Omoro sōshi*, p. 563.
10. *kochaguchi*	'Storage entrance'.
11. *shu*	'Master'.
12. *Jana-Uebaru*	Place name.
13. *keyagetaru*	*Keyage*, related to Japanese *keage* 'to kick up'. *Taru* denotes completed action.
14. *tsuyo*	'Dew,' related to Japanese *tsuyu*.
15. *kabasha*	Derived form of the cognate of Japanese *kanbashii* 'sweet, fragrant, aromatic, balmy'.

The general prosperity of the kingdom brought about by such factors as uninterrupted peace, the introduction of iron agricultural implements and the resultant increase in food production, and brisk overseas trade, was also reflected in rural life, as seen in the next *omoro.*

Banquet at the Castle Town[52]

Shimo[1] no, okite,[2] netote,[3]	Junior chief as the leader,
Tsuki no kazu,[4] natsu no yani[5]	Every month, like summer,
Amaeru,[6] kiyora ya.	Making merry and gay! How beautiful!
Monoinisha,[7] netote	Our speaker as the leader,
(Tsuki no kazu, natsu no yani)	(Every month, like summer,)
(Amaeru, kiyora ya.)	(Making merry and gay! How beautiful!)
Kume no Nakagusuku,	At Nakagusuku of Kume,
Tsuki no kazu, (natsu no yani)	Every month, (like summer,)
(Amaeru, kiyora ya.)	(Making merry and gay! How beautiful!)
Toyomu, Nakagusuku	At the renowned Nakagusuku
(Tsuki no kazu, natsu no yani)	(Every month, like summer,)
(Amaeru, kiyora ya.)	(Making merry and gay! How beautiful!)
Fuyo,[8] natsu mu,[9] shirazu[10]	There is no winter or summer,
Natsu, fuyo mu, shirazu	There is no summer or winter,
Fuyo wa, ozakemoru[11]	In the winter, we have feasting,
Natsu wa, shigechimoru.[12]	In summer, we have banqueting.
Anji kara ru,[13] kaniaru[14]	It's so since our lord's reign.
Teda[15] kara ru kaniaru.	It's so since our master's reign.

1. *shimo*	'Below, down, junior'.
2. *okite*	Head of the village, who collects taxes and pays them to the lord. *Okite*, in Okinawan pronounced /utchi/, literally means 'rule', 'law'.
3. *netote*	*Ne* 'sound, tone, note, ring, strain, voice'. *Tote* 'to take, to lead'. Therefore, to lead in music or singing or in general to lead.

4. *tsuki no kazu*	*Tsuki* 'moon' or 'month' + *no* 'of' + *kazu* 'number'. Hence, every month, each month.
5. *natsu no yani*	*Natsu* 'summer'. Like (a) summer, *natsu no yoni.*
6. *amaeru*	'To make merry and gay'.
7. *monoinisha*	'Speaker'. Synonym for *okite. Mono* 'matter' + *i* 'to speak', 'to tell' + *nisha* 'mister'.
8. *fuyo*	'Winter'.
9. *natsu mu*	*Natsu* 'summer' + *mo* 'and', 'as well as', 'both ... and'. Winter as well as summer, both winter and summer.
10. *shirazu*	*Shiru* 'to know'. *Shirazu* is negative, 'without knowing', 'not knowing'.
11. *ozakemoru*	Verb related to Japanese *osakemori* 'to have a drinking bout (party, feast, banquet)'.
12. *shigechi*	Synonym for *sake* 'wine'.
13. *anji kara ru*	*Anji* 'lord' + *kara* 'since', 'from' + *ru*, emphatic particle.
14. *kaniaru*	'It is thus', 'it is so'.
15. *teda*	'Sun'. Synonym for *anji* 'lord'.

This *omoro* is from Nakagusuku (later renamed Uegusuku in deference to the crown prince or king, also called prince of Nakagusuku), Kumejima. In days gone by, people used to have a banquet or feast only in summer immediately after the harvest. It was affordable only once a year, and then only if there was a rich harvest. All other months were months of hardship and toil. But now, making merry and gay, every month is like summer! Though we are working as hard as ever, we are happy, for the fields and paddies are giving us more food than ever. All the granaries are full. When there is a little extra rice, we'll brew wine with which to forget the day's hard work or to simply enjoy with our friends. It's all started since our lord's reign. Isn't it wonderful? From the way we live, no one can tell whether it's summer or winter. Nowadays, not a month goes by without one ceremony or another when people can rest and have fun.

Feasting is a joyous time; however, when everyone has had his fill, when everyone has sung and danced unto exhaustion, the feasting comes to an end and, one by one or in twos and threes, the villagers take leave and stagger homeward. And one step outside the feast, where it was so lively and gay, the countryside is quiet, lonely, and as rural as ever. The following *omoro* describes just such a scene. The sun is about to set in the western sea, and it is getting dark in the village and over the hills. In the twilight, groups of people are seen on their way home from some kind of festival or banquet. The priestess in her ceremonial white robe is on her way home too. Overhead, an *ankwena* bird (said to be a snipe or a kingfisher) cries "kwei! kwei!" as she flies home from the shore in the dusk. She may be following the people because she is lonesome. Someone calls out, "*Ankwena* bird! Long-beaked bird! What are you coming after? Who are you coming after? You saw the priestess in her white robe, and you are following her, aren't you?"

Evening When the *Ankwena* Was Crying[53]

Akurena[1] no, tori[2] no	*Ankwena* bird,
Kuchinaka[3] no, tori no	Long-beaked bird,
Eke,[4] koino,[5]	There! *Koino!*
No,[6] micheka,[7] oikyoru[8]	What are you following?
Ikyamicheka,[9] oikyoru	Who are you coming after?
Kimi,[10] michesu, oikyore	Following the priestess,
Nushi,[11] michesu, oikyore	Coming after the priestess.

1, 2. *akurena no tori*	*Tori* is 'bird'. *Akurena* is an onomatopoeical name of a bird that cries "ankwena!" or "kwena!" in the evening as it flies landward from the beach to its nest.
3. *kuchinaka*	*Kuchi* 'mouth', 'beak', 'bill' + *naka* 'long'.
4. *eke*	A refrain.
5. *koino*	*Omoro* style transcription of *kwena*.
6. *no*	'What'. Pronounced /nu/.
7. *micheka*	Alternate form of *miteka* (from *mi-* 'to see' + an interrogative ending).
8. *oikyoru*	*Oi* 'to follow' + *kyoru* or *kiyoru* 'to come'. The line "*no, micheka, oikyoru*" literally means "What did you see that you are coming after?"
9. *ikya*	Alternate form of *ika* 'who'.
10, 11. *kimi, nushi*	Both refer to the priestess.

CHAPTER 4

Life of the Ruling Class

With respect to the history of Ryūkyū, the reader of formal histories such as the *Chūzan sekan* or *Chūzan seifu* receives the impression that in the beginning everything was ideal—the country was united under one king and one dynasty and only later, when an unvirtuous king ascended the throne, did the central government decline and the country become divided into the three small kingdoms of the north, the center, and the south, still later to be reunited under a great and illustrious king.[1] Indeed, this is the view reiterated by some historians such as Shidehara Hiroshi[2] in his *Nantō enkaku shiron*.

In the beginning, Ryūkyū was governed by the legendary dynasty of Tensonshi which lasted until 1186, when the rebellious Riyū usurped the throne by poisoning the king. Riyū was in turn killed shortly thereafter by the army of Sonton, the alleged son of the renowned Japanese warrior, Minatomo-no-Tametomo. Although Sonton, at that time the lord of Urasoe, thrice refused to ascend the throne, he was finally prevailed upon to become king, calling himself King Shunten. His dynasty was the first historical dynasty. It lasted three generations, for a total of 73 years ending in 1259 in the reign of King Gihon. Gihon, seeing the country suffer from a series of epidemics, famines, and other natural disasters, felt that he did not have a mandate from heaven and therefore voluntarily abdicated in favor of Eiso, lord of Izu (or Ezu), Urasoe. The latter, said to be a descendant of the original Tenson dynasty, was well known, for he ruled his domain well and brought prosperity to his people. The second and third kings of the Eiso dynasty ruled the country well enough; however, the fourth, King Tamagusuku (reigned 1314–1336), was too addicted to worldly pleasures to look after the matters of state.

Thus, the country fell into decay. The local lords became more and more independent, and civil wars ensued. Out of the continuous internal warfare emerged Hokuzan (Northern Mountain Kingdom) and Nanzan (Southern Mountain Kingdom), which were considered rebels. There was also Chūzan (Central Mountain Kingdom), the legitimate dynasty. All the small villages or domains belonged to one of the three kingdoms which fought among themselves for supremacy over the whole of Okinawa.

In the meantime, the power and prestige of the Eiso dynasty fell to its lowest ebb during the reign of young King Seii (reigned 1337–1349) who ascended the throne when he was only ten years old. His mother, the queen dowager, actively intervened in the affairs of state, making matters worse. When King Seii died in 1349 at the age of 23, the government officials, who were weary of King Seii, or more specifically, the queen dowager, rejected the heir to the throne and instead chose Satto, the lord of Urasoe who was famous for his wisdom and statesmanship. His reign (1350–1395) restored prosperity to the kingdom. It was during his reign that for the first time, the islands of Miyako and Yaeyama pledged loyalty to Chūzan and began sending tribute. It was also during his reign that Chūzan established official contact with Ming China (1363), commenced trade (1372), and received the so-called thirty-six families from China who, settling in Naha, served the kingdom in various capacities as scholars, diplomats, and technicians. It was also during his reign in the year 1392 that the kingdom began sending students to the Chinese National Academy. Chūzan was the wealthiest and most powerful of the three kingdoms, but the Satto dynasty quickly alienated itself when the second king, King Bunei (reigned 1396–1405) wallowed in a life of dissipation and debauchery, rejecting those who would give him the bitter medicine of good advice and approving those who would give him sweet words of flattery.

In the meanwhile, the lord of Sashiki, Shō Hashi, in the southeast corner of Okinawa, was rapidly rising to fame as a great and spirited ruler who placed the welfare of his subjects above everything else. In 1402, without much difficulty, he defeated his powerful neighbor, the lord of Yaesu of East Osato. The *Chūzan sekan* states that his virtue and blessings extended even to the birds and beasts, and even to the dead, and that half of Chūzan and Hokuzan were just as good as his. In 1405, he attacked and defeated the unpopular King Bunei of Chūzan. After taking some years to consolidate his power, in 1416, he managed to defeat his powerful enemy to the north, King Haneji of Hokuzan. In 1422, King Taromai of Nanzan followed the fate of King Haneji. Thus Shō Hashi completed the long-cherished reunification of Okinawa, under his hegemony.

From this time on, peace reigned continuously with the exception of the occasional rebellion of the outlying islands, but there were no major internal wars. There was a change of dynasty in 1469, but it was completed without bloodshed and the next dynasty assumed the same dynastical name, Shō, implying continuation of the previous dynasty. Thus, as stated earlier, the political history, or history of the ruling class and their struggle for supremacy, appears to have begun with an "ideal" united Okinawa under one king. It split into three kingdoms in the first quarter of the fourteenth century. In 1422, it was again united after about one hundred years of internal warfare.

However, it is what the official scholar historians, who were thoroughly steeped in the traditional Confucian ideology, would have the reader accept: an ideal ancient state which could always be looked back on with pride, the withdrawal of the mandate of heaven from a king without virtue, and the emergence of the virtuous king on whom the mandate of heaven is now bestowed.

It must be assumed that the unification of 1422 by Shō Hashi was in fact not a reunification at all, but rather a unification for the first time. That is to say, until about the tenth or even the twelfth century, the society that existed on Okinawa was that of the *makyo* consanguineous village community which was in the process of transformation to the *mura* village community. There was no lord or king at this time. As the *mura* village communities grew larger and larger in area and more powerful militarily and economically, they came in contact with others in their area. Peacefully or otherwise, the more active and powerful *mura* village communities gradually expanded to include other *mura* villages within their domain. Thus the *nebito* of the conquering *mura* villages gave rise to a class of local lords called *anji* or *aji*.

The central region of Okinawa, which includes roughly Naha, Shuri, and Urasoe and adjacent areas, was the earliest and most highly developed part of Okinawa; it encompassed the important ports of Naha, Tomari, and Makiminato on the China Sea coast and the port of Yagi on the Pacific coast where overseas trade was carried on from earliest times. Naturally, the lord who controlled this area was first and foremost over the lesser lords. The Shunten and Eiso dynasties (1187–1259 and 1260–1349, respectively) did not rule Okinawa per se, but controlled the most advanced region with its excellent natural harbors which were centers of foreign trade. Easier access to overseas trade meant superior tools and armaments as well as economic advantages, as a result of which Chūzan became the economic, political, and cultural center of Okinawa.

Although it is recorded in the formal histories that during the reign of King Tamagusuku (1314–1336) the country became divided into three warring kingdoms, it should be noted that the regions of the north and the south (later called Hokuzan and Nanzan, respectively) which began their development later than the central region of Chūzan, had just caught up with Chūzan, forming their own small states under the leadership of the lord of Nakijin in Hokuzan and the lord of Ozato in Nanzan. As the three came into contact with each other, conflicts started and wars of expansion and conquest followed. It was not that one country had been divided into three, with the three fighting among themselves, but that though one began to develop earlier than the other two, they all developed independently, and when all three became strong, they began fighting for hegemony. The official record in the formal histories merely reflects the biased view of the historians of the later Chūzan kingdom who insisted that their dynasty was the only legitimate line on Okinawa.[3]

In the early Omoro era, the center of Chūzan was Urasoe; in the late Omoro era, it was Shuri. It is no coincidence that the founders of the first three (of the total of five) Okinawan dynasties had come from this region.

The following *omoro* describe the castle in Ezo in the neighborhood of Urasoe which was the residence of Eiso before he ascended the throne in 1260 at the age of 31, succeeding King Gihon who, as mentioned above, was alleged to have voluntarily abdicated after a series of misfortunes beset the country.

Castle of Ezo[4]

Ezo[1] Ezo no, ishigusuku,[2]	Ezo, the Stone Castle in Ezo
Amamikyo[3] ga, takudaru[4] gusuku	Castle that Amamikyo has built
Ezo Ezo no, kanagusuku.[5]	Ezo, the Iron Castle in Ezo.

1. *Ezo*	Name of the place where Eiso's father was lord. Also written Izo or Eiso, it is located in the neighborhood of Urasoe Castle.
2. *ishigusuku*	*Ishi* 'stone' + *gusuku* 'castle'.
3. *Amamikyo*	Creator goddess. Also, by extension, 'ancient time' or 'in ancient times'.
4. *takudaru*	A descriptive word formed from the past tense of *takumu* 'to plan', 'to devise', 'to make', 'to build'.
5. *kanagusuku*	*Kana* 'iron, metal' + *gusuku* 'castle'.

The second line, "Castle that Amamikyo has built" means by inference "the castle built long ago in the age of the gods." Even in the 1260s, this castle was considered to be very old. Also indicated is the still earlier transition in this region from the *nebito*-ruled *makyo* and *mura*—self-sufficient, isolated, and independent villages—to the *anji*-ruled small state comprising one or more *magiri* (in turn comprising about ten to fifteen *makyo* or *mura* hamlets).

Castle of Ezo[5]

Ezo no ishigusuku	[Ezo,] the Stone Castle in Ezo.
Nobote[1] micharu[2] masari[3]	The impregnability that is seen upon climbing to the top.
Ezo no kanagusuku.	[Ezo,] the Iron Castle in Ezo.

1. *nobote*	'Climbing on top, ascending'.
2. *micharu*	A past tense form of the verb 'to see', here used descriptively.
3. *masari*	Superior, surpassing, impregnable.

Castle of Ezo[6]

Ezo Ezo no, ishigusuku	Ezo, the Stone Castle in Ezo.
Iyoya[1] ni osote[2] choware[3]	Prevail, and rule for ever and more.
Ezo Ezo no, kanagusuku.	Ezo, the Iron Castle in Ezo.

1. *iyoya*	Equivalent to Japanese *iyamashini* 'more and more', 'still further', 'further and further'.
2. *osote*	'To rule, to attack, to cover'.
3. *choware*	Elegant and emphatic word for 'to be', translated as 'prevail'.

Though history relates that King Gihon abdicated voluntarily and that Eiso was begged by all, including King Gihon himself, to ascend the throne—these *omoro* seem to indicate that if Eiso was a virtuous and benevolent statesman, he was also an able military leader. He was also very prosperous, as seen in the following *omoro.*

Young Lord of Ezo[7]

Ezo no, Ikusamoi,[1]	Ikusamoi of Ezo,
Tsuki no kazu, asubi,[2] tachi,[3]	Giving a banquet as often as the number of full moons.
Tomomo to,[4] wakateda,[5] hayase.[6]	May the young Sun be praised for eternity.
Ijeki,[7] Ikusamoi	Sagacious Ikusamoi!
Natsu wa, shigechi,[8] moru[9]	Giving a feast in summer,
Fuyo wa, ozake.[10]	Giving a banquet in winter.

1. *Ikusamoi*	Eiso's name. *Ikusa* 'war' + *moi*, a suffix of endearment.
2. *asubi*	'Play, game, diversion'.
3. tachi	Literally, 'to stand, to raise'. Here it means to give or throw a party.

4. *tomomo*	Tens of hundreds. *To* 'ten' + *momo* 'hundred'.
5. *wakateda*	*Waka* 'young' + *teda* 'sun'. An epithet of the young lord Eiso.
6. *hayase*	'To cheer, to praise'.
7. *ijeki*	'Spirit, will, spirited'.
8. *shigechi*	Synonym for *ozake* or *osake* 'wine drinking', 'feast'.
9. *moru*	'To serve, to fill, to hold'.
10. *ozake*	*Sake* 'wine'.

The *Chūzan sekan* states that in ancient times, the forefathers of the legendary Tenson dynasty selected the place where the royal castle is now located as the best site for building a castle, and that is why it is called Shuri *(shu* 'the first', 'the head', *ri* 'village').[8] Thus it seems that from the beginning Shuri had always been the capital of Chūzan.

However, scholars are divided on this question. Higaonna and Iha believe that the capital was transferred from Urasoe (formerly called Tokashiki) to Shuri in the time of King Shō Hashi (reigned 1422–1439).[9] Majikina Ankō and Shimabukuro Zenpatsu disagree and insist that Shuri had always been the capital of Chūzan.[10] Lastly, Okuzato Shōken has made public his view that though Urasoe was the old capital as Higaonna and Iha have said, the time of transfer of the capital from Urasoe to Shuri is not during the time of King Shō Hashi but earlier than that—in the time of King Satto (reigned 1350–1394).[11]

Iha relies mainly on the strength of the etymology of the word *urasoe* for support of his theory. *Urasoe* is a contraction of *uraosoi* which appears in many places in the *Omoro sōshi*. In the *Omoro sōshi*, Urasoe is praised as "the fair country from which the lords have come," suggesting that Urasoe was very likely the capital of the central region or Chūzan. *Uraosoi* consists of *ura*, inlets or beaches, and *osoi*, noun form of *osou* 'to take', 'to attack', 'to fall on'. *Ura* here is used as in *tsutsu-ura'ura-ni* 'throughout the length and breadth of the land' or 'in every nook and cranny of the land'. Thus, *uraosoi* or *urasoe* means 'that which takes and covers the whole land'. Interestingly enough, later, when the royal castle was built at Shuri, the main building was called Mondasoi, derived from *momo-ura-osoi*, 'ruler of the hundred *ura*'. Nakahara suggests that the word Shuri (Okinawan /sui/) might have originated from a stylized transcription of *soi* or *osoi* 'attack', 'rule'.[12]

Okuzato accepts Iha's explanation above, but seeks further evidence. First, he points out the fact that the Gokuraku-ji Temple, built for the Japanese priest Zenkan under the patronage of King Eiso, was built immediately beyond a cliff at the northwest corner of Urasoe Castle and not Shuri Castle. Secondly, in a folktale related to King Satto's mother, who was said to be a celestial angel, the action takes place in the Urasoe area, not Shuri. Thirdly, when King Satto was still young, Japanese trading ships came to Makiminato which was the port for Urasoe, not Tomari which would have been the port used had the royal castle been in Shuri. All of the aforegoing indicates that early in the reign of King Satto, the capital was in Urasoe. That it was moved to Shuri later in his reign is supported by the following evidence. First, when the chief of Miyako Island and his party came to Okinawa to pay tribute in the forty-first year of the reign of King Satto in 1390, they stayed three years at Tomari, the port for Shuri. Had the capital still been in Urasoe, they would have stayed at Makiminato. Secondly, the Japanese priest Yorishige, who was the protege of King Satto, built the Gogoku-ji Temple and the Manju-ji Temple (the exact dates of the building of these temples are not known, but Priest Yorishige died in 1384) in the Naha area and not Urasoe. Thirdly, the so-called thirty-six Chinese immigrant families who came to Okinawa in 1392 were granted residence in Naha. On the strength of these factors, Okuzato contends that King Satto transferred the capital immediately after he ascended the throne in 1350. In any event, there is no doubt that Urasoe was an important town in earlier times.

To the Renowned Urasoe[13]

Kikoe,[1] Uraosoi ni	To the renowned Urasoe,
Nishi higa no kamae,[2]	Tributes from the East and the West,
Mochiyosete,[3]	Have been brought,
Toyomu[4] Uraosoi ni.	To the glorious Urasoe.

1. *kikoe*	Related to Japanese *kiku* 'to hear', *kikoe* means 'well heard about' or 'well known'.
2. *kamae*	'Tribute, tax'. In modern Okinawan, *kaneye* is a tenant fee or farm rent.
3. *mochiyosete*	'To bring something over together'.
4. *toyomu*	Literally, 'resounding, reechoing, shouting loudly'.

For the Renowned Urasoe[14]

Kikoe, Uraosoi ya	For the renowned Urasoe is
Shima[1] no oya[2] yareba	The capital of the country.
Momochara[3] no, kamae,	Let the hundred lords their tributes
Tsudemioyase,[4]	Offer
Toyomu Uraosoi ya.	For the glorious Urasoe.

1. *shima*	'Village, home village, one's territory, island'. Here, it is used collectively to mean the whole country.
2. *oya*	'Parent(s)'; figuratively, 'the capital'.
3. *momochara*	*Momo* 'hundred' + *chara*, a synonym for *anji* 'lord'. *Chara* may be related to *ki-aru* 'one who has spiritual power'.
4. *tsudemioyase*	*Tsude* is a contraction of *tunde*, a conjugated form of *tsumu* 'to pile up', 'to load', 'to heap up'. *Mioyase* is an elegant term.

At this time, besides Urasoe, there were other smaller ports which also carried on trade with the outside—mainly Japan. One of these was Yagi on the Pacific coast of central Okinawa.

Imported Folding Screen[15]

Yagi no Kanamori ni	In the Kanamori Grove of Yagi
Mimono, myabu,[1] oroche	A magnificent folding screen was unloaded
Kamishimo[2] no,	The high and low
Mimono suru,[3] kiyora ya,[4]	Flocked to see its beauty.
Higa no, Kanamori ni	In the Kanamori Grove of the East
(Mimono, myabu, oroche)	(A magnificent folding screen was unloaded)
(Kamishimo no,)	(The high and low)
(Mimono suru, kiyora ya.)	(Flocked to see its beauty.)

1. *myabu*	Cognate to Japanese *byobu*, 'folding screen'.
2. *kamishimo*	*Kami* '[the] high' + *shimo* '[the] low', i.e., the multitude of people.
3. *mimono suru*	A verb construction that means 'to look upon a sight to see'. In this context: '[a beauty that] is a spectacle, a sight to see'.
4. *kiyora ya*	"What a beautiful sight!" Said by the people who flocked to admire the beautiful folding screen.

Armor and Shoulderpiece[16]

Yagi kara, noboru,	Shoulder piece and armor
Shitatari[1] ya, yoroi,[2]	That came up from Yagi,
Taru[3] ga, kiche,[4] niseru,[5]	Who is becoming in them?

Ajiosoi,[6] tedasu,[7]	Our Lord, the Sun
Meshowache,[8] nisere	Is most becoming in them.
Higa kara, noboru	Shoulder piece and armor
(Shitatari ya, yoroi,)	(That landed in the East,)
(Taru ga, kiche, niseru,)	(Who is becoming in them?)
(Ajiosoi, tedasu,)	(Our Lord, the Sun)
(Meshowache, nisere.)	(Is most becoming in them.)

1. *shitatari*	Cognate to Japanese *hitatare* 'shoulder piece'.
2. *yoroi*	'Armor'.
3. *taru*	'Who'.
4. *kiche*	Cognate to *kite, a* conjugated form of *kiru* 'to wear', 'to put on' (a dress or an armor).
5. *niseru*	'To fit, to become'.
6. *ajiosoi*	Ruler of the lords.
7. *tedasu*	Epithet, "Master of the Sun."
8. *meshowache*	Polite term for 'to wear'.

The following *omoro* relates that in those days even the petty lord of Makabe in southern Okinawa was trading with Japan which sent her own ships from the port of Ishiki. Several things may be surmised from this *omoro*. First, since Makabe was a rather insignificant territory, and the port of Ishiki not particularly outstanding, if Makabe was trading with Japan with her own ships, how many lords who were in a better position than the lord of Makabe must have been trading with Japan? Secondly, the main items of import from Japan were, significantly, hammers (for the obvious purpose of construction) and jewels, notably comma-shaped jades with a hole in the head (known as *magatama* in Japanese) used by the priestesses for religious and ceremonial purposes. The secular and the religious were equally important in Okinawan culture, and the two coexisted harmoniously and supported each other. Thirdly, it would appear that the Okinawans possessed (possibly having built them themselves) good ships built of camphorwood (camphor considered the best material for shipbuilding) in Japanese style, perhaps even of better design and quality.

Trade at Lower Ishiki[17]

Ishikeshita,[1] yo,[2] gaho,[3]	Lower Ishiki is a port
Yosetsukeru, tomari[5]	That invites an abundant year.
Kaneshi, kane,[6] dono yo	Dear Master Kaneshi
Ishihetsu wa, konode	Was fond of stone hammers,
Kanahetsu wa, konode	Was fond of metal hammers,
Ishike, yori, naoche[7]	Built Ishiki Port,
Natara,[8] yori,[9] naoche	Built Natara Port,
Kusunoki wa,[10] konode	Was fond of camphorwood ships,
Yamato,[11] fune, konode	Was fond of Japanese style ships,
Yamato, tabi, nobote	Has gone on a journey up to Yamato
Yashiro,[12] tabi, nobote	Has gone on a journey up to Yashiro
Kawara,[13] kai ni, nobote	Gone up to buy necklace jewels,
Temochi,[14] kai ni, nobote	Gone up to buy wristlet jewels,
Omoigwa no, tamesu	For the beloved prince
Warigane ga, tamesu.	For the Prince Warigane.

1. *Ishikeshita* — Ishiki is a village in what is now Makabe-son in southern Okinawa. Ishikeshita means Lower Ishiki.

2, 3. *yo gaho* — 'Fortunate or blessed world'.

4. *yosetsukeru* — 'That which invites, brings together'.

5. *tomari* — 'Port'.

6. *kane* — Cognate of archaic Japanese *kanashi* 'to love', 'to cherish'. It is a term of endearment.

7. *naoche* — 'To repair, to build'.

8. *Natara* — Another name for Ishiki, probably meaning 'gentle slope' or 'flat land'.

9. *yori* — 'A gathering or stop'. Synonym for port.

10. *kusunoki* — 'Camphor tree', which is supposed to be an excellent material for shipbuilding.

11. *Yamato* — Another name for Japan; name of an old province (present Nara area).

12. *Yashiro*	Name of an old province, southern part of the present Kyoto area.
13. *kawara*	Ornamental or ceremonial jewelry made of mother-of-pearl, stone, metal, or ceramic. *Kawara* is pronounced /gaara/. *OS*, pp. 357–361.
14. *temochi*	Also a kind of ornamental or ceremonial jewelry, especially that worn as a wristlet. *Te* means hand, *mochi* means to have.

With respect to shipbuilding, it seems there were quite a few immigrants from Japan who were craftsmen and artisans such as shipwrights, blacksmiths, goldsmiths, and folding-screen makers.[18] The following *omoro* sings the praises of an able young shipwright named Kotarō on the island of Ike near Katsuren Peninsula, Okinawa.

Shipbuilding[19]

Ike no, Morigusuku,	At Mori Castle on Ike Island
Kyayose,[1] hakiagarya[2]	The *Kyayose* has been completed
Nami osou,[3] haya mioune[4]	A fast ship to rule over the waves.
Jakuni,[5] Morigusuku	At Mori Castle on the Fair Island,
(Kyayose, hakiagarya)	(The *Kyayose* has been completed)
(Nami osou, haya mioune)	(A fast ship to rule over the waves.)
Kotara, waka saiku.[6]	What a shipwright, young Kotarō!

1. *Kyayose*	Name of the ship. Though Nakahara says its meaning is not clear, it may be a compound of *kyo*, capital city of Kyoto, and *yose*, to bring hither, namely, 'one who brings the culture of Kyoto hither'.
2. *hakiagarya*	Literally, to complete tearing off, peeling off, or ripping off. Here, it means to complete the building of the ship. It seems to be reminiscent of making dugout type boats.
3. *nami osou*	An adjective meaning 'to rule over the waves'. *Nami* 'wave' + *osou* 'to attack', 'to rule'.
4. *haya mioune*	*Haya* 'swift', 'quick' + *mi-o*, a double honorific + *(f)une* 'boat', 'ship' (f of *fune* is dropped).

5. *Jakuni* Another word for 'country', here, Ike Island.

6. *waka saiku* *Waka*, 'young', *saiku*, 'craftsman' such as a carpenter or smith.

In 1264, in the fifth year of the reign of King Eiso, outlying islands such as Kume, Kerama, and Iheya began paying tribute to Chūzan. This seems to indicate that though there might have been some private intercourse previously, King Eiso began exercising control over some ports in his region at this time. It is also indicative of the extent of economic development in these islands which enabled them to trade with Okinawa. In the eighth year of the reign of King Eiso in 1267 the northeastern islands of Amami-Ōshima came to Chūzan and paid tribute. An official document records the following exchange between King Eiso and the envoy from the Amami-Ōshima Islands.[20] "Your islands lie beyond the boundaries of my country," said the king. "Why then have you come here to pay tribute?" The envoy replied, "Of recent years there have been no natural disasters such as typhoons or floods on our islands and the five grains have given us rich harvests. We felt that this must be because of the influence of your benevolent rule which favorably affects the heaven and earth. That is why we have come all the way to pay you tribute." The king accepted the tribute with pleasure, rewarded them well, and sent them back. Thereafter, they paid tribute every year. In reality, this must be considered the same relationship as Chūzan, under the reign of King Satto, came to have later with Ming China—an officially sanctioned trade relationship under the guise of tribute payment, an arrangement flattering to the powerful and profitable to the small. At this time there had already been considerable trade between Okinawa and Japan proper and the islands of the Amami-Ōshima group. The following *omoro* describes the departure of a ship from Yoron in the Amami-Ōshima Islands. It begs the gods for favorable winds and invokes a blessing on the voyage.

Ship from Yoron Island[21]

Kaefuta[1] no, oyanoro,	Chief *noro* priestess of Yoron
Tokara-asobi,[2] takabete,	Venerate Tokara'asobi,
Urako-shiche,[3]	With impatience
Sodetarete, haryase.	And with sleeves down, let it sail!
Nenoshima[4] no, oyanoro,	Chief *noro* priestess of Nenoshima!
(Tokara-asobi, takabete,)	(Venerate Tokara-asobi)
(Urako-shiche)	(With impatience)

(Sodetarete, haryase)	(And with sleeves down, let it sail!)
Noronoro[5] wa, takabete	Priestesses praying
Kamikami wa,[6] takabete	Goddesses worshipping,
Nishi kowaba,[7] nishi-nare	Let it be the northerly wind if they wish.
Hae kowaba,[8] hae-nare.	Let it be the southerly wind if they wish.

1. *Kaefuta*	Kae is the old name of a Yoron Island village and Kaefuta, meaning Kae Village, also refers to Yoron Island itself. *Futa* is a synonym for *makyo* consanguineous village.
2. *Takara-asobi*	Divine name of Yoron Island.
3. *urako-shiche*	*Shiche* is cognate to Japanese *shite* (from *suru*, a verb comparable to 'to do' in English). *Urako-shiche* means to be weary of, to be impatient with. *Urako* means, literally, to itch in the mind.
4. *Nenoshima*	*Ne* 'root' + *no* 'if' + *shima* 'island', thus, Root Island, an epithet for Yoron Island.
5. *noronoro*	Plural of *noro* 'priestess'.
6. *kamikami*	Plural of *kami* 'god', 'goddess', here, the priestesses.
7. *nishi kowaba*	*Nishi* 'northerly wind', *kowaba*, a conditional form of *kou* 'to beg', 'to request'; namely, 'if begged, if requested'.
8. *hae kowaba*	*Hae* 'southerly wind'.

The first line of the above *omoro* from Yoron Island reveals an interesting fact. That is, it describes the village of Kae as Kae-*futa*. *Futa* is a synonym for *makyo* a consanguineous kinship village, the oldest and most primitive type of village, in which religious functions were under the control of the brother-sister pair, the *nebito* and *negami*, the root man and root *kami*. On Okinawa Island, when the *makyo* villages developed into *mura* villages composed of multiple *makyo* villages, the central government appeared. Out of the necessity of replacing or at least controlling the influence of the *nebito* and *negami*, the government introduced and superimposed a system of *noro* priestesses. Therefore, the *noro* priestess was a feature of the *mura* village system and the *negami* priestess was a feature of the *makyo* village system. But here on Yoron, although the village structure is still that of the *makyo*, the religious system is that of *noro* priestesses, most likely imposed by the government of Chūzan in Okinawa as a part of the system of control of the former by the latter.

The next *omoro* describes a trade ship making her maiden voyage from Erabu Island in the Amami-Ōshima Islands to Naha. Priestess Mizerikyo of Erabu Island is aboard as spiritual leader and protector.

Voyage of the Priestess of Erabu Island[22]

Micherikyo[1] ga, Mochoro[2]	Mizerikyo's *Mochoro*
Kaminisha[3] ga, Mochoro	Priestess's *Mochoro*
De wan,[4] koreiche,[5] haryani[6]	Now, let me praise it and sail it.
Erabu,[7] Erabu, Erabu	Chosen and chosen from Erabu
Momoerabi[8] no, oyaoune [9]	Hundred times chosen our great ship
Erabu, Erabu, Erabu	Chosen and chosen from Erabu
Yasoerabi no, oyaoune,	Eighty times chosen our great ship
Momoso, noru,[10] funako,[11]	Hundred sailors aboard
Nanaso, noru, funako,	Seventy sailors aboard
Iyaya[12] makoroku[13] ga	Well! A man among men
Ichi no kaji[14] machyoku	Is strong at the first rudder!
Kobashima[15] no kamikami[16]	May the gods of Kubashima
Osanshiche,[17] maburyowa[18]	Watch over them from afar!
Tsureshima[19] no, kamikami	May the gods of Tsureshima
Osanshiche, maburyowa	Look after them from afar!
Nahadomari, nukiatete	Straight to Naha Port
Oyadomari,[20] nuki, atete.[21]	Straight to the Great Port.

1. *Micherikyo* Name of the priestess of Erabu Island.
2. *Mochoro* Name of the ship. It means beautiful, bright, clean.
3. *kaminisha* *Kami* 'god', 'goddess', 'priestess' + *nisha*, an honorific. Here it refers to the priestess.
4. *de wan* *De* is an interjection, *wan* is a cognate of Japanese *wa* or *ware*, meaning 'I', 'me'. "Let me. . . ."
5. *koreiche* *Kore* 'this' + *iche* 'saying', 'speaking', 'announcing'.

6. *haryani*	'Let it sail'. In modern Okinawan, *harasun* is to let something go, sail, run.
7. *Erabu*	Erabu is the name of the island, but the word 'to choose' is also *erabu;* hence, it is a play on the two words.
8. *momoerabi*	*Momo* 'hundred' *erabi*, a derived form of *erabu* 'to choose'.
9. *oyaoune*	*Oya* 'parent', 'great' *ofune (o*, honorific *fune* 'ship', 'boat').
10. *noru*	'To board, get aboard'.
11. *funako*	'Sailor(s)'.
12. *iyaya*	Interjection.
13. *makoroku*	'True man, man among men'.
14. *ichi no kaji*	Literally, the number one or first rudder. This seems to be not only a rudder for determining the direction of the boat but also a scull for propulsion.
15. *Kobashima*	Island of Fountain Palms, another name for Kudaka Island. The fountain palm is one of the symbolic trees of a sacred grove, and Kudaka has one of the most sacred groves in Okinawa.
16. *kamikami*	Repetition of *kami* 'god', conveying plurality.
17. *osan*	'To look down from a high place'.
18. *maburyowa*	Imperative of 'to protect'.
19. *Tsureshima*	Literally, 'islands in company'. Since Tsuken and Kudaka are located close by and form twin islands, they are called Tsureshima.
20. *oyadomari*	*Oya* 'parent', 'great' + *domari, tomari* 'port'.
21. *atete*	'To point to directly'.

If it is a valid premise that a course of traffic, whether on land or sea, tends to converge in and connect regions that are most highly developed, namely, regions of greater population, wealth, culture, and so on, the course of the voyage made by the priestess of Erabu poses a question contradictory to that premise.

Historically, all the towns and cities of any importance developed on the China Sea coast, and this tendency has continued even until today. For instance, the historical Makiminato and Urasoe, historical as well as modern Shuri and Naha, and recent Motobu, Nago, and Itoman are all located on the China Sea coast. In comparison, there are only two towns, Yonabaru and Ishikawa, on the Pacific coast. However, since Ishikawa is a town created relatively recently in 1945 in connection with World War II, it will not be considered here. That leaves only one town of any size on the Pacific coast, one that was developed only in this century. Clearly the China Sea coast of Okinawa Island has been much better developed than the Pacific coast and, relatedly, Okinawa has been oriented toward the west.

Since this *omoro* mentions prayers for safekeeping to the gods of Kudaka Island and Tsuken Island which lie on the Pacific coast of Okinawa, there is no doubt that the ship has taken the Pacific coast route to Naha. But since Naha is located on the southwestern coast of Okinawa, the ship has to go all the way around the southern end of Okinawa to get there, a much longer route than by the China Sea coast.

These seemingly illogical facts have made me reconsider conditions and possibilities on the Pacific coast. Although there is hardly a large town on the Pacific coast, the most sacred groves connected with the creation of Okinawa and the introduction and cultivation of grains such as rice, wheat, and millet are located there. According to the *Chūzan seifu*, three grains, *mugi* (wheat), *awa* (millet), and *kibi* (millet; *Panicum miliaceum)* appeared on Kudaka Island by themselves, and rice started to grow in the area of Chinen and Tamagusuku, on the southeastern coast of Okinawa.[23] Every king paid an annual visit to Kudaka Island in the second month and to Chinen and Tamagusuku in the fourth month to participate in the sacred ceremonies. Perhaps as a result, there are more *omoro* of voyages along the southeastern coast of Okinawa than along any other coasts.

Springtime on the Coast of Hyakuna[24]

Hyakuna,[1] urashiro[2] fukeba	On Hyakuna coast, when the southerly wind blows,
Uraura to,[3] Wakakimi,[4] tsukai[5]	The *Wakakimi* sails gently and softly.
Waga ura ni,[6] urashiro, fukeba	On our coast, when the southerly breeze comes,
(Uraura to, wakakimi, tsukai)	(The *Wakakimi* sails gently and softly.)
Tekazu wa,[7] koba no hana. [8] sakyora[9]	At the hand rudder bloom fountain palm flowers.
Kaiyaru wa,[10] nami hana.[11]	At the oars bloom flowers of waves.

1. *Hyakuna*	Southeast coast of Okinawa facing Kudaka Island.
2. *shiro*	There are three kinds of southerly winds: *ara'hae* 'new southerly wind (at the start of the rainy season); *kuro'bae* 'black southerly wind (in the middle of the rainy season); and *shiro'hae*, 'white southerly wind (when the rainy season has ended)'. *Shiro*, here is an abbrevation for *shiro'hae*, the wind that blows when the long rainy season has stopped and early summer has begun.
3. *uraura to*	An adjective roughly equal to 'gently', 'serenely', or 'softly'.
4. *Wakakimi*	The name of the ship, literally, 'The young Lord'.
5. *tsukai*	Literally, 'to employ, to use, to drive'.
6. *waga ura*	*Waga* 'my' or 'our' + *ura* 'coast'.
7. *tekazu*	The 'hand rudder' or 'one who steers'. Here seemingly a reference to a senior sailor. But Hokama and Saigo's *Omoro sōshi* (1972, p. 395) defines it as 'every-time they ply an oar'.
8. *kobanohana*	*Koba, kuba* 'fountain palm' + *hana* 'flower'.
9. *sakyora*	Derived from *saku* 'to bloom', it expresses a sense of wonder. The poet sees the white wave break at the rudder or oar and says, "I wonder if it is the fountain palm flower that breaks at the rudder?"
10. *kaiyaru*	*Kai* 'oar'. *Kaiyaru* 'to use an oar'.
11. *namihana*	*Nami* 'wave' + *hana* 'flower'.

Springtime on the Coast of Hyakuna[25]

Kikoe, Akeshino[1] ga	The famed Akeshino,
Agarui[2] no, kobamori[3]	In Kubamori Grove in the east
Kobano, hana no	When the fountain palm
Sakiyoreba,[4]	Blooms,
Uraura to,	Serenely
Wakakimi,[5] tsukai	Sails the Young Lord.
Toyomu, Akeshino ga	The renowned Akeshino,
(Agarui no, kobamori)	(In Kubamori Grove in the east)
(Kobano, hana no)	(When the fountain palm)

(Sakiyoreba,)	(Blooms,)
(Uraura to,)	(Serenely)
(Wakakimi, tsukai.)	(Sails the Young Lord.)

1. *Akeshino* Name of the priestess, *noro.*
2. *agarui* *Agaru* 'to rise'. Hence the direction where the sun rises, the east.
3. *kobamori* Literally, 'fountain palm grove'. This sacred grove on Kudaka Island was visited by the king every year (later, every other year).
4. *sakiyoreba* *Saku* 'to bloom'; *sakiyoreba* means 'if or when it is in bloom'.
5. *Wakakimi* Literally, 'The Young Lord' (ship's name).

Springtime on the Coast of Hyakuna[26]

Kikoe, Akeshino ga	The famed Akeshino
Sayahadake,[1] orewache[2]	Has descended from Sayaha Grove,
Akezu miso,[3] meshowache[4]	In a butterfly wing [gossamer] dress,
Kazanaori,[5] sashowache[6]	With an eagle feather pinned on her forehead.
Namitodoro,[7] Umitodoro[8]	She sails the Roaring Wave, the Roaring Sea.
Oshiukete, Hyakuna no	Pushing through off the coast of Hyakuna
Urahari[9] ga, mimon	What a sight to see her sail!
Toyomu, Akeshino ga	The renowned Akeshino
(Sayahadake, orewache)	(Has descended from Sayaha Grove,)
(Akezu miso, meshowache)	(In a butterfly wing dress,)
(Kazanaori, sashowache)	(With an eagle feather pinned on her forehead.)
(Namitodoro, Umitodoro)	(She sails the Roaring Wave, the Roaring Sea.)
(Oshiukete, Hyakunano)	(Pushing through off the coast of Hyakuna)
(Urahari ga, mimon)	(What a sight to see her sail!)

1. *Sayahadake*	Located in Chinen, in the southeastern corner of Okinawa, Sayahadake (modern Okinawan *Seifa utaki*) is considered the holiest of all the holy groves in all Ryūkyū. It was customary for a new *kikoe-ōgimi*, the highest priestess in the kingdom, to pay a visit personally. The *kikoe-ōgimi* was also appointed the head of Chinen village with an annual stipend of 200 *koku*.
2. *orewache*	Polite term for *oriru* 'to descend'.
3. *akezu miso*	*Akezu* 'butterfly', *miso* a polite term for 'dress, costume'. *Akezu miso* is a gown as thin and beautiful as a butterfly wing.
4. *meshowache*	Polite term for *mesu* 'to use', 'to put on'.
5. *kazanaori*	Literally, 'wind setter' or 'wind corrector', it is an eagle feather pinned on the headband worn by the priestess.
6. *sashowache*	Polite term for *sasu* or *sashi* 'to stick' or 'to pin'.
7. *Namitodoro*	Ship's name. *Nami* 'wave' + *todoro* 'roaring'.
8. *Umitodoro*	Also the ship's name. *Umi* 'sea', 'ocean'.
9. *urahari*	*Ura* 'beach', 'coast' + *hari* 'to run', 'to sail'.

The *omoro* "Shipbuilding" attests to the fact that even the people of an island as small as Ike were capable of building fast, seaworthy vessels. The five *omoro* immediately above, "Ship from Yoron Island," "Voyage of the Priestess of Erabu Island," and the three entitled "Springtime on the Coast of Hyakuna," clearly indicate that there was considerable traffic along the Pacific coast at this time.

In considering factors which determine a given course of traffic, we have briefly discussed the economic premise of convergence in and connection of highly developed regions by the shortest direct line. What cannot be ignored, what is probably even more important than the economic premise, especially in the primitive stage of the development of transportation, is natural and physical conditions. That is to say, the ancients were much more at the mercy of nature than are the moderns who have far more effective means of overcoming natural obstacles.

In my opinion, the history of shipbuilding and navigation in Okinawa is divisible into three stages or periods. The first is the period prior to 1185 when watercraft were of the simplest design—probably mostly dugout canoes with sails. The second period, which covers about two centuries beginning around

1185, was introduced by a chance factor in history. That is, in 1185, the Taira clan, one of the two greatest military clans in Japan and one which had long held supremacy on the sea, lost the decisive sea battle of Dan-no-ura at the western extreme of Honshū, the main island of Japan. Many of the defeated Taira fled to the numerous southwestern islands encompassing the entire Ryūkyū archipelago in search of refuge. Undoubtedly, they brought with them advanced techniques in shipbuilding and navigation, for the Taira clan was known for its naval power. The Japanese-style ship mentioned in the *omoro* "Trade at Lower Ishiki" or the speedy ship built by the young shipwright Kotaro of Ike Island may have been introduced by the Taira refugees. The third period began in 1392, marked by a deliberate policy for the introduction of advanced techniques when the so-called thirty-six Chinese families, many of whom were shipwrights and navigators, were transplanted to Naha. Ever since this time, great transoceanic ships began to be built on Okinawa. Indeed, during this period, navigational terminology was dominated by Chinese vocabulary.[27]

The significance of advancements in shipbuilding and navigation technology for a country like Okinawa, limited in natural resources and consequently dependent on trade with the outside world for her development, is clear. Shipbuilding, navigation, and other aspects of transportation technology are so important, in fact, that it is possible to redefine the historical eras in the light of these functions.

In the earliest period, from prehistoric times to 1185, the country was oriented primarily toward the north. It made little progress of its own and most of what it had was transplanted from Kyūshū and other northern islands. The population must have been very small, and the predominant social structure must have been the small, isolated, and independent *makyo* consanguineous villages. Most of the *makyo* villages at that time were probably located along the seacoast or around the inlets in the southeastern part of Okinawa or adjacent offshore islands. People made their livelihood from simple agriculture and shallow sea fishing.

The second period extended from approximately 1185 to 1392. It was during this period that, with the introduction of advanced shipbuilding and navigational technologies and with the relative isolation afforded by the internal wars in Japan, the heretofore separate regions of Okinawa began to be conscious of their belonging to a single cultural entity and thus to grope toward political unification. By this time, natural increases in population made people spread and move, transforming the small, isolated *makyo* villages into larger *mura* villages and stimulating travel to and contacts with other islands. Coastal dwellers pushed inland and across the seas to other islands. Letters were introduced.

Greater use of iron farm implements raised agricultural productivity considerably. The surplus of wealth created by higher agricultural productivity was accompanied by the emergence of a class of local lords *(anji)* who fought among themselves for supremacy. The port towns of Urasoe and Naha were established. The kingdom of Chūzan, which possessed the best natural harbors and hinterlands, gradually emerged from the chaos of internal warfare. This was a period of nascent national consciousness and development.

During the third period, from approximately 1392 to 1609, superior navigational and shipbuilding technology was imported from Ming China. With the use of transoceanic ships, the Okinawans succeeded in transforming the vast expanse of isolating ocean into bridges to all nations. They were trading with literally all of the nations in East and Southeast Asia, and Okinawa's reputation was such that it was compared to Milan in Europe. With trade came contact with advanced civilizations, especially that of China, civilizing the barbarous island kingdom. This period was the first golden age in the history of Okinawa, and Okinawa was very conscious of the outside world, especially China and the South Seas. The spirit of the times is reflected in the following words inscribed upon a great bell cast and hung at Shuri Castle in 1458 during the reign of King Shō Taikyū: "Ships are means of communication with all nations; the country is full of rare products and precious treasures."[28]

Throughout each of these periods or stages in the development of shipbuilding and navigation, people continued to depend mainly upon wind and human energy for propulsion: namely, sail, oar, and scull. It seems only in the last stage that they were able to travel continuously for any number of days without sighting land. By contrast, in the first stage, that is, from earliest times until about the end of the twelfth century, when boats were crude dugout canoes made either of pine or pasania wood with some sort of sail,[29] people must have travelled from one island to another depending upon the wind and weather, always keeping land in sight (from Kyūshū, Japan to Okinawa, some headlands are always within sight from any point en route).

At this stage, wind, current, and coastal topography were the three most important factors in determining the route of sea traffic. In winter, the Ryūkyū Islands, together with the greater Japanese archipelago, are under the influence of the predominantly westerly and northwesterly winds that blow from the northern interior of Asia. In summer, the winds shift, notably to the south and southeast. The coasts of the Ryūkyūs are washed by the Black Current, a strong, warm current which moves steadily north-eastward from the seas of Melanesia up along the Philippines and the Taiwan coast, serving as a natural belt conveyer carrying everything from the south to the shores of Ryūkyū and southern

Japan.[30] As borne out by many *omoro* on the subject of trading voyages, it seems that from time immemorial the islanders were familiar with and utilized the monsoon winds, leaving for the north in summer and returning in winter, or leaving for the south in winter, and returning home in summer.

However, in earlier times—definitely before the twelfth century, sea traffic from Okinawa appears to have been restricted mainly to the islands in the north and Japan for a geographical reason which George Kerr, in his *Okinawa: The History of an Island People*, correctly points out as an important factor "which had some bearing upon the distribution of prehistoric settlements and upon the rate of cultural change (and its direction) within historic times."[31] That is to say, "when traveling northward from Okinawa toward Japan on good days, land is always in sight. When moving south, however, it is necessary to cross a stretch of turbulent sea in which no land may be seen in any direction at the midway point; it is 175 miles from Okinawa to the nearest islands in the Miyako group."[32] In addition to the question of sheer distance, there is the factor of climate—"modern records indicate that a minimum of twelve and a maximum of forty-five typhoons may be experienced in Okinawan waters in the course of any year. At least three pass directly over the main island; others linger nearby. A small storm may be only forty or fifty miles in diameter revolving about the baleful eye; the greater storms sometimes have a two-hundred-mile diameter and a wind velocity in excess of 150 miles per hour."[33]

In the first stage, then, distance and climate precluded to a considerable extent trade or other traffic between Okinawa and the islands that lie farther south. However, even in the absence of a well-developed navigational technology, migration southward from Japan as far as Okinawa or trade and other traffic between the two was quite possible and indeed relatively easy. Indications are that ancient Okinawa faced northward to Japan.

On the question of the Pacific coast versus the China Sea coast as the center of culture during this early period, the singular topography of Okinawa, in combination with the aforementioned factors of wind and current, seems to have made it far easier for a small boat to travel on the Pacific coast than on the China Sea coast. As the map of Okinawa clearly illustrates, the northern part of Okinawa is gently convex on the Pacific coast, making it easier for a small boat to traverse it. About half-way down the coast of Okinawa, there is a series of small offshore islands. The first or northernmost is Ike Island which has already been mentioned as having an excellent young shipwright (could it be that its ideal location made it a sort of aid station for boats coming down from the north?). The last or southernmost is Kudaka Island, site of the Kubamori sacred grove, one of the two holiest groves in Ryūkyū. (The other is Seifa utaki, a grove located just across the strait in Chinen on Okinawa Island.) A little below Ike Island, the Katsuren Peninsula of Okinawa Island juts out into the sea like an outstretched arm to receive the newcomers from the north. A little way below Katsuren peninsula is another peninsula, Chinen. The indented coastline between Katsuren and Chinen forms an ideal bay, Nakagusuku Bay. The port of Yagi is located within this bay. At the entrance to the bay lie the islands of Tsuken and Kudaka, forming a natural breakwater. If a boat takes the Pacific coast route down from the north, it will be under the lee of Okinawa Island, protected against the strong rough winds from the north and against the strong steady northward flow of the Black Current. Ike, Miyagi, Heanza, Tsuken, Kudaka, and other smaller islands serve as an effective breakwater. None of these conditions exist on the China Sea coast.

We noted in the discussion above how the Okinawan center of culture moved with time and changing conditions. Although there seems to be little doubt that ancient Okinawa faced northward to Japan, history gives one to suspect that it sprang up suddenly on the China Sea coast[34] in about the mid-twelfth and thirteenth centuries. On the basis of the evidence presented so far, it is hypothesized that the center of Okinawan culture at its earliest stage (until about the tenth, eleventh, or even twelfth centuries) was located on the Pacific southeast coast, a region roughly encompassing the Katsuren Peninsula southward to the Chinen area. This hypothesis is supported not only by this region's connections with the outside world to the north, just discussed, but also by its topography. That is, northern Okinawa is dominated by steep mountains and hills which are definitely unfit for primitive agriculture. Even on the coast, steep hills suddenly drop into the Pacific Ocean, and there is hardly any coastal plain to permit development of a fair-sized agricultural community. In comparison with the northeastern coast, the southeastern coast has ample coastal plains conducive to agriculture and settlement. Its hinterlands are not steep hills as in the northern region but are gentle slopes and plains.

In the light of this hypothesis, the myth related in the *Chūzan sekan* to the effect that the creator-goddess Amamiku (Amamikyo) brought the seeds of five kinds of grains from heaven, and that she sowed the rice seeds in Tamagusuku, Chinen, and sowed the rest on Kudaka Island,[35] may be interpreted as the story of strangers from the north bringing with them new fruits and grains and advanced agricultural techniques. This also explains the strength of King Shō Hashi who rose to power in the area of Sashiki and Chinen on the southeast coast, which forms the southern part of the early cultural center of our hypothesis. Also explained is the unusual power and prosperity of Amawari, lord of Katsuren, a hero who came too late and failed. According to traditional accounts,[36] he was a cunning traitor to King Shō Taikyū (1454–1460), historically a villain, but the following *omoro* seems to tell a different story.

Katsuren and Kamakura[37]

Katsuren wa,	Katsuren
Naonigya,[1] tatoeru,[2]	To what can we compare it?
Yamato no,	Let us compare it
Kamakura[3] ni, tatoeru	To Kamakura in Japan.
Kimutaka[4] wa,	High spirited (Katsuren),
Naonigya, tatoeru,	To what can we compare it?
(Yamato no,)	(Let us compare it)
(Kamakura ni, tatoeru.)	(To Kamakura in Japan.)

1. *naonigya* — Equivalent to Japanese *nani-nika. Nao* 'what', 'where'. *Naonigya* literally means 'to what?'.

2. *tatoeru* — 'To compare, to make comparison to'.

3. *Kamakura* — City of Kamakura in eastern Japan near present Yokohama. It was the seat of government of the Kamakura shogunate from 1185 to 1333.

4. *kimutaka* — *Kimu* 'liver', 'gall bladder' + *taka* 'high'. Courage was considered to reside in the liver; hence, *kimutaka* means courageous, bold, or brave. Though Iha takes this word to be an adjectival epithet for Amawari, lord of Katsuren, Nakahara believes this to be an epithet for Katsuren. The writer follows Nakahara whose interpretation gives consistency in this context.

This *omoro* reveals two interesting things. First, at this time (approximately, from the end of the fourteenth century to the beginning of the fifteenth century), there must have been considerable traffic, trade or otherwise, with Japan, for the people or at least the author of this *omoro* seems quite well acquainted with the situation in Japan—that of Kyoto being the nominal capital but Kamakura the real seat of power and government. Nakahara remarks that it is very impressive that while the Shuri *omoro* consistently refer to Kyoto, the Katsuren *omoro* consistently refer to Kamakura for purposes of comparison.[38] Second, since, as this *omoro* shows, Katsuren was comparable to Kamakura in Japan, Katsuren must have been very powerful—perhaps as powerful or even more powerful than Shuri. At the time of Amawari, lord of Katsuren, the great warrior king Shō Hashi was long dead and after a rapid succession of three short-lived kings (from 1440 to 1454, only fourteen years) each of which entailed enormous expenditures connected with the three investiture missions from China and a war of succession in 1453, the Shuri administration of King Shō Taikyū was quite weak. In fact, the marriage of Princess Momoto-fumiagari, daughter of King Shō Taikyū, to Lord Amawari seems to have been a political alliance with the local lord, a potential rival to the king. The rise of Katsuren coincided with the gradual decline of Shuri.

In Praise of Katsuren[39]

Katsuren wa, teda,[1] mukate,[2]	In Katsuren, the Jade Palace
Jyō,[3] akete,[4]	A gate was built
Madama,[5] kogane, yoriyou,[6]	Facing the sun
Tama no, miuchi[7]	Pearl and gold
	Have gathered together.
Kimutaka no, tsuki,[8] mukate,	In Kimutaka, the Jade Palace,
(Jyō, akete,)	(A gate was built)
(Madama, kogane, yoriyou,)	(Facing the moon,)
(Tama no, miuchi)	(Pearl and gold
	Have gathered together.)
Katsuren wa,	Katsuren,
Kesa[9] mu, mya[10] mo,	In the present as in the past,
Anji, erabu.	Has chosen her lord.

1. *teda* — 'Sun'. The word is pronounced */tida/.* Nakahara explains that *teriya* 'that which shines', has become *tera*, which in turn corrupted to *tida.*

2. *mukate* — 'Facing forward'.

3. *jyō* — 'Gate'.

4. *akete* — A conjugated form of *akeru* 'to open'. Here it also means 'to make or build (a gate).'

5. *madama* — *Ma*, prefix meaning 'true, genuine' + *dama* or *tama*, 'jade, precious stone'.

6. *yoriyou* — 'To come together or to gather together'.

7. *miuchi* — *Mi*, honorific + *uchi* 'house, building'. Here, *tama no miuchi* is translated as 'Jade Palace'.

8. *tsuki* — 'Moon'.

9. *kesa* — Though in modern Japanese *kesa* means 'this morning', here it means the past, and not necessarily this morning only.

10. *mya* — 'The present time, now'. It is derived from *imya*, a cognate of Japanese *ima*, meaning 'now, the present'. Dropping of the initial 'i' is found in some other instances also.

Amawari, Lord of Katsuren[40]

Katsuren no Amawari	Amawari, lord of Katsuren,
Tamamishaku,[1] ariyona[2]	They say, has a jeweled ladle.
Kya, Kamakura,	To even Kyoto and Kamakura
Koredo,[3] iche,[4] toyoma	Let this be known and reechoed.
Kimutaka no Amawari	Amawari, lord of Kimutaka,
(Tamamishaku, ariyona)	(They say, has a jeweled ladle.)
(Kya, Kamakura,)	(To even Kyoto and Kamakura)
(Koredo, iche, toyoma) Shimajiri[5] no, misode[6]	(Let this be known and reechoed.)
no anji	Revered lord, who governs the island
Kunishiri no, misode no anji,	Revered lord, who governs the country,
Shori, owaru, teda kosu[7]	It is the king who resides in Shuri
Tamamishaku, aryoware[8]	That has the jeweled ladle.

1. *tamamishaku* — *Tama* 'jade', 'jewel' + *mishaku* or *hishaku* 'ladle', 'scoop'.

2. *Ariyona* — *Ari* 'to have', 'to possess' + *yona*, a mildly emphatic article.

3. *kore* — 'This'. It refers to the fact that Amawari owns the jeweled ladle.

4. *iche* — Equivalent to Japanese *itte* 'speaking thus'. *Koredo iche* 'saying this', 'telling this'.

5. *shimajiri*	*Shima* 'island', 'country' + *jiri* or *shiri* 'to know and to rule'.
6. *misode*	*Mi*, an honorific + *sode* or *sude* 'superior'. It is derived from *sudaru*, which means 'to be born again and again (with eternal life, symbolically, just as a snake exuviates again and again, casting off its old skin)'.
7. *teda kosu*	*Teda* 'the sun', epithet for the king in Shuri + emphatic *kosu* or *koso*.
8. *aryoware*	'To possess' (polite term).

Both of these *omoro* praise Katsuren and Lord Amawari. "In Praise of Katsuren" boasts of the wealth of Katsuren derived from overseas trade and of the people's pride in their able lord. "Amawari, Lord of Katsuren" may express childish vanity—i.e., "Amawari, lord of Katsuren, has a jeweled ladle, the like of which is owned only by the king in Shuri. Therefore, let's tell this all over Japan and be proud of our lord"—but for all its pride, it suggests that the wealth of Katsuren approached that of Shuri. The wealth and power of Katsuren, which threatened the hegemony of Shuri, was amassed through Amawari's able leadership and the advantageous location of Katsuren, which lay in the northern part of the primary culture center. Though Katsuren was rather out of the way, it possessed considerable farmland and controlled some smaller strategic islands nearby. Therefore, it was comparatively rich in both agricultural and marine products and enjoyed brisk trade with distant islands in the north such as Yoron, Oki-erabu, Tokunoshima, Amami-Ōshima, and even Kyūshū, Japan.

However, Lord Amawari was born about a century too late. For Hashi, later known as King Shō Hashi, the first to unify Okinawa, had been born in Sashiki in the southeastern corner of Okinawa. Still more important was the occasion on which King Satto of Chūzan, who was located then at Urasoe, received an imperial envoy from Ming China and began trading at enormous profit with that vast empire in 1372. After a series of trade missions to China, when the thirty-six Chinese families migrated to Okinawa and settled in Naha in 1392 under the protection of Chūzan, the center of culture and power in Okinawa moved from the southeast or Pacific coast to the southwest coast facing the China Sea. Just as the Chinese empire by its power and wealth dominated East Asia, the southwest coastal region of Okinawa, having overcome the isolating sea barrier and having connected itself with China, was bound to assert its hegemony over other areas in the small island society.

The following *omoro* is from the area of Urasoe, center of Chūzan during the early Omoro period.

Ezo's Housewarming[41]

Ezonya[1] no uchi[2] ya	At the mansion of Lord Ezo
Amae[3] yabera[4]	Let us make merry.
Hokori[5] yabera	Let us all be happy.
Teda ga uchi yareba[6]	Because it's the mansion of our Sun (lord),
(Amae yabera)	(Let us make merry.)
(Hokori yabera)	(Let us all be proud.)

1. *Ezonya* — Master of Ezo, lord of Ezo. Ezo (or Iso, Ishu, Izu, or Eiso variously) is a village in the Urasoe area.
2. *uchi* — 'House, building'.
3. *amae* — 'To make merry'.
4. *yabera* — 'Let's do . . . ', related to archaic Japanese *haberu* or *haberan*, it is a polite form for 'let . . . be or do'.
5. *hokori* — 'Happiness or pride'.
6. *uchi yareba* — *Uchi* 'house', 'mansion' + *yareba* 'because it is'.

They Have Wine in Urasoe[42]

Uraosoi ya, Uraosoi ya	In Urasoe, in Urasoe,
Mikii do,[1] aruna,[2]	They offer sacred wine.
Sake[3] do, aruna,	They have wine.
Tasha,[4] tasha,	To shieh! To shieh! [Thanks! Thanks!]
Kyo[5] ya, kyo ya,	Today is the day
Yoyosenyo[6] ga, kachi,[7] tsukai[8]	Yoyosenyo has sent for me.
Tokashiki[9] ya, Tokashiki ya Sake do, aruna	In Tokashiki, in Tokashiki, they have wine.
Mikii do, aruna,	They offer sacred wine.
(Tasha, tasha,)	(To shieh! To shieh!)
(Kyo ya, kyo ya,)	(Today is the day)
(Yoyosenyo ga, kachi, tsukai)	(Yoyosenyo has sent for me.)

1. *mikii do*	*Miki(i)* 'sacred wine (offered to the gods)' + *ido* or *do*, an emphatic particle.
2. *aruna*	'There is or there are'. *Na* has no meaning but expresses an idea of confirming something to oneself.
3. *sake*	'Wine'.
4. *tasha*	Chinese *to shieh* 'thanks'.
5. *kyo*	'Today'.
6. *Yoyosenyo*	A man's name.
7. *kachi*	'In the direction of'.
8. *tsukai*	'Messenger, to send a messenger', later having the meaning 'to invite'.
9. *Tokashiki*	Older name for Urasoe.

The first of the two *omoro* above celebrates the housewarming of the new mansion of the lord of Ezo (or Eiso). There is evidence that Japanese trade ships frequented the port of Makiminato during the reign of Eiso. At this time also, the priest Zenkan, believed to be a Japanese, built Gokurakuji Temple. People must have been attracted to Urasoe by its prosperity. With growing wealth and population, the number of mansions and buildings naturally increased. Perhaps more elaborate buildings were built than ever before with the improved technology introduced from abroad.[43]

When a mansion was built, the owner would throw a housewarming party to which townspeople and out-of-town guests were invited. The second *omoro*, "They Have Wine in Urasoe," depicts just such a scene. The poet, who lives outside of Urasoe (formerly Tokashiki), has been invited to a party given by Yoyosenyo, where he knows (perhaps he was told by the messenger) that there will be an offering of wine. After the sacred wine has been offered to the gods, there will be a big feast. Thinking of the delicious wine, the poet's heart is happy and light, and he sings an impromptu *omoro* on his way. The remarkable thing about this *omoro* is that it is the only one which includes Chinese vocabulary. The poet says (in lines four and ten) "*to shieh! to shieh!*"—'thanks! thanks!'.

From the inception of formal trade with China in 1372, Chinese cultural influence was increasingly felt in Okinawa. One of the most obvious examples of Chinese influence was the adoption of certain Chinese vocabulary terms. It's no wonder that some simple expressions such as *to shieh* should be popular—especially so, perhaps, among the educated class and townspeople of

Urasoe, Naha, and Shuri, which were the focal points of contact with China. Conversely, the fact that a foreign phrase such as *to shieh* was popular in the Chūzan area is indicative of that area's having been the cultural center of Okinawa at the time, for generally speaking, according to the usual pattern of cultural dissemination, the highly developed urban port town is most sensitive to foreign cultural influence.

The following *omoro* affirms that the lord of Urasoe reigned supreme over all other lords, and that Urasoe was the original capital of the kingdom of Chūzan before the capital was transferred to Shuri. It describes a scene at a party where the lord of Urasoe proudly displays his jeweled ladle to the many guests in attendance.[44] Note that the word Yonotsuji is used as a synonym for Urasoe. It literally means 'the top of the world', referring, no doubt, to the capital of the kingdom.

Jeweled Ladle[45]

Urasoe ni, chowache[1]	One who resides in Urasoe
Tamamishaku,[2] sashiyuwareba[3]	Ladled [wine] with a jeweled ladle.
Momochara[4] wa, michedo[5]	How envious the hundred lords may be to see it!
Urayami[6] yoru	May be to see it!
Yonotsuji[7] ni, chowache	One who resides in Yonotsuji
(Tamamishaku, sashiyuwareba)	(Ladled [wine] with a jeweled ladle.)
(Momochara wa, michedo)	(How envious the hundred lords)
(Urayamiyoru.)	(May be to see it!)

1. *chowache*	Polite term for 'to be, to exist'.
2. *tamamishaku*	*Tama* 'jade', 'jewel' + *mishaku* 'ladle', 'scoop'.
3. *sashiyuwaru*	Polite term for *sasu* 'to pour into', 'to fill (a cup)', 'to offer (a cup)'.
4. *momochara*	*Momo* 'hundred' + *chara*, synonym for *anji* 'lord'.
5. *michedo*	'To see, and. . . . '
6. *urayamu*	'To be envious, to be jealous'.
7. *yonotsuji*	*Yo* 'the world' + *no* 'of' + *tsuji* 'top'. Top of the world, used as a synonym for Urasoe.

The next two *omoro* constitute simple vignettes on the subject of taxation. Apparently, up until the time of King Eiso there had been no systematic mode of taxation. Whenever there was need, a head tax, a bundle of rice about the size of a man's head called *tsuka-kanai*, was collected. According to the *Chūzan sekan*, Eiso ascended the throne in 1260, and the next year, following the tax system of Chou (of ancient China), he corrected boundaries and divided the land according to the well-field system. Owing to the improved system, there were abundant harvests, taxes were fully paid, and the country prospered.[46] Even if the *Chūzan sekan* is to be trusted, there is no way to know to what extent King Eiso actually adopted and practiced the system of taxation. However, it seems reasonable to assume that by the time of King Satto, about a century later, a system of taxation was fairly well established.

That a system of regular taxation, based not upon the sporadic needs of the king but upon the yearly yield of the land, collected regularly, was instituted sometime between the latter half of the thirteenth century and the first half of the fourteenth century indicates that during this period the structure of government and state became developed and established in place of the old tribal government, for it is only with an estimable regular income that the various functions of state can be performed. It also indicates that the level of production was sufficient to support such a system of taxation. This period also coincides with my hypothetical second stage of development in the technology of navigation discussed earlier.

Rejoicing over the Payment of Taxes[47]

Oeyafuso[1] no ōya[2]	As chief of Oyafuso,
Ōyako[3] ga, kanai,[4]	Ōyako has offered
Nobote, ikeba[5]	As one has gone up, [to carry taxes to the king],
Teda ga, hokori, yowache	The king was proud and happy.
Matayoshi[6] no ōya,	As chief of Matayoshi,
Ōyako ga sasage,[7]	Ōyako has presented
(Nobote, ikeba)	(Taxes to the king,)
(Teda ga, hokori, yowache)	(The king was proud and happy.)
Kyo no, yokaru hi[8] ni,	On this day of good omen,
Ōyako ga, sasage	Ōyako presented them,
Kyo no kyakaru[9] hi ni.	On this day of brilliance.

1. *Oeyafuso*	A village in Urasoe. Present day Oyafuso.
2. *ōya*	Literally, 'the big house', another name for the root house or main house of the village. The root man, the eldest son of the root house, was also called *ōya* and represented the village.
3. *ōyako*	Same as *ōya* 'root man' above.
4. *kanai*	'Tax goods.' It now means 'tenant fee' or 'rent'.
5. *nobote, ikeba*	'As one goes up, or as one takes something up', referring to taking or presenting the tax to king.
6. *Matayoshi*	Another name for Gusukuma village in Urasoe.
7. *sasage*	From *sasageru* 'to lift up, offer, devote'.
8. *yokaru hi*	*Yokaru* 'good, auspicious' + *hi* 'day'.
9. *kyakaru*	'Bright, shining'.

The next *omoro*, "Tribute Tax from the Sea," relates that a wise man called Hyaryomoi of Jana village leased a fishing ground from the lord of the region, and that as a tax payment he presented the lord some of his catch, thereby winning the lord's favor. Nakahara believes that this Hyaryomoi may be the one who, later called Janamoi, eventually became King Satto[48].

Tribute Tax from the Sea[49]

Jana no, Hyaryomoi,	Hyaryomoi of Jana,
Ijeki,[1] Hyaryomoi,[2]	Splendid Hyaryomoi,
Kanate,[3] anji ni, omowarete[4]	Favored by the lord
	And leased [the fishing ground].
Jana no, yokari shima[5]	Jana, the good village,
Umi chikasa,[6] amon[7]	Is near the ocean.
Togya[8] wa, iyo[9] tsuku[10]	The spear to pierce the fish,
Igyo[11] mo, tako[12] tsuku	The harpoon to pierce the octopus,
Umi mu,[13] oyamon,[14]	The sea, too, belongs to the lord.
Takya[15] mo, oyamon.	The ocean, too, belongs to the lord.

1. *ijeki*	'Spirited, superior, splendid'.
2. *Hyaryomoi*	*Hyari*, a childhood name + *omoi* 'to think' (used as a suffix of endearment).
3. *kanate*	'To lease, to rent'.
4. *omowarete*	'To be thought of, to be loved, to be favored'.
5. *yokarishima*	*Yokari* 'good' + *shima* 'village'.
6. *umi chikasa*	*Umi* 'sea' + *chikasa* 'near'.
7. *amon*	Contraction of *aru mono* 'to be', 'to exist'. *Umi chikasa amon* 'the sea is near'.
8. *togya*	'Spear [to catch fish]'. Today it is called *tuja*.
9. *iyo*	'Fish'.
10. *tsuku*	'To push, to pierce'.
11. *igyo*	'[A dull-pointed] spear [used to catch octopus]'.
12. *tako*	'Octopus'.
13. *umi mu*	*Umi* 'sea', 'ocean' + *mu* 'also', 'too'.
14. *oyamon*	*Oya* 'parent' + *mon[o]* 'thing or matter'. That which belongs to a superior or noble.
15. *takya*	Synonym for *umi* 'sea' (Pronounced /tagya/ or /taja/).

In an island nation such as Okinawa, poor in natural resources, the extent of development of overseas trade, especially during the period under study, is a direct measure of the wealth and power of society, or that segment of it that engaged in such trade. In 1372, long ahead of the kingdoms of Hokuzan and Nanzan, King Satto of Chūzan sent a tributary mission to China headed by his younger brother Taiki.[50]

This was an economic as well as political move which yielded King Satto not only great profits but also tremendous political prestige and recognition from the emperor of the greatest empire then known.

First Trade Ship[51]

Oza[1] no Tachomoi[2] ya,	Master Tachi of Uza!
Tō akinai,[3] haerache[4]	Pioneer the trade with China
Anji ni omowarere[5]	And stand high in the lord's favor.

Ijeki, Tachomoi ya,	Master Tachi, the great!
(Tō akinai, haerache)	(Pioneer the trade with China)
(Anji ni omowarere.)	(And stand high in the lord's favor.)

1. *Oza* — A village in present day Yomitan near Urasoe. The modern pronunciation is /uza/.
2. *Tachomoi* — *Tachi* + *omoi* = *Tachomoi*. *Tachi* is a personal name, written in the official records as *Taiki*, and *yomoi* or *omoi* is a suffix of endearment. Nakahara is of the opinion that Tachi or Taiki was probably not a younger brother of King Satto but a powerful retainer and a lesser lord of Oza under Satto. It may be a sort of assimilated temporary rank given to envoys.
3. *Tō akinai* — *Tō* 'T'ang, China'; *akinai* 'business, trade'.
4. *haerache* — Derived form of *hayaru* 'to become fashionable or current'. *Haerache* is a causative: 'he has made it fashionable or current'.
5. *omowarere* — *Omoware* means 'to be well thought of, or to stand high in someone's favor'; the final *re* is for emphasis.

The *omoro* above, "First Trade Ship," apparently celebrates Tachi, or Taiki's departure for China. The main items of trade he took with him on this mission are as follows: horses, swords, gold, silver, wine, agate, ivory, mother-of-pearl, gold- and silver-dusted fans, copper, zinc, fabrics, cowhides, sandalwood, sappanwood, and other perfume materials, peppers, sulphur, and grinding stones.[52] Most of these items are not native products of the Ryūkyū Islands. They appear to have been imported from Japan and the countries bordering the seas to the south, leading to the conclusion that trade with these countries was already well established. When Taiki returned, having accomplished his mission, a big feast was held in his honor. The following *omoro* describes the sight of the chiefs of nearby villages coming to the party bringing wine-jars carried by their servants.

To Welcome the Returning Trade Ship[53]

Oza no, Tachomoi ya,	To Master Tachi of Uza,
Ijeki, Tachomoi ya,	To Master Tachi, the great,
Kagami,[1] iro[2] no,	Let us offer the mirror-like

Sudemizu[3] yo, mioyase,[4]	Water of rejuvenation [wine].
Oza Tokesu,[5] umata,[6]	Chiefs of Tokeshi and Uza
Shigechikame,[7] hawate,[8]	Taking their wine-jar carriers along,
Oza Tokesu, asuta,[9]	Chiefs of Uza and Tokeshi,
Osake, mochi, hawate.	With their liquor-jar carriers along.

1. *kagami*	'Mirror'.
2. *iro*	'Color'.
3. *sudemizu*	*Mizu* 'water' + *sude* 'to rejuvenate'.
4. *mioyase*	Polite term for 'to offer'.
5. *Tokesu*	Village of Tokeshi in present day Yomitan near Urasoe.
6. *umata*	Literally, 'a groom'. However, here it means some important person of the village. It is the same person as the root man of the village, for it is his duty in a religious ceremony to drive the horse of the *noro* priestess.
7. *shigechikame*	*Shigechi* 'a kind of wine' + *kame* 'jar'.
8. *hawate*	'To take someone along'.
9. *asuta*	*Asu* means the 'upper class, the leaders of the village', and *ta* is a plural suffix.

In the light of the very active trade with China during King Satto's reign (Taiki went to China in 1373, 1374, 1376, and 1382, and there were other missions as well), the lines in the *omoro* "In Praise of King Satto," quoted earlier, "The Treasure House door that / All the lords were weary of waiting / Lord Janamoi has opened" begin to take on another meaning. That is, "the Treasure House door that Lord Janamoi has opened" seems to refer not only to the great agricultural improvement that he introduced but also to his pioneering trade with China to bring the wealth and civilization of China to Okinawa.

As the kingdom of Chūzan under the able rule of King Satto prospered, remote areas on Okinawa and other, lesser, islands also began to develop. In the process, there were inevitable rivalries among the lords resulting in wars and unrest all over Okinawa and on the outlying islands. For instance, the following *omoro* from Kume Island portrays the priestess Senokimi desperately seeking the aid of the gods and Buddha for the safety and protection of a lord in crisis. It's interesting to note that by this time, the concepts of Japanese *kami* and the Buddha had been integrated into the life of the priestess. Can the fact that the *kami* and *hotoke* (Buddha) appear only in this *omoro*, in which the priestess seems desperate, mean that she was resorting to the *kami* and *hotoke*, foreign deities, as higher authorities than the native *kami?*

Lord and Priestess[54]

Kikoe, Senokimi ya	Well known Senokimi praying,
Kami hotoke	Gods and Buddha!
Imya[1] no anshiosoi[2]	Let us protect
Mabura[3]	Our present lord.
Toyomu, Senokimi ya	Renowned Senokimi praying,
(Kami hotoke)	(Gods and Buddha!)
(Imya no anshiosoi)	(Let us protect)
(Mabura)	(Our present lord.)
Mashikesu[4] ga, miuchi[5] ni,	Within the sanctuary,
Kawarume[6] ga, miuchi ni.	Within the sanctum sanctorum.

1. *imya* 'now', 'present'.
2. *anshiosoi* *anji osoi* 'lord'.
3. *mabura* Varient of *mamora* 'let's protect'.
4. *mashikesu* *Ma* is a prefix meaning 'true, genuine', and *shikesu* or *shike* is a 'sacred place of worship'.
5. *miuchi* 'Within, inside'.
6. *kawarume* The actual meaning of this word is 'something strange or spectacular or beautiful.' Since it is used here as a synonym for the sanctuary rather than applied adjectivally, it has been translated as 'sanctum sanctorum'.

Although King Satto was an able statesman who brought great prosperity to Chūzan, he was not able to unify the whole of Okinawa during his lifetime. After he died in 1395 at the age of 75, his heir, King Bunei, neglecting the affairs of state, quickly dissipated on personal pleasure the wealth his father had accumulated.

In the meanwhile, in 1372, about twenty years before the death of King Satto, in Nawashiro, Sashiki, in the southeast corner of Okinawa, a baby boy named

Hashi was born to Nawashiro Ōya, the root man of Nawashiro. The birth of the future king is described in the following *omoro:*

The Birth of King Shō Hashi[55]

Sashiki, Nawashiru ni,	At Nawashiro, Sashiki
Sudemono,[1] mamono,[2]	Was born a holy one, divine one,
madama[3] no,	Like a true jewel,
Tomoyagaru,[4] mishako[5]	Like an ossifrage taking to the sky.
Motai, Nawashiro ni,	At prosperous Nawashiro
(Sudemono, mamono,	(Was born a holy one, divine one,)
madama no,)	(Like a true jewel,)
(Torimoyagaru, mishako.)	(Like an ossifrage taking to the sky.)

1. *sudemono* — *Sude* 'to hatch, to exuviate, appearance of new life' + *mono* 'matter, thing'. Literally translated 'one who has been born', it applies only to one who is greatly superior or divine.

2. *mamono* — *Ma* is a prefix denoting 'trueness, genuineness'. *Mono* is explained above. *Mamono*, like *sudemono*, refers to an exceptional, even superhuman person, a god, or equal to a god.

3. *madama* — 'True jewel'.

4. *tomoyagaru* — 'To jump up, to fly up'. *Tobi* 'to fly' + *agaru* 'to rise'. In one version, *'toriyakaru'*.

5. *mishako* — A large bird of prey, such as the eagle fisher, osprey, or ossifrage, *Pandion haliaetus*, or even more likely, the lammergeier (also called ossifrage), *Gypaetus barbatus.* Said to be the largest European bird of prey, it is characterized by a wingspan as large as ten feet and a droopy black feather 'moustache' under the beak. The lammergeier ranges as far as China

A talented general, Hashi conquered neighboring villages and expanded his domains. In about 1403, he took over nearby Nanzan. Two years later, in 1405, he defeated King Bunei of Chūzan and placed his own father on the throne. In 1422, succeeding his father, he finally conquered Hokuzan in the north, thus uniting the whole of Okinawa.[56]

Shō Hashi's Attack[57]

Sashiki, ijeki, aji	Spirited lord of Sashiki
Masano,[1] ijeki, aji ya	Truly spirited lord
Oya shinate,[2]	Allied with his father
Shimauchi,[3] masari,[4] yowache	Attacked and conquered the country.
Sashiki, jakuni,[6] aji,	High lord of fair Sashiki
(Masano, ijeki, aji ya)	(Truly spirited lord)
(Oya shinate,)	(Allied with his father)
(Shimauchi, masari, yowache.)	(Attached and conquered the country.)

1. *masano* 'True, genuine'.
2. *oya shinate* *Oya* 'parent'; *shinate* 'to be harmonious with', 'to be friendly with'. Here, reference is made to the fact that Hashi and his father cooperated in the conquest.
3. *shimauchi* *Shima* 'village', 'country'. *Uchi* 'to hit', 'to attack'.
4. *masari* 'To be superior to, to surpass'.
5. *yowache* Polite term modifying the preceding words.
6. *jakuni* 'Fair country, big country'.

The Priestess Leads the Army[58]

Kikoe ōkimigya[1]	The well known chief priestess
Ake[2] no, yoroi,[3] meshowache	Put on a scarlet armor,
Katana, uchisu,[4]	[And] with a sword at her side,
	[Went to war.]
Jakuni, toyomiyoware	Her fame resounded in the country.
Toyomu sedakako[5] ga	The illustrious king has made
Tsukishiro[6] wa, sadakete[7]	Tsukishiro his guide
Monoshiri[8] wa, sadakete	The priestess his leader.

1. *kikoe ōgimi* 'Chief priestess'.
2. *ake* 'Red, scarlet'.
3. *yoroi* 'Armor'.

4. *uchisu*	Possibly a variant of *uchisoe*, an emphatic term for hitching a sword to one's side. In Nakahara and Hokama's *Kōhon Omoro sōshi* it appears as *uchii* (p. 62).
5. *sedakako*	*Se* 'spiritual power' + *daka* or *taka* 'high', meaning one who is high (strong) in spiritual power, such as king Shō Hashi.
6. *tsukishiro*	Literally, 'white moon', an adjective to praise the beautiful moon. It is the name of guardian god or spirit of Lord Sashiki, that is, Shō Hashi.
7. *sadake*	'To lead, to guide'.
8. *monoshiri*	Literally, 'one who knows things', i.e., a shaman or a priestess

Nawashiro Ōya, Hashi's father, perceived his son's military ability early on, and gave his position to Hashi. With his father's assistance and support, Hashi was able to conquer the whole island. "Shō Hashi's Attack" tells of this father-son alliance. The second *omoro*, "The Priestess Leads the Army," describes Hashi's army as it marched on Chūzan. As will be seen in several *omoro*, magic was believed to be as potent as military might, and it seems a war of incantation preceded the actual fighting. In the *omoro* above, Hashi's priestess and shaman appear to be in front of the advancing army as guides and protectors against the evil enemy spirits.

The next two *omoro*, "First Envoy to China" and "Chinen-mori Castle," show clearly how Hashi was able to build up his economic and military power. His birthplace of Sashiki located on the southeast coast of Okinawa was advantageous for trade with Japan, but Hashi had also succeeded in luring Chinese ships to his Grove Castle of Chinen, where he could trade with China independently of Chūzan. It must have been from this trading activity that he acquired the means to finance his military ventures. When Hashi became king of Chūzan in 1405, he dispatched his nephew, chief of Tedokon (1372–1439) as his envoy to the Ming court to request investiture. Tedokon succeeded not only in obtaining Ming recognition of Hashi as king of Chūzan, but also received an official rank in the Chinese court. His success was indeed worthy of recounting all over Japan.

First Envoy to China[59]

Tedokon[1] no, ōyako	Chief of Tedokon
Tō[2] no, michi,[3] akewache[4]	Has opened the way to China
Tedokon-su	Master Tedokon,
Nihon-uchi[5] ni, toyome[6]	Let his name resound all over Japan
Tedokon-su, satonuchi.[7]	Village chief of Tedokon.

1. *Tedokon*	A place name in Sashiki.
2. *Tō*	'T'ang, China'.
3. *michi*	'Way, road, path'.
4. *akewache*	A polite term for *akeru* 'to open'.
5. *Nihon-uchi*	*Nihon* 'Japan', *uchi* 'inside'.
6. *toyome*	'To resound, to echo'.
7. *satonushi*	*Sato* 'village' + *nushi* 'chief'.

Chinen-mori Castle[60]

Chenen morigusuku[1]	Grove Castle of Chinen
Tō no fune	Is the castle where
Kokora[2] yoru[3] gusuku	Many Chinese ships gather
Jakuni morigusuku	Grove Castle of the fair country
(Tō no fune)	Is the castle where
(Kokora yoru gusuku)	(Numerous Chinese ships come together.)

1. *morigusuku*	*Mori* 'grove' + *gusuku* 'castle'. This castle was originally the site of a holy grove.
2. *kokora*	A variant of *kokoda* 'many, numerous'.
3. *yoru*	'To gather, to come together'.

The following *omoro*, though not related to Hashi, best describes the attire of a lord of this era:

Mounted Young Lord[61]

Chibana[1] owaru,[2]	Lord of Chibana
Memayo,[3] kiyora,[4] anji[5] no	Who has fair eyes and brows,
Chibana, owaru,	Lord of Chibana
Hakuki,[6] kiyora anji,	Who has fair teeth and mouth,
Mihachimaki,[7] techiyoku[8]	Has a headband tied
Maki,[9] showache[10]	And tied around tightly,
Shirakake,[11] misho[12]	Has on a white silken gown

Kasabemisho,[13] showache	And on top of many clothes,
Toikikiobi[14]	Has a ten-fold sash around
Mayashi,[15] hikishimete,[16]	And around tight and secure,
Ōkatana[17] yo,	Has a great sword
Kakesashi,[18] showache	Hitched to his side,
Koshikatana[19] yo,	Has a waist dagger
Ikasa,[20] sachishowache	Clasped fast and firm,
Higya,[21] kawasaba[22]	Has goathide sandals
Uchikake, kumi[23] showache	On his feet,
Umahiki[24] no	Has his horse
Michahiki[25] no, Kotara	Led by a groom-boy, Kotaro,
Mashiraha[26] ni,	Has a pure white horse
Koganekura,[27] kakete,	With a golden saddle on,
Maekura ni	On the front of the saddle
Teda no kata,[28] ekache[29]	The sun is painted,
Shiruikura[30] ni	On the back of the saddle
Tsuki no kata egache.	The moon is painted.

1. *Chibana* — Name of a village in present day Misato-son, in central Okinawa.
2. *owaru* — 'To be, to reside' (polite).
3. *memayo* — *Me* 'eye', *mayo* 'brows'.
4. *kiyora* — 'Beautiful, clean, pretty'.
5. *anji* — 'Lord'.
6. *hakuki* — *Ha* 'tooth', 'teeth' + *kuki*, a mistranscription of *kuchi* 'mouth'.
7. *mihachimaki* — *Mi*, honorific + *hachimaki* 'headband'. In those days, men tied their heads with headbands of red, white, or black cloth about 13 feet in length. Later in King Shō Shin's time, it was changed to a form of cap.
8. *techiyoku* — *Te* 'hand' + *chiyoku* 'strong'. Tied tightly with the hand.

9. *maki* 'To tie around'.

10. *showache* 'To do (polite)'.

11. *shirakake* 'Made of white silk'.

12. *misho* *Misho, miso* 'dress', 'costume'.

13. *kasabemisho* *Kasabe* 'to pile up on top [of another], put or place [upon another], in layers, one over the other'. *Misho* 'dress', 'costume'. Many layers of dress or costume.

14. *toikikiobi* *Toi, toe* 'ten-fold' + *kikiobi* 'a sash worn around the waist'.

15. *mayashi* 'To turn around, to pass [a sash around oneself]'.

16. *hikishimete* 'To tie tightly and securely'.

17. *ōkatana* 'Great sword'.

18. *kakesashi* 'To wear [a sword, by hitching it to one's side]'.

19. *koshikatana* *Koshi* 'waist' + *katana* 'sword'.

20. *ikasa* 'Fast and firm'.

21. *higya* 'Goat'. It is pronounced /hijaa/. It means one who has a beard.

22. *kawasaba* *Kawa* 'hide' + *saba* 'sandal', 'slipper'.

23. *kumi* 'To wear [on the foot]'. *Uchikake* appears as *uchioke* in the *Kōhon Omoro sōshi* by Nakahara and Hokama, p. 565.

24. *umahiki* *Uma* 'horse'; *hiki* 'to pull', 'to drive'.

25. *michahiki* 'Groom'.

26. *mashiraha* Ma 'pure', 'true'; *shira, shiro* 'white'; *ha, ba* 'horse'.

27. *koganekura* *Kogane* 'gold' + *kura* 'saddle'.

28. *kata* 'Figure, picture'. *Teda no kata* 'picture of the sun'.

29. *ekache* 'To draw, to paint'.

30. *shiruikura* *Shirui, shiri* 'the back' + *kura* 'saddle'.

With a lord as handsomely dressed and equipped as the lord of Chibana, the army of Shuri advanced to the north and the south, conquering its enemies.

Lord Aorikumo at War[62]

Aorikumo[1] no, anji	Lord Aorikumo,
Jakuni, shirataru	Famed throughout the fair country,
Uchichesu,[2] modore	Conquered them and came back.
Teorikumo[3] no, anji,	Lord Teorikumo,
(Jakuni, shirataru)	(Famed throughout the fair country,)
(Uchichesu, modore)	(Conquered them and came back.)
Shori, oya, ikusa[4]	Great Shuri army,
Gusuku,[5] oya, ikusa	Great royal army,
Itaja,[6] seme, tsukete[7]	Attacked the wooden gate,
Kanaja,[8] seme, tsukete	Assaulted the iron gate,
Itaja, seme, ijache[9]	Drove them out of the wooden gate,
Kanaja, seme, ijache	Routed them out of the iron gate,
Mashiki,[10] oi, tsumete[11]	Chased them into the sanctuary,
Teraho,[12] oi, tsumete	Followed them into the temple,
Momoso,[13] kiri, fusete	Cut down a hundred of them,
Nanaso, kiri, fusete	Slew seventy of them.

1. *Aorikumo*	Name of the lord in charge of the army of Shuri.
2. *uchichiesu*	'To hit, to defeat'.
3. *Teorikumo*	Another name for Lord Aorikumo.
4. *oya ikusa*	*Ikusa* means 'army', and *oya*, as used here, is an honorific rather than in its usual meaning, 'parent'.
5. *gusuku*	Refers to Shuri Castle.
6. *itaja*	*Ita* 'wooden board' + *ja, jyo* 'gate'.
7. *seme tsuke*	'To attack hard'.
8. *kanaja*	'Iron gate'. *Kana* 'metal', 'iron'.
9. *ijache*	'To let out, to chase out'; *seme ijache* 'attacked the enemy and chased him out'.
10. *mashiki*	'Sanctuary'. Here, it means within the compound of a temple. *Mamaki* in some versions, but *mashiki* is correct.

11. *oi tsume*	'To drive to bay, to corner'.
12. *teraho*	*Tera* 'temple', *ho, he* 'corner'.
13. *momoso*	'Hundred persons'; *momo* 'hundred', *so* 'person'.

Thus the army of Shuri led by Shō Hashi fought and conquered the whole of Okinawa. In correspondence with the Ashikaga shoguns of Japan around this time, the king used the same title for himself as he used in addressing Ashikaga Yoshimochi (1386–1428) and Ashikaga Yoshinori (1393–1441): he called himself *Ryūkyūkoku no Yononushi* (Master of the Country of Ryūkyū) and in the same manner called the shoguns *Nihonkoku no Yononushi* (Master of the Country of Japan).[63] After the unification of Okinawa in 1422, Shō Hashi followed the policy of King Satto, actively engaging in foreign trade with Japan, Korea, and China, as well as with the countries of the seas to the south. In the 1430s, the merchant ships of Ryūkyū, competing with the Portuguese, were already seen as far as Java, Sumatra, Malaya, Siam, Annam, Luzon, and adjacent areas.[64] According to the *Rekidai Hōan* (Valuable records of successive generations), during the period of 45 years from 1425 to 1470, 45 trade ships departed for the south: 27 for Siam, one for Palembang, five for Java, one of unknown destination, eight for Malacca, and three for Sumatra. They carried such items as silk and satin damasks, figured satin, swords, gold-dusted fans, and great quantities of ceramics and sulphur.[65]

In exchange, Okinawan trade ships brought back such items as pepper, sappanwood, various fabrics, perfumes, and exotic wines. For instance, in 1431, King Shō Hashi sent a mission to Korea, presenting the king a gift of 2,000 *kin* (2,646 lbs.) of sappanwood and 100 *kin* (132 lbs.) of alum.[66] Okinawan ships often took these goods to Korea and Japan for trade (Hakata, in northern Kyūshū, was described as a port where Ryūkyūan and southern sea ships gathered together),[67] but just as often, Japanese and Korean ships went down to Naha to purchase rare and valuable goods imported from China and the countries of the southern seas. In 1471, Ashikaga Shogun Yoshimasa sent an official to Shimazu, lord of Satsuma (present Kagoshima, at the southern end of Kyūshū) to tell the latter, "In recent years there has been an increasingly greater number of ships leaving the port of Sakai for Ryūkyū. From now on, absolutely no ship is allowed to go without an official permit from the shogunate. If any ship is found carrying coins, all coins must be confiscated and sent to the shogunate at once."[68] Apparently, numerous ships were attracted to Ryūkyū by stories of the profitable trade center at Naha.

In the *Haedong Chogukki* (Account of countries east of the sea), written in 1471 by the Korean scholar Shin Suk-ju, Ryūkyū is described as follows: "The land is small and the population is great. Their business is to trade by ship. In the west, they go as far as China and the seas to the south, and in the east, they reach Japan and our country. Ships of our country, Japan, and the seas to the south congregate at the seaport of its capital. Therefore, its countrymen set up a market near the coast and trade with each other."[69]

Port of Naha[70]

Shori, owaru tedako[1] ga,	Son of the Sun in Shuri
Ukishima[2] wa, geraete	Built the Floating Island
Tō,[3] Naban,[4] yoriyou,[5]	Where the Chinese and southern seas ships come and gather
Naha, tomari	Into the port of Naha.
Gusuku, owaru,	In the castle resides
Tedako ga.	Son of the Sun.

1. *tedako*	*Teda* 'sun', *ko* 'son'. Epithet of the king.
2. *ukishima*	*Uki* 'to float' + *shima* 'island'. An elegant old name for Naha, which in those days was a delta island in the Kokuba River.
3. *Tō*	'T'ang, China'.
4. *naban*	Contraction of *namban*, referring to the southern barbarians or countries of the seas to the south (including Southeast Asia) in general.
5. *yoriyō*	'To come together'.

Son of the Sun is an epithet for King Shō Hashi, who resided in his castle in Shuri overlooking the port of Naha. Though the port of Tomari adjacent to Naha was the older port, as trade expanded and many ships from China and the South Seas began coming in, the port of Tomari became too small to accommodate them, and in the 1450s extensive construction was begun on a larger port at Naha.

The kingdom and dynasty founded by Shō Hashi seemed destined to prosper forever. But unfortunately, after Shō Hashi died in 1439 at the ripe age of 67, all of his successors (as many as four in about fifteen years) were short-lived and quarrelsome. The rapid succession of kings entailed tremendous expenditure (especially in connection with the visits of Chinese ambassadors for the investiture of the new king) and the internal wars of succession and rebellion of Lord Amawari dissipated the treasury of the kingdom more quickly than foreign trade was able to replenish it. By the time King Shō Toku ascended the throne in 1461, the economic foundation of the kingdom was already shaky. In addition, the hard-headed young king insisted upon sending several expeditions against rebellious Kikai Island of the Amami-Ōshima Island group. Finally, he himself headed a great army and subdued the rebels in 1466. These expeditions caused conditions to deteriorate further, and upon Shō Toku's demise in 1469, officials led a coup d'etat which saw the Shō Hashi dynasty overthrown with little bloodshed.

The First Shō Dynasty had achieved its hegemony by military power and unfortunately remained a military power and not more. That is, after Shō Hashi conquered his rivals, he failed to devise an effective political system which would assimilate his former enemies and stabilize and perpetuate the dynasty. Because of the failure to replace military power with political power, the First Shō Dynasty was forced to use military might against all kinds of rebellious activities (in the seven generations of the dynasty, about sixty years, there were nine wars). It became a great political and economic burden which eventually led to the fall of the dynasty.

Kanemaru, former royal treasurer and mayor of Naha, who had retired earlier in disgust over the rash conduct of the young King Shō Toku, was prevailed upon to accept the throne by popular acclaim, or so it is recorded in the official history of his dynasty.[71] To ease the transition, Kanemaru chose the dynastic name Shō, the very same as the one just replaced, and called himself King Shō En. Shō En proved himself a mature statesman, and under his rule the government of a gifted individual began to shift to an institutional basis. It is small wonder that his dynasty, later called the Second Shō Dynasty, lasted longer than any other, that is, for about four hundred years till the end of the kingdom of Ryūkyū in 1879 when Ryūkyū became Okinawa Prefecture of the Japanese empire.

The following *omoro* is said to celebrate Shō En's coronation in 1470.

Coronation of the King[72]

Shori chowache kara wa,[1]	Since coming to Shuri,
Shima no, nushi[2] teda[3] yo	You are the king and the sun
Imya do,[4] kamishimo[5]	Now, indeed, over the high and low
Toyomu.[6]	Let it ring out.
Gusuku, chowache kara wa,	Since coming to the castle,

(Shima no, nushi teda yo)	(You are the king and the sun over the islands.)
(Imya do, kamishimo)	(Now is the time, over the high and the low)
(Toyomu.)	(To let it ring out.)

1. *chowache kara wa*	*Chowache* 'to be', 'to reside' (polite), *karawa* 'since', 'hence'.
2. *nushi*	'Master, owner', synonym for king.
3. *teda*	'Sun', synonym for king.
4. *imya do*	*Imya* = *ima* 'now', 'present'; *do*, emphatic particle.
5. *kamishimo*	*Kami* 'high', *shimo* 'low'.
6. *toyomu*	'Resound, ring out, sound out'.

After ascending the throne at the age of fifty-six, Shō En worked assiduously to save the kingdom from the near ruin brought about by the reckless government of King Shō Toku. In spite of the obvious incongruity in age (Shō En was older than Shō Toku by twenty-six years), Shō En succeeded in receiving investiture from China as the son and heir of Shō Toku, which meant not only recognition as the rightful ruler of the kingdom but also an official license to trade in Chinese ports and elsewhere in southern Asia where much business was done through the overseas Chinese merchant communities.

Shō En died in 1476. After a brief and bloodless struggle for power,[73] Shō En's young son, Shō Shin, ascended the throne in 1478, beginning a fifty-year reign in which Okinawa reached the peak of its prosperity. From 1506 on, Okinawan trade with China annually brought in huge profits to the kingdom. The social classes were becoming more firmly delineated. The government was centralized in 1526. According to George H. Kerr, Okinawa "had perfected in general terms the institutions and social forms which were to remain intact until the late nineteenth century. The islands were independent. They were in constant communication and at peace with neighboring states. The Okinawans were in a happy position of freedom to adopt what they wanted, and to remain indifferent—or at best only mildly curious—about foreign artifacts and institutions for which they felt no pressing need. China loomed as the neighbor of unquestioned superiority and they were in close and constant communication with Japan, but were overwhelmed by neither."[74]

Shō Shin's reign was the golden era of Okinawan history. It is commemorated by the following *omoro* in simple words of praise.

In Praise of Shuri[75]

Shorimori,[1] nobote[2] ikeba[3]	Going up to Shuri Grove,
Yo no akete[4]	It's like the dawn is breaking,
Teda no, teriyoruyani[5]	Like the sun is shining.
Madamamori,[6] nobote ikeba	Going up to Madama Grove,
(Yo no akete)	(It's like the dawn is breaking,)
(Teda no, teriyoruyani.)	(Like the sun is shining.)

1, 6. *Shorimori, Madamamori*	Both Shuri Grove and Madama Grove are located on the Shuri Castle grounds. They are often treated as synonymous with either Shuri Castle or the town of Shuri. Here, it refers to the latter.
2. *nobote*	'To rise, to go up'.
3. *ikeba*	'As (one) goes'.
4. *yo no akete*	*Yo* 'night' + *akete*, a conjugated form of *akeru* 'to open' or 'to dawn'.
5. *teriyoruyani*	*Teri* means 'to shine'. *Teriyoruyani* 'like . . . is shining'.

Enjoying unprecedented prosperity, King Shō Shin vigorously set out to improve the various governmental systems: he rebuilt and expanded the royal palaces and parks, erected temples to propagate Buddhism, and built bridges, roads, and ponds. It was planning after a Chinese fashion, and someone coming from the countryside to Shuri could not fail to be impressed.

Among the many monuments erected during the reign of King Shō Shin is one established in 1509 on the palace grounds in commemoration of the expansion and beautification of the main palace, Momourasoe Hall. Inscribed upon the front balustrade is a list of the Eleven Great Achievements of the Age, quoted in full here:

> Our King Shō Shin's natural appearance is superior and distinguished, and he is intelligent and bright. His virtue is equal to the three kings [Yao, Yu, and Wen of ancient China], and his name is known in the four quarters of the world. He indeed deserves to be called a wise ruler. The king's

compassion flows like a river and is as broad as an ocean. The prosperity of his court is a sight for awe and wonder for all eternity. On careful reflection, the humble subject reverently finds that there are eleven superior achievements of the present generation, surpassing the previous generations.

1. He believes in Buddha and has the image of Buddha made. He has temples built and plated in gold. Buddhist temples, chambers for the priests, libraries for the sutras, and towers for the bells stand side by side in rows in architectural magnificence. The reigning ruler makes devotion in [lit., makes as his mind] the Three Treasures of the Buddha, the Law, and the Priesthood. His is the mind of Emperor Ming Ti of Han and Emperor Wu Ti of Liang in ancient China.
2. He has established the correct decorum in meeting with his officials and he has lightened taxes for the benefit of his people. There is not a single day that he does not apply himself to the task of managing the family and governing the country. Therefore, the masses of people look up to him like the sun and moon and the hundreds of officials adore him like their parents. This is indeed a case of a harmonious and intimate relationship between the high and the low.
3. To the southwest lay a country named Taipingshan [present-day Yaeyama Islands]. In the year of the Monkey [AD 1500], he dispatched an expedition of one hundred warships to chastise them. The countrymen raised a flag of surrender and submitted themselves to him. In the following year they came and paid a tribute of grains, textiles, and corvee labor. Our country is more powerful and prosperous than ever before.
4. Brocade and embroidered silk are used for garments and gold and silver are used for utensils. Swords and bows and arrows exclusively are accumulated as weapons in the protection of the country. In the matter of finances and armament, this country excels other countries.
5. One thousand officials are awarded court ranks and one hundred officials are appointed to posts. The noble and the mean, the high and the low, their ranks are regulated by the yellow and red colors of their caps and the gold and silver pins in their hair. This is the model for the noble and for men of later generations.
6. Exotic flowers are grown in pots and rare trees are made into hedges. Gold and silver are used in building small boats, and Yao's vermillion and Shun's purple are put aboard. Copper is used in decorating small spiral shellfishes, and flowers from the hedges are placed in

their holes. In the front palace and the rear chamber there is spring throughout the four seasons. It is fragrant for the royal inspection.

7. Within the inner garden there is a temple with a man-made landscape of hills and waters. This is an exquisite area for the royal pleasure.
8. Feasts with eight exotic foods and nine vessels are given, and treasures of coins, silks, garments, and sashes are bestowed. There is fragrant tea in pots and excellent wine in barrels. Scrolls are hung on the wall and music is played on the floor. All are for the honor of the guests and the pleasure of the subjects. Is this not prosperous?
9. Our travel to and submission to the Great Ming is owing to the fact that we paid tribute during the Hungwu period and received the royal investiture during the Yunglo period. Since then, an envoy was dispatched to present tribute once every three years. When the reigning emperor ascended the throne, our king dispatched an envoy to offer congratulations upon his coronation and showed sincerity in presenting the tribute with proper decorum. At this time, the frequency of the tribute was changed from once every three years to once a year. The reason is that our national bond is strengthened by more contact with China.
10. Chinese customs have been transmitted with a view toward changing the ways of this land. It is for this reason that court ceremonies are held on the first and fifteenth of the month, and an order of precedence has been established by making two rows of officials on the left and right sides of the court. Specifically, they are to wish the king long life.
11. In emulation of the system of the imperial palaces of China, blue stones have been carved to make the balustrades which span the lower section of the palace. This is a sign of prosperity which was not seen in ancient times.

The eleven achievements listed above are owing to the mighty virtue of our king and the great merit of the loyal subjects. In ancient times, emperors with great virtue and subjects with great merit were all listed in the books of history so that they might serve as a model for later generations. Now, the lord of Chūzan is a sage with virtue and his subjects are loyal and with merit. There is no reason why it should not be inscribed on stone to keep later generations informed. Accordingly, next to the balustrades, words were chosen to describe the eleven achievements, and an inscription was made on a pillar of the balustrades.[76]

The following *omoro* relate respectively to the building of Shuri Castle, the fountain in Shuri Castle, the castle walls, and Enkakuji Temple.

Building Shuri Castle[77]

Shorimori,[1] Madamamori[2]	Shuri Grove, Madama Grove
Geraete,[3]	Have been built.
Nochimasaru,[4] yokake hyashi,[5] Mioyase[6]	Applause for eternal rule Has been offered.
Shimoashi kara,[7] motoashi kara[8]	From the bottom and from the foundation
Oriagete,[9]	Have been piled up high,
Take takaku,[10] hari hiroku,[11]	High in height, wide in width,
Oriagete.	Have been piled up high.

1, 2. *Shorimori, Madamamori*	Shuri Castle is built on top of a hill and surrounded by stone walls. It seems that before the castle was built, these two groves, Shuri Grove and Madama Grove, were the holy groves of Shuri. Here they mean Shuri Castle.
3. *geraeru*	'To build, to repair'.
4. *nochimasaru*	*Nochi* 'in the end, in the future', *masaru* 'to surpass, to better'.
5. *yokake hyashi*	*Yo* 'the world', *yokake* 'ruling the world'. *Hyashi* refers to beating time by clapping hands; that is, music, a tune. It means to sing an auspicious *omoro* to pray for the prosperity of the kingdom.
6. *mioyase*	'To serve, to offer'.
7. *shimoashi kara*	*Shimo* 'lower', *ashi* 'legs', *kara* 'from'; from the bottom.
8. *motoashi kara*	*Moto* means 'base'; therefore, from the foundation or base.
9. *oriage*	'To pile up'.
10. *take takaku*	*Take* 'height', *takaku* 'high'.
11. *hari hiroku*	*Hari* 'width', *hiroku* 'wide, broad'.

In Celebration of the August Fountain[78]

Aka no, Oetsuki[1] ya	Let Oetsuki of Aka,
Neha no, Oetsuki ya	Let Oetsuki of Neha [celebrate],
Shori shu[2]	"Shuri is the castle
Momoura[3] hiku, gusuku,	That leads all the villages."
Shori, oya,[4] higawa[5]	"The water of the august Shuri Fountain
Mizu kara do, yo kakeru[6]	Is the water that feeds the world."
Gusuku, oya, higawa.	The castle! The august fountain!

1. *Oetsuki*	Name of an *omoro* poet.
2. *Shori shu*	*Shu* is an emphatic form of 'is' or 'are'. 'It is Shuri that (leads . . .)'.
3. *momoura*	*Momo* 'hundred' + *ura* 'coasts,'villages'.
4. *oya*	Literally, 'parent', but used here as an honorific.
5. *higawa*	'Fountain, spring'.
6. *yo kakeru*	*Yo* 'the world', *kakeru* 'to rule'.

Within the castle grounds there was a fountain called Ryūhi, or Dragon Fountain, which supplied clear, cool drinking water all year round. The *omoro* above sings of this fountain, as does the *omoro* which follows. It may be that each *omoro* poet invited to the ceremony sang his own composition, perhaps in competition.

August Fountain[79]

Omoro neyagari[1] ya	Let Omoro Neyagari [celebrate]
Yo[2] no sōzu[3] ijache	The release of pure water for the king
Kami, teda no, sorote[5]	With the god and the sun together protecting.
Maburi,[6] yowache[7]	Let Serumu Neyagari [celebrate]
Serumu neyagari ya	(The release of pure water for the king)
(Yo no sōzu ijache)	(With the god and the sun together)
(Kami, teda no, sorote)	With the god and the sun together.
(Maburi, yowache.)	(Protecting.)

1. *Omoro neyagari*	Name of an *omoro* poet, same person as Serumu Neyagari, who is the author and singer of this *omoro.*
2. *yo*	'The world'.
3. *sōzu*	'Pure water, clean water'.
4. *ijache*	'To let out, to flow out'.
5. *sorote*	'Together'.
6. *maburi*	'To protect'.
7. *yowache*	Polite term of respect modifying *maburi.*

The following *omoro* commemorates the building of the walls of Shuri Castle.

Walls of Shuri Castle[80]

Shori owaru, tedako[1] ga,	The king who dwells in Shuri
Tama ishigaki,[2] geraete,	Had precious stone walls built
Tama kogane,	For the castle
Mochi,[3] micheru,[4] gusuku[5]	That is full of gems and gold.
Gusuku, owaru, tedako ga,	The king who dwells in the castle
Tama ishigaki, geraete	Had precious stone walls built
(Tama kogane,)	(For the castle)
(Mochi, micheru, gusuku.)	(That is full of gems and gold.)

1. *tedako*	*Teda* 'sun'; *tedako* 'son of the sun', that is, the king.
2. *tama ishigaki*	*Tama* 'gem', 'precious stone' + *ishigaki* 'stone wall'.
3. *mochi*	'To have, to possess'.
4. *micheru*	'To be full of, to fill'.
5. *gusuku*	'Castle'.

Buddhism was favored by all the royal dynasties ever since it was introduced to Okinawa in the thirteenth century by Priest Zenkan. Beginning with the reign of Shō Taikyū (1450–1460), a devout Buddhist who erected several temples, it became increasingly prosperous. King Shō Shin, also a staunch believer, had Enkakuji Temple built to the north immediately beyond the walls of Shuri Castle in 1492 in memory of his father, King Shō En. Its compound covered 1,080 *tsubo* and it was granted a stipend of 100 *koku* of rice as the royal family temple of the Shō dynasty.[81] It took three years to complete and its magnificence was such that even the Chinese ambassador, Chen Kan, who came in 1534, was astonished. Noting that its main building contained a golden statue of the Buddha and several thousand volumes of Buddhist canons, he commented that its excellence and beauty were second only to the royal palace. In the same breath, he also noted the fact that not a single commoner was allowed inside the temple compound.[82] At this time, Buddhism was not for the salvation of the masses as much as for the protection and prosperity of the state and the ruling elite. The following *omoro* was composed on the occasion of the completion of Enkakuji Temple in 1492.

Enkakuji Temple[83]

Ogyakamoi[1] ga, okonomi,[2]	Under the plan of King Shō Shin
Enkakuji, geraete,	Enkakuji Temple was built.
Inori, yoreha,[3]	As the prayers are offered,
Teda ga, hokori,[4] yowache	How proud our king is!
Ajiosoi[5] ga, okonomi	Under the plan of the king.
(Enkakuji, geraite,)	(Enkakuji Temple was built.)
(Inori, yoreba,)	(As the prayers are offered,)
(Teda ga, hokori, yowache)	(How happy our king is!)
Ōkimi[6] wa, takabete[7]	The high priestess is venerated,
Miyatera[8] wa, geraete	And the temple is built,
Kimikimi wa, takabete,	The priestesses are venerated,
Kamishimu wa, soroete,	The high and the low are in harmony,
Jihanare[9] wa, soroete,	Far off islands are in harmony,
Miyatera no, sudemizu[10]	Let the holy water of the temple
Ogyakamoi ni, mioyase	Be offered to King Shō Shin
Tomomosue,[11] tohyakusasu[12] choware.[13]	So he may live tens and hundreds of years!

1. *Ogyakamoi*	Divine name of King Shō Shin.
2. *okonomi*	'To plan, to devise'.
3. *inori yoreha*	*Inori* 'prayer', *yoreha* (*yoreba*) 'as [the prayers] are said'.
4. *hokori*	'To be proud of, to be happy for'.
5. *ajiosoi*	'Ruler of the *anji*, ruler of rulers, the king'.
6. *Ōkimi (Ōgimi)*	'High priestess'.
7. *takabete*	Derived form of *takaberu* 'to venerate, to worship, to respect'.
8. *miyatera*	*Miya* 'shrine' + *tera* 'temple'. Refers to Enkakuji. No distinction was made between a temple and a shrine.
9. *jihanare*	*Ji* 'land' + *hanare* 'separate', 'disconnected'. *Jihanare* refers to the smaller islands other than Okinawa.
10. *sudemizu*	*Sude*[*ru*] 'to hatch', *mizu* 'water'. *Sudemizu* means the holy water of eternal life.
11. *tomomosue*	*To* 'ten' + *momo* 'hundred' + *sue* 'future', tens of hundreds of years.
12. *tohyakusasu*	*To* 'ten' + *hyaku* 'hundred' + *sasu* 'age'.
13. *choware*	'To be' (polite term). Here, 'may the king 'be' for tens of hundreds of years'.

Significantly, although the kingdom or at least the royal dynasty had wholeheartedly adopted the new religion of Buddhism and many temples were built during the reign of King Shō Shin, the new religion never completely replaced the old indigenous faith, as evidenced in the role of the priestesses and the use of the holy water. The new religion of Buddhism was merely superimposed on ancient beliefs in the Sun God, high priestess, and others. On one hand, it shows the persistence of the old native beliefs, and on the other, it indicates the freedom to adopt only what was needed. Okinawan culture during this period was remarkably cosmopolitan.[85]

Another important event at this time was the centralization of the government proclaimed in 1478 when Shō Shin ascended the throne. Gradually completed over the long years of his reign, it required each lord to take up permanent residence in Shuri. There is no doubt that the effect of this step in promoting the urbanization of Shuri and Naha was similar to that of the centralization of the Tokugawa shogunate in Edo nearly a century later. However, besides the urbanization of the administrative and commercial center of Shuri and Naha, the concentration of the gentry in Shuri and Naha served to stimulate the rural economy, for each lord was dependent upon the resources of his own domain for the maintenance of his town establishment. New lands were cleared for cultivation and various products from land and sea moved steadily into the urban areas of Shuri and Naha.

According to the account of three shipwrecked Korean sailors,[86] farmers were growing mainly rice, wheat, millet, beans, and other vegetables. They were already double-cropping rice and millet and their agricultural techniques were fairly well advanced. Domestic animals included the cow, horse, goat, pig, chicken, and duck. Horses, which were ridden or used as draft animals, had long been exported to China.

The following *omoro* depict scenes of farmers going to Shuri to serve the king or to pay taxes.

Hyakuna Villagers' Attendance at Shuri Castle[87]

Hyakuna,[1] kara,[2] nobote[3]	From Hyakuna, we have come up,
Nekuni, kara, nobote	From the fair country, we have come,
Shima,[4] sorote	All of us villagers together
Tomomosue, mioyase[5]	Are honored in your service forever.
Shorimori,[6] chowaru	Our King Shō Shin
Ogyakamoi,[7] ganashi.[8]	Who dwells at Shuri Castle.

1. *Hyakuna*	Name of a village in southeast Okinawa.
2. *kara*	'From'.
3. *noboru*	'To rise, to come up, to go up'.
4. *shima*	'Island, village'. Here it refers to the villagers.
5. *mioyase*	'To serve, to offer'.
6. *Shorimori*	Shuri Grove, a synonym for Shuri Castle.
7. *Ogyakamoi*	Divine name of King Shō Shin.
8. *ganashi*	Suffix of endearment.

Carrying in the Tribute Tax[88]

Nakamine,[1] kyomon[2]	Nakamine has come,
Kanetsuki,[3] kyomon	With the tribute, he has come,
Shori, kyan'uchi[4]	To make happy

Amayakase[5]	Shuri and the castle.
Kanai,[6] shiche,[7] kyomon	Tax goods have come,
Sasage,[8] shiche, kyomon	Tribute goods have come
(Shori, kyan'uchi)	(To make happy)
(Amayakase.)	(Shuri and the castle.)

1. *Nakamine*	The name of a person, possibly the head of a village in Gushikawa.
2. *kyomon*	'Has (have) come'.
3. *Kanetsuki*	*Kanetsuki, kane, kanai, kamae* all mean 'tax' or 'tributes'. They can also mean 'trade goods'.
4. *Kyan'uchi*	*Kya, kyo* 'capital', *uchi* 'inside'; within Shuri Castle.
5. *amayakasu*	'To make happy, to make animated'.
6. *kanai*	'Taxes'. See item 3 above.
7. *shiche*	'To do'. *Kanai shiche* 'to pay a tax'.
8. *sasage*	'Offering, tribute'. Here used as a synonym for *kanai.*

The centralization policy of Shō Shin was in a sense more complete than that of Tokugawa Japan. Whereas under Tokugawa centralization each lord still had control of his own fief and by residing there every other year maintained close ties with the people and the land, under Shō Shin, each lord, together with his family, was made to stay permanently in Shuri, while the actual control of his domain was in the hands of an official appointed by the king. Undoubtedly, it was easier for the king to control the entire kingdom than it was for the Tokugawa. But it also had the effect, probably unintended, to make the communication between the rural areas and the urban areas one way: farmers produced food and other goods needed by the urban gentry but they received little in return. They were happy if they could pay their taxes and still have something left over for themselves.[89] Contact with the urban lifestyle was probably very limited.

While the rural areas were lagging far behind, reaping little benefit from what they produced, Shuri and Naha, supported by agriculture and enriched by the foreign trade they monopolized, flourished as never before. Considerable improvements were made to the port of Naha as trade expanded.

The following account appears in *Nantō Shi*, from the early eighteenth century, by the noted Japanese scholar Arai Hakuseki:

> The port of Naha lies in the southwest. It is located at a distance of a little more than a *li* from the capital. The port is congested with ships from many nations overseas. The depth of the port is twenty-two *cho* and its width is one *cho* and twenty *ken*. It can accommodate thirty great ships.[90]

According to still another source, the largest Okinawan trade ships had a capacity of 238 crew members and the smallest, a capacity of 90.[91]

The growing port city of Naha comprised four sub-districts at this time: Kume, Tomari, Higashi, and Nishi. At the Tenshi-kan, the Mansion for Heavenly Ambassadors (from China), erected in 1396, Chinese ambassadors of high rank were received and entertained. Its splendor rivaled that of the royal palace. The Oyamise, pronounced /wyeemishi/, a foreign trade office near the harbor, was already in existence by the mid-fifteenth century. Later, especially after 1609, it evolved into a sort of city office for Naha as well as an office for foreign affairs and trade. The aforementioned shipwrecked Korean sailors observed Japanese, Chinese, southern Chinese, and southern barbarians operating prosperous business houses in Naha, and markets full of food, clothing, porcelain, and other necessities and luxury goods.[92]

The importance of overseas trade cannot be overemphasized. Principal return cargoes from Southeast Asia were sappanwood and pepper. Sappanwood "sold in China for one hundred times the prevailing price in Ryūkyū and many hundred times the purchase price in Southeast Asia. Pepper sold in China for 750 to 1500 times the original price. Other goods brought from Southeast Asia included cloves and nutmeg, camphor, gold, tin, ivory, sandalwood, perfumes and incense, coral, mercury, opium, saffron, Malacca wine, cotton prints, muslin, silk goods, olibanum, eaglewood, costusroot, rose water, rhinoceros horn, exotic animals and birds, ebony, agate, resin, ship's timber, musical instruments, and other products of Southeast and South Asian arts and crafts."[93]

According to Shunzo Sakamaki,

> . . . the period of trade with Southeast Asia, from roughly 1385 to 1570, gave birth to a golden age in Ryūkyū. The tremendous profits that were realized went primarily into the royal coffers, strengthening the king's government as against the former regional lords of the islands. The country was unified under a central authority, which was strong enough to enforce an edict banning the private possession of weapons of war. The king's castle and the surrounding capital city of Shuri were rebuilt in a splendor that reflected the wealth that accrued from the overseas trade.

> Many temples, bridges, and other structures were built. Roads were constructed and improved, and the port of Naha was developed. Books, scrolls, paintings, and other luxuries were imported from China, Japan, and Korea.[94]

The vitality of the young maritime state is expressed in several *omoro* that follow.

Let Them All Serve Our King[95]

Kikoe owamori[1] ya,	Renowned Owamori!
Kya, Kamakura,[2]	Kyōtō and Kamakura,
Kawara,[3] naban,[4] gyame,[5]	Java and the South Seas,
Tō[6] Miyako, soroete,[7]	China and Miyako,
Kanawashoware,[8]	Let them all serve our king.
Toyomu owamori ya.	O famed Owamori!

1. *owamori*	Name of one of the thirty-three high priestesses under Kikoe Ōgimi.
2. *Kya, Kamakura*	'Kyōtō and Kamakura', in Japan.
3. *Kawara*	'Java'.
4. *naban*	Contraction of *nanban*, islands or countries of the southern seas.
5. *gyame*	'Till, even as far as'.
6. *Tō*	'T'ang or China'.
7. *soroe*	'Together, uniformly'.
8. *kanawashore*	'Let . . . be as you wish, let . . . serve you'. *Kanau* refers to fulfilling one's wish.

The following *omoro* "Departure of the *Sejiaratomi*" illustrates even more dramatically than the preceding "Let Them All Serve Our King" the vital importance of foreign trade to the kingdom. For it is the *omoro* that King Shō Shin himself sang at the pier of Naha port on the 25th day of the 11th month of 1517, in farewell to the trade ship *Sejiaratomi* on its departure for the South Seas. Even the king himself was not too august a personage to sing an *omoro* of farewell to the trade ship.

Departure of the *Sejiaratomi*[96]

Ōkimi wa, takabete,[1]	With an invocation, the high priestess
Sejiaratomi,[2] oshiukete,[3]	Launched the *Sejiaratomi.*
Ōkimi ni,	Let the high priestess pray
Oeche,[4] koute,[5] haryase[6]	For the fair wind to sail.
Sedakako[7] wa, takabete	With the prayer, the high priestess said,
Ajiosoigya,[8] osouze[9] ya	"May the wisdom of our king
Mukou,[10] kata, shinate[11]	Be accomplished everywhere she goes!"
Ogyakamoi[12] ga, osouze ya	"May the wisdom of King Shō Shin
Mukou, kata, shinate	Be realized everywhere she goes!"
Ajiosoigya	King of the lords
Oyaoune,[13] oshiuke,	Launched the greatest ship.
Kazu maburyo[14] wa	Winds! Protect her!
Gerae,[15] Sejiaratomi, kuriuke,	Sublime *Sejiaratomi* is afloat.
Kazu, maburyo wa	Winds! Protect her!
Bureshima[16] no, kamigami	Gods of isles and islands,
Ayosorote,[17] maburyo wa	Be one in mind and protect her!
Kimihae wa, takabete,	With the prayer of Priestess Kimihae,
Sejiaratomi, oshiukete	The *Sejiaratomi* is on her way.
Noronoro wa, takabete.	Pray, priestesses!

1. *takaberu* — 'To worship, to pray, to offer an invocation'.
2. *Sejiaratomi* — Name of the trade ship. *Seji* means 'spirit', hence, a ship endowed with spiritual power.
3. *oshiukeru* — 'To push forward, to launch (a ship)'.
4. *oeche* — 'Tailwind, favorable wind'.
5. *kou* — 'To beg, to request'.
6. *haryase* — 'Let . . . run, let . . . sail'.
7. *Sedakako* — One who is elevated in spirit, another name for the high priestess.
8. *Ajiosoigya* — One who rules the lords, synonym for the king.

9. *osouze* — 'King's will or wish, king's wisdom'.

10. *mukou kata* — *Mukou* means 'to face front', and *kata* "direction'. *Mukou kata* means 'whatever direction faced'.

11. *shinate* — Derived from the verb *shinau* 'to be harmonious', 'to be well received', 'to become well adjusted'.

12. *Ogyakamoi* — Divine name of King Shō Shin.

13. *oyaoune* — *Oya* 'parent, great' + *o*, an honorific, + *(f)une* 'ship'.

14. *kazu maburyo* — *Kazu*, variant of *kaze* 'wind' + *maburyo* 'to protect'.

15. *gerae* — As a verb, it means to 'build' or to 'repair', but here it is used as an adjective: 'beautiful, pretty'.

16. *bureshima* — *Bure* 'group' + *shima* 'island(s)'.

17. *ayosorote* — *Ayo* 'mind', 'soul' + *sorou* 'to be uniform, to be one'.

Southbound trade ships always left in winter, taking advantage of the strong northerly winds from the northern Asiatic continent, and always returned in spring or early summer with the steady monsoon winds blowing northward and the strong Black Current carrying the ships northeastward to Ryūkyū. The risks at sea were terribly high, and there are many *omoro* that sing of the anxiety and impatience, through the winter months, and the joy when spring comes around, of those who wait at home for their loved ones far away in the southern sea areas.

Monsoon Wind in Spring[97]

Orezumu[1] ga, tachiyoreha[2]	As March has come around,
Aga,[3] ashage,[4] kamiashage[5]	At my sacred hut, ceremonial hut
Onarigami,[6] tezuriyora[7]	My sister goddess must be praying,
Ōkimi[8] ni,	"Beg the great god
Mahae,[9] koute,[10] haryase	For the straight southern wind So you can set out your ship for home."
Wakanatsu[11] ga, tachiyoreha	As the early summer has come around,
(Aga, ashage, kamiashage)	(At my sacred hut, ceremonial hut)
(Onarigami, tezuriyora)	(My sister goddess must be praying,)
(Ōkimi ni,)	("Beg the great god)
(Mahae, koute, haryase.)	(For the straight southern wind) (So you can set out your ship for home.")

1. *orezumu*	March in the lunar calendar. It is pronounced /urijin/ or /urijim/. It falls at the beginning of the rainy season. The moistening of the land by rain is called *urii* (cognate to Japanese *uruou*). Perhaps *urijin* or *orezumu* is a contraction of *urihajimu* 'to begin to be moistened'.
2. *tachiyoreha*	*Tachi* or *tatsu* 'to begin, to start'; *tachiyoreha* or more usually *tachiyoreba* adds the notion of causation: 'because something has started'.
3. *aga*	*A* 'I or me'; *aga* 'my'.
4. *ashage*	A village hut in which religious ceremonies are held. It appears as *ashatsu* in one version but this is probably a scribal error.
5. *kamłashage*	Same as above.
6. *onarigami*	*Onari* means 'sister', and the *onarigami* or the spirit of a sister was believed to protect her brother who was away on a journey.
7. *tezuriyora*	*Tezuri* 'to rub the hands together [in prayer]'. *Tezuriyora* means someone must be praying.
8. *Ōkimi*	'Great god' (no particular god specified).
9. *mahae*	*Ma* is a prefix denoting 'true' or 'straight', and *hae* means 'southern wind'.
10. *kou*	'To beg, to request'.
11. *wakanatsu*	*Waka* 'young', and *natsu* 'summer'. Ergo, 'early summer'.

The *omoro* above is sung by someone who is far away on a trade journey to the south. When spring comes around, he thinks of his home and sings that his sister must be praying at the village ceremonial hut, begging for favorable winds so that her brother may soon come home safely.[98]

When the Southern Wind Whispers[99]

Mahae, sutsunari[1] kya	Straight southern wind!
Mahai, saramekeba[2]	When the southern wind whispers,
Tō, naban	Let the *Suzunari* bring back
Kamae,[3] tsude,[4] mioyase[5]	The trade goods from China and the South Seas [to our king].

Oeche,[6] sutsunari ga	Straight tailwind!
Oeche, saramekeba	When the tailwind begins whispering,
(Tō, naban)	(Let the Suzunari bring back)
(Kamae, tsude, mioyase.)	(The trade goods from China and the South Seas [to our king].)

1. *Sutsunari*	Name of the ship. *Sutsu* is *suzu*, 'bell', and *nari*, 'tinkle'.
2. *sarameku*	'To begin rustling, whispering'.
3. *kamae*	'Tribute, tax, trade goods'.
4. *tsude*	From *tsumu* 'to pile', 'to load'.
5. *mioyase*	Polite term for to 'make an offering to the king'.
6. *oeche*	Variant of *oite* 'tailwind'.

This *omoro* was composed by someone waiting at home. Spring has come, and with it the warm southern wind, rustling the fresh green leaves of the trees. It's time for the *Suzunari*, which left for the ocean areas to the south last winter, to come home. Come home, *Suzunari*, and offer your cargo of precious and exotic merchandise to the king!

> Ships putting in at Naha after a voyage to the south, or coming from China or Japan or Korea, provided occasions of holiday interest and excitement in the town. Returning seamen told of adventures on the high seas and in distant ports. Curios and fine objects brought back for the king's court went up to Shuri under the watchful eyes of port officers and the ship's commandant. The chief of mission and the vice-chief, together with the principal officers, made reports, delivered documents, and escorted distinguished visitors to the castle on the hill. Goods for transshipment were offloaded to be stored near the quay until the next fleet was ready to set out. Objects too damaged for the royal palace or for shipment onward became available for barter and trade among the seamen and their friends. Who could tell what strange birds, plants, or animals might be brought ashore, what new musical instruments might be among the souvenirs, or what colorful bales and bolts of cloth might be disclosed in the cargo? We read of shipment of parrots and peacocks sent up to the king of Korea, who in time sent back in exchange a great bronze bell. Monkeys and bright-plumaged chickens were brought in. Earthenware from the south and glazed ceramics from the China coast were imported

in quantity, some to be used in Okinawa and some to be sent on to Kyoto, where it was in great vogue among the tea masters at the shogun's court.[100]

As mentioned previously, Naha, though small, was a well-known international trade center where people of different nationalities flocked together in pursuit of opportunities for trade and profit. There were communities of Chinese and Koreans. At least one scholar even suggests there might have been some Arabs at Naha as merchant seamen, some of whom apparently served on the king's trade ships as guides to the countries to the south, such as Siam, Malacca, Vietnam, Sunda Islands, and Patani during the fifteenth and sixteenth centuries.[101]

The fifty-year reign of Shō Shin was a golden era in the history of Okinawa. As in centuries past, the lot of the farmers and fishermen was hard, but now that internal wars among the petty lords had ceased, life was at least more stable. Ceremonies and festivals were celebrated with food, wine, and dance by commonfolk and gentry alike. In Naha and Shuri, the gentry and nobles lived a comfortable life supported by stipends from the king or by taxes from their own fiefs. Ordinary townspeople had to earn their own livelihood but were empted from taxation. And in general, those who lived in town, whether noble, gentry, or commoner, shared in benefits accrued from the thriving overseas trade. That the following *omoro* was composed seems only natural.

The King and the Sun[102]

Shori no teda to,	The Sun (king) in Shuri,
Ten ni teru[1] teda to,	The Sun shining in heaven,
Majuni,[2] choware,[3]	May prosper together forever.
Mikanashi[4] teda to	The beloved Sun,
Teni ni teru teda to	The Sun shining in heaven,
(Majuni, choware,)	(May flourish together forever.)
Teda, ichiroku[5] to	The living Sun and
Teni ni teru teda to	The Sun shining in heaven.
Teda hachiroku[6] to	The Sun on earth and
Teni ni teru teda to.	The Sun shining in heaven.

1. *teru*	'To shine'.
2. *majuni*	'Together, in the company of'.
3. *choware*	'To be, to prevail' (polite).

4. *mikanashi*	*Mi*, honorific, plus *kanashi* 'to love'.
5. *ichiroku*	Synonym for king.
6. *hachiroku*	Synonym for king.

However, even as the poet was eulogizing the king, dark clouds were gathering on the horizon, for although the Okinawans were enjoying unprecedented prosperity under the reign of Shō Shin, there were already signs of trouble within the kingdom, and abroad the international situation was turning ominous.

The beautification of Shuri and Naha with elaborate parks and bridges and the building of many splendid palaces, temples, and shrines and other public buildings were financed mainly by the profits that came from foreign trade. However, these undertakings, in addition to the rising standard of living of the gentry class, undoubtedly made heavier taxation of the farmers necessary and inevitable. The fact that several rebellions broke out in the outlying islands from about the middle of the reign of Shō Shin seems to have resulted from the harsh exploitation of the farmers in these islands by the Shuri government because of the latter's financial difficulties. When the Yaeyama Islands in the south rebelled against Shuri about 1496 or 1497 and stopped sending tribute to Okinawa, King Shō Shin sent nine generals with about three thousand soldiers in forty-six ships to put down the rebellion in 1500, the twenty-fourth year of his reign.[103] About thirty years later, in 1537, yet another rebellion on Ōshima Island in the north, was also suppressed.[105]

The following rather long *omoro*, "Chastisement of Yaeyama," was composed in 1500 when King Shō Shin sent his army to quell the rebellion in Yaeyama. The repeated lines, "Ruler of the lords, / May you not sorrow in your heart, / For you shall be granted spiritual power" seem to forebode the decline and dark future of the kingdom.

Chastisement of Yaeyama[106]

Anjiosoi ya	Ruler of the lords,
Kogane uchi[1] ni, choware	May you be in the Golden Palace,
Yo no, souze[2] showare	May you govern the country with wisdom,
Ōkimi su,[3] kei[4] yaryoware	For you shall be granted spiritual power.
Anjiosoi ya	Ruler of the lords,
Kyō no uchi[5] ni chowache	May you be in the castle,

Yo[6] no, souze, showare	May you rule the country with wisdom,
Setakako su,[7] kei yaryowame	For you shall be granted spiritual power.
Anjiosoi ya	Ruler of the lords,
Ogimouchi[8] wa, nakekuna[9]	May you not sorrow in your heart,
Ōkimi su, kei yaryowame	For you shall be granted spiritual power.
Tatamikyo[10] wa	Ruler of the lords,
Ayo ka, uchi wa, nakekuna	May you not grieve in your bosom,
Shurimori, ōgoro[11] ka	Warriors of Shuri Castle
Shima hiroku,[12] soete	Conquer the whole island,
Anjiosoi ni	Offer the whole country
Yo soete, mioyase	To the ruler of the lords.
Mishimakasu[13] korokoro	Strong men of all Shuri
Kuni hiroku, soete	Conquer the whole country.
Kimihae ka	Priestess Kimihae
Miyakoshima, hacheoware	Hastens to Miyako Island,
Shima hiroku, soete	Pacifies the whole island,
Kyo no sho[14] ka	Venerable Kimihae
Yaemashima hacheowache	Hastening to Yaeyama Island,
Kuni hiroku soete	Conquering the whole country.
Yaemashima izuko[15]	If the Yaeyama soldiers
Asera[16] tameyaraha[17]	And generals are pacified,
Ōkimi su, yoshirame[18]	May the chief priestess govern them.
Hatarashima[19] kuhara	If the Hateruma soldiers
Chikawa,[20] tameyaraha	Are pacified,
Setakako su, yoshirame	May the spiritual chief govern them.
Asera, tameyaraha,	As the Yaeyama chiefs are defeated,
Okinamasu,[21] sumoran[22]	Slice them like namasu
Ōkimi su, yoshirame.	So the chief priestess might govern them.

1. *kogane uchi*	*Kogane* 'gold', *uchi* 'house', 'building'.
2. *souze*	To think about. King's thought, wisdom. *Yo no souze* means to think about the world, viz., to govern, government.
3. *Ōkim isu*	*Ōkimi* means the chief priestess, *su* is an emphatic article.
4. *kei*	Also *ke* or *ki.* Spiritual power, synonymous with *se* or *seji.*
5. *kyo no uchi*	Specifically, the sanctuary located in the southwest corner of Shuri Castle. It also refers, in a broader sense, to the castle itself.
6. *yo*	The world, the country.
7. *Setakako*	One who is high in spirit, namely, the chief priestess.
8. *ogimouchi*	*O* is an honorific. *Gimo* or *kimo* is the liver where the soul was supposed to reside. *Uchi* means inside.
9. *nakekuna*	*Nakeku* 'to be saddened', 'to grieve' + *na*, a negative particle.
10. *tatamikyo*	Literally, noble man, viz., the king.
11. *ōgoro*	*Koro (goro)* means a man in his prime; *ō* means big, great.
12. *shima hiroku*	*Shima* 'island' + *hiroku* 'wide'; the whole island.
13. *mishimakasu*	*Mishima* literally means three villages of Shuri, *kasu* means number; *mishimakasu,* all three villages of Shuri.
14. *kyo no sho*	Spiritual person, another name of Priestess Kimihae.
15. *izuko*	Soldier, youth.
16. asera	*Ase* means a senior or leading group of men; *ra* is a suffix indicating plural.
17. *tameyaraha*	*Tameyaru* or *tameru* means to bend, twist, correct, pacify, defeat. *Tameyaraha* or tameyaraha 'if pacified'.
18. *yoshirame*	To govern, to rule. *Yo* 'the world' + *shiru* 'to know'.
19. *hatarashima*	Another name of Yaeyama Island.
20. *chikawa*	Lower class of soldiers under the *asera.*
21. *okinamasu*	A kind of food—sliced raw fish.
22. *sumoran*	Perhaps a mistranscription of *shimeran* 'to let do'.

Although the royal army of Shuri was powerful enough to crush all domestic rebellions, there was little anyone, even the king, could do to keep external affairs from turning against the kingdom.

With the intrusion of the European powers into Southeast Asia, beginning with the Portuguese conquest of Malacca in 1511, Okinawan traders began losing their favorite trade ports one by one. From the fourteenth to the sixteenth century, Okinawan trade ships visited Siam, Palembang, Java, Malacca, Sumatra, Patani, Annam, and Sunda. But after 1511, when Albuquerque occupied Malacca and monopolized the trade, the Okinawans stopped visiting there. After 1520 (the forty-fifth year of the reign of Shō Shin), the Okinawans traded only with Siam and Patani. And in 1541, they retreated from Patani and traded only with Siam.[107]

From the north came the dreaded Japanese pirates (*wakō)* who terrorized the coasts of southern Korea and China. Earlier in the fourteenth century their main targets were the coastal towns of southern Korea which they raided as often as 376 times during the thirteen-year period from 1375 to 1388.[108] They gradually shifted their targets to the coast of southern China along Fukien and Hangchow. They were swift, deadly, and thorough: it was said that where they had passed through, the land was emptied of people and property. For the peaceable Okinawans it meant losing the command of the sea upon which their overseas trade depended. In a record dated 1534, Chinese ambassador to Okinawa Chen Kan mentions the great annoyance of Okinawan officials with the cunning and haughty Japanese.[109]

In such troubled times, the maritime risks were high even in the Inland Sea of Japan, especially after the civil war of Ōnin (1467–1477) when the power of the Ashikaga shogunate in Kyoto became too weak to effectively control the restive feudal lords. When the Okinawan trade ships gradually began withdrawing from the ports of Hyogo and Sakai despite an invitation from the Ashikaga shogun (1480), Sakai merchants, whose major source of profits was from the trade with Okinawan ships, decided to go to Okinawa themselves. When the merchants from Sakai (near present-day Osaka), Hakata, and Hirado in northern Kyūshū began vying with each other for the opportunity to trade at Naha, they faced a tremendous obstacle in the person of Shimazu, lord of Satsuma, whose territorial coast they had to pass in order to reach Okinawa. Lord Shimazu wanted to control, and if possible to monopolize, the lucrative trade with Okinawa.[110]

It was when the greedy eyes of the Japanese feudal lords were turned impatiently on Okinawa—actually there were two attempts by different Japanese feudal lords to conquer Okinawa in 1516 and 1591, and there were several attacks by pirates—that the ill-fated Shō Nei ascended the throne in 1589.

In Congratulation on the Coronation of King Shō Nei[111]

Shori, Ōkimi kya	As the Shuri high priestess
Shorimori, orewache	Has descended on Shuri Grove
Ajiosoi sho,[1]	May the ruler of the lords
Seji,[2] masate,[3] choware	Be blessed with divine power.
Toyomu, kuniosoi[4] kya	Renowned Kuniosoi
Matamamori, orewache	Has descended on Madama Grove,
(Ajiosoi sho,)	(May the ruler of the lords)
(Seji, masate, choware)	(Be blessed with divine power.)
Ajiosoi ka, oyori,[5]	For the sake of the ruler of the lords,
Wonise[6] ka, oyori	For the sake of the king,
Kira no kasu,[7] orewache	Every auspicious day, she descends
Eka no kasu, orewache	Every day of good omen, she descends
Orerakasu,[8] mimafura	Whenever she descends, let's guard him.
Asubakasu,[9] mimafura.[10]	Whenever, divine, she dances, let's protect him.

1. *sho*	Emphatic article.
2. *seji*	Spiritual power.
3. *masate*	*Masaru* 'to surpass, excel'. *Seji masate choware*, literally, 'excellent in spiritual power'.
4. *Kuniosoi*	Another name of the Shuri high priestess.
5. *oyori*	For the sake of.
6. *Wonise*	King.
7. *kira no kasu*	*Kira* (and *eka* in the following line) 'an auspicious day', *kasu* 'number, time'. *Kira no kasu* means 'on every auspicious day'.
8. *orerakasu*	*Orera* or *oreru* 'to descend'. 'Every time she descends'.
9. *asubakasu*	*Asuba* is a form of *asobu* 'to play', 'to dance'.
10. *mimafura*	Cognate of *mimamora* 'to protect', 'to guard'.

This *omoro* was actually composed in 1607, about sixteen years after Shō Nei ascended the throne, on the occasion of a great ceremony in which the high priestess appeared as a living goddess to confirm and celebrate the reign of the king. Although the high priestess, praying that the king be blessed with divine power, promised always to protect him, it seems his reign was doomed from the outset. In 1592, only three years after his ascent to the throne, the Jana clan rebelled right in the capital city of Shuri.[112] An inauspicious incident was recorded in the *Ryūkyū shintōki* wherein sometime before 1606 but after Shō Nei ascended the throne, a disparagement of the king and the high officials was written in large characters on the wall of a building. The one who wrote it was later discovered and he and his family were exiled to a distant island.[113]

The Chinese sage Lao Tzu said, "When bronze and jade fill your hall, it can no longer be guarded. Wealth and honor breed insolence that brings ruin in its train." The combination of the aforementioned factors, domestic and foreign, plus the ill-advised judgment (an underestimate of the intent and power of Japan, and overdependence on China) of the prime minister, Jana Teidō, in connection with Japan's Korean expedition and its aftermath, culminated in the disastrous Satsuma invasion of Ryūkyū in 1609. With this fatal event, the vitality of the kingdom of Ryūkyū was extinguished, and there were no *omoro* composed after the following one. The army of Satsuma captured King Shō Nei and took him back to Satsuma as a hostage. The saddened queen, anxiously awaiting her husband, composed this *omoro*. Since King Shō Nei was taken to Satsuma in the fifth month of 1609 and returned in the tenth month of 1611, it is likely that this *omoro* was composed in the winter of 1610.

Sorrow of the Queen[114]

Manishi[1] ga, manemane,[2] fukeba	When the northerly wind blows,
Anjiosoiteda[3] no	I wait only for the ship
Oune do[4] machoru[5]	Of my king, the ruler of lords.
Oeche[6] ga, oeche do, fukeba	When the tailwind, tailwind blows,
(Anjiosoiteda no)	(I long only for the ship)
(Oune do machoru.)	(Of my king, the ruler of lords.)

1. *manishi*	'Straight northerly wind'.
2. *manemane*	'With (the wind)', describing the way the wind blows, 'at the mercy of (the wind)'.

3. *anjiosoiteda*	'King'.
4. *ounedo*	*Oune* = *ofune* 'ship'; *do* is emphatic—it is *his ship* that I am awaiting.
5. *machoru*	'[I am] waiting'.
6. *oeche*	'Tailwind', related to Japanese *oite*.

CHAPTER 5

Conclusion

In the history of any nation or cultural entity, there always exists a period of transition from the primitive stage, when there was yet no nation but numerous independent and isolated tribal groups, to the recent, when the nation or state was formed with full consciousness of its cultural and national oneness and distinctiveness. This period of transition stamps its full impression upon later development, giving the latter its distinctive characteristics and determining to a large degree the course of that development. This book, *A Brief History of Early Okinawa Based on the Omoro sōshi*, is a study of the period of transition from the primitive era to the recent in the history of Okinawa.

There has been a tendency in the past to treat the history of Okinawa as though it suddenly commenced in about the twelfth or thirteenth century with whatever preceded in the realm of vague legend. The same tendency makes the history of Okinawa look as if it began with the prosperous port towns of Urasoe and Naha on the southwestern coast with no preceding agricultural period. Moreover, there has been an overdependence on and uncritical trust of official histories which tend to follow a Confucian moralistic bias and which in turn place too much emphasis on the fortunes and vicissitudes of the succeeding dynasties and a series of great heroes, disregarding the life of the common people.

In order to shed more light on this period in Okinawan history, and particularly on the questions above, I have attempted to reconstruct the period from about the tenth century to the beginning of the seventeenth century. For my main source material, I have used the *Omoro sōshi*, the book of *omoro* poems composed by priestesses, poets, anonymous commoners, and even a queen, compiled by the order of the royal court at Shuri during the sixteenth and seventeenth centuries. Since the *Omoro sōshi* comprises largely spontaneous poems sung by people from many walks of life, it is remarkably free of the embellishments which often distort the official histories. For this reason, the *Omoro sōshi* offers an advantage over the traditional historical accounts. But, at the same time, because of the fact that it is composed largely of free and spontaneous poems, it lacks order and systematization, which makes it necessary to consult supplementary sources.

Analysis of various versions of the creation mythology and of some *omoro* reveals that long before the course of written history (which begins with the Shunten dynasty in 1187), there existed first the primitive *makyo* (consanguineous kinship group) village under the leadership of the brother-sister pair of the main household (which persisted throughout the history of Okinawa), and then the *mura* village made up of two or more *makyo* groups, the growth of which eventually produced the *anji*, or local lord, with whom written history began. Although the original migration to the Ryūkyū Islands is estimated to have taken place sometime before the third or fourth century CE, there were still later migrations—most likely from the north—within the people's memory. On the basis of evidence in the *omoro* poems, together with other geographical and cultural factors, I have hypothesized that the primary cultural center of the nation was located on the southeastern coast of Okinawa, and that it later moved during approximately the thirteenth and fourteenth centuries to a secondary center on the southwestern coast. This means that the primary center faced northward to Japan, but the later secondary center faced mainly westward to China and southward to the South Seas.

I have also proposed that the history of a nation such as Okinawa, poor in natural resources and consequently dependent upon intercourse with the outside world, be examined in the context of the development of improved techniques of transportation.

Limited in natural resources and agricultural potential, the Ryūkyū Islands themselves have never been able to support a great population. Population movement was rigidly restricted by legislation and the most primitive kind of population control was practiced to keep the population down. According to one estimate, the population of the Ryūkyū Islands in about the fifteenth through seventeenth centuries "did not exceed 200,000 of which perhaps 125,000 lived on Okinawa. And of these it has been estimated that more than half lived in the four towns of Shuri, Naha, Tomari and Kune."[1] That the islands were able to support this population was due mainly to active overseas trade (the heavy concentration of population in the urban areas also attests to the fact that an increase of population was made possible only by the benefits from foreign trade). Thus, it was natural that the one consistent policy of all the dynasties in Okinawa was to break the isolating barrier of the ocean and to make it instead the bridge over which the wealth of all nations was to be brought in. In this sense, improved techniques of transportation, specifically, in navigation and shipbuilding, significantly influenced the development and history of Okinawa.

Accordingly, I have divided the history of Okinawa up to 1609 into three periods. The first period is from time immemorial to the end of the twelfth century. During this period, the primitive stage of shipbuilding and navigation—namely, that of the dugout canoe—gave inhabitants only one choice in traffic with the outside world, that is, with the northern islands of Amami-Ōshima and Kyūshū, Japan. The second period extends from the end of the twelfth century—when defeated Japanese seagoing warriors who took refuge in the Ryūkyū Islands brought with them advanced navigation and shipbuilding technology—to the end of the fourteenth century. During this period, there seems to have been more interisland intercourse including the Miyako and Yaeyama groups than before. Perhaps it was at this time that the Miyako and Yaeyama Islands began to form a loose federation or alliance with Okinawa. The third period begins at the end of the fourteenth century when Chinese maritime technology was introduced together with the possibility of acquiring great wealth overseas. As China became increasingly important to Okinawa, the Miyako and Yaeyama Islands also increased in importance as way stations for Okinawan ships bound for China and the South Seas. The Chūzan kingdom of Ryūkyū therefore tried to bring Miyako and Yaeyama more fully under its control. The rebellion of Yaeyama in 1500 could probably be viewed as an indication of the resistance of the native ruling class of Yaeyama against such efforts by Okinawa.

This hypothesis, by pointing out the importance of communication with the outside world, also explains the ascendancy of central Okinawa, with its superior natural harbors and hinterlands, throughout history. Whoever controlled communication with the outside world was probably always able to obtain the best arms and the best agricultural implements. Military supremacy based upon superior arms was supported and enhanced by increased agricultural productivity made possible by the use of iron implements. This is clearly illustrated by the stories of how King Satto and King Shō Hashi, founders of the fourteenth and fifteenth century dynasties, respectively, derived their initial popularity and power by distributing iron implements to the farmers.

In agreement with a number of scholars of Okinawan history, I reject the view which states that the unification of Okinawa in 1422 by Shō Hashi was a *re*unification. It seems to be an obvious example of the Confucian scholar-historian's bias which distorted facts in order to idealize the past and legitimize the reigning dynasty of Chūzan. Shō Hashi's unification of Okinawa in 1422 must be regarded as the first; prior to that time the three small kingdoms or principalities enjoyed equal sovereignty and legitimacy.

Finally, because of the basic affinity of Okinawan culture to that of Japan, Japan has continually exerted a strong influence upon Okinawa. And, from about the twelfth and thirteenth centuries, Okinawans assiduously studied under Chinese tutelage, for China had the greatest empire and civilization in East Asia. Okinawa drew freely from all around her; adopting and assimilating borrowed elements into her own distinctive culture. Sometimes efforts were made to emulate China, notably in the matter of urban planning under the reign of King Shō Shin. In architectural designs and motifs such as the dragon or castle arch-gate, Chinese influence may be clearly detected, but Shuri Castle, with only the royal family and its attendants living within, and with the majority of retainers and townsmen living outside, more closely resembles a Japanese castle town than a Chinese one. In fact, the old capital of Japan, Heiankyō, with its square city blocks, is a much more faithful replica of a Chinese capital than Shuri ever was. Reading the official histories of Ryūkyū, one cannot but be surprised at the scrupulous application of Chinese doctrine of the mandate of heaven related to dynastical changes, but one is even more surprised to find that at the Sogenji Temple where the royal ancestral spirits are enshrined, all previous kings are treated as though of one lineage, preserving in Japanese fashion the fiction of one unbroken line. Government officials were given Chinese titles and their ranking seems to reflect the correct Confucian ideology, yet in actual practice the native aristocracy maintained their privileged positions to the exclusion of commoners. It was quite in contrast to the Chinese egalitarianism expressed in the civil service examination system. Ryūkyū did in due time acquire its own civil service examination system based on the Confucian classics in the Chinese fashion, but its spirit was closer to the Japanese because commoners were excluded. In government, the dualism of government and religion as symbolized in the sovereignty of the brother-sister pair persisted throughout, in spite of some official attempts to eradicate the influence of women from the court. In religion, though Buddhism was introduced from Japan and attracted the attention of the elite, the indigenous religion, Shintoism, was never completely displaced and continued to ert an influence upon people. In the realm of poetry, from the mid-seventeenth century onward, Japan began to ercise strong influence and Ryūkyū did produce a fair number of poets versatile in the Japanese *waka* short poem, but the Ryūkyūans continued to keep alive the tradition of the *omoro* in the later *ryūka* Ryūkyūan poem, as distinct in the number of syllables required and in the pathos that was revealed. Finally, in the area of music and dance, in spite of the clearly discernable influence from both China and Japan, Ryūkyū remained most distinctly Ryūkyūan. In fact, it is in the area of music, dance, and drama that the Ryūkyūan language and literature have been preserved faithfully until today.

Appendix

History of the Study of the *Omoro Sōshi*

The third and final compilation of the *Omoro sōshi* was completed in 1623. About a century later, in 1709, there was a huge fire which destroyed the royal castle and its priceless records, necessitating massive restoration work. As a part of this restoration work, the royal government made copies of the *Omoro sōshi* in 1710 from a set preserved in the Gushikawa family. When they did so, the officials concerned discovered themselves hardly able to understand much of the language of the *Omoro sōshi*. Apparently, since the Satsuma conquest of Ryūkyū in 1609, such radical changes had taken place in Ryūkyūan society, with concomitant changes in the language, that the *Omoro sōshi*, written barely a century earlier, had now, in 1710, become largely incomprehensible. Alarmed officials sought out an old court lady of remarkable memory who had served three generations of kings since King Shō Ken (1641–1647), and with her assistance the board of compilers, probably under the direction of Shikina Seimei (1651–1715), a distinguished scholar-official versed in Japanese learning, completed compilation of the *Konkōkenshū* in 1711. The *Konkōkenshū* is practically a dictionary of ancient terms in the *Omoro sōshi*, and hence marks the preliminary for the study of the *Omoro sōshi*.

After a lapse of about two hundred years, Professor Basil Hall Chamberlain, the first professor of modern philology at the Imperial Tokyo University, visited Okinawa in 1893 and came across the *Omoro sōshi*. He described it as "a collection of ancient hymns or liturgical chants, used in the religious services of the royal household." However, he abandoned any attempt to decipher the manuscript as "great difficulties necessarily attend the study of such texts, whose obscurity is doubled by their transcription in a foreign and ill-adapted system of writing."

In the same year, 1893, Tajima Risaburō arrived in Okinawa to teach Japanese literature at the Prefectural Okinawa Middle School. Prior to his arrival, he was told by a friend who had been to Okinawa that there were enigmatic manuscripts of about fifty volumes written in Ryūkyūan which no one could decipher.

After considerable time and effort, he finally found the twenty-two volumes of the *Omoro sōshi*, and thus began his laborious study of this work, the first ever undertaken. Before leaving Okinawa in 1897, he had made personal copies of the *Omoro sōshi* and *Konkōkenshū* and a manuscript entitled "Ryūkyū-go kenkyū shiryō" [Materials for the study of the Ryūkyūan language]. It was published in Tokyo in a magazine called *Kokkō*, the New Year's edition of 1898, and was later republished in 1924 as a book called *Ryūkyū bungaku kenkyū* [Studies in Ryūkyūan literature]. The *Ryūkyū bungaku kenkyū* is important as the first attempt to present an overview of Okinawan literature with emphasis on the *omoro*.

In 1903, while still in Tokyo, Tajima gave all of his manuscript materials to Iha Fuyū, a former student of his at the Okinawa Middle School who was then a student of philology at the Imperial Tokyo University, with the plea that Iha continue the study of the *Omoro sōshi*. A few days thereafter, Tajima suddenly left Tokyo for Taiwan and other lands, never to return to Japan.

Iha was now forced to study the *Omoro sōshi* all by himself. Reflecting on his first attempt in those days, years later, in 1924, Iha mused that it was like trying to study a foreign literature; at one point he even considered abandoning the attempt altogether. It was only with the utmost will power and by telling himself over and over that no matter how difficult it might be, it was, after all, a literature left by his own ancestors, that he was able to persist. With the help of the *Konkōkenshū*, the only dictionary of the ancient Ryūkyūan language, he finally began to decipher, little by little.

In 1911, he published his monumental work, *Ko Ryūkyū* [Ancient Ryūkyū], which immediately established his reputation as a scholar in the study of ancient Ryūkyū. *Ko Ryūkyū* contains an article entitled "Omoro shichishu" [Seven kinds of *omoro*] and a second edition, in 1916, also contains the *Konkōkenshū as* an appendix. However, it was not until 1924 that his first major work on the *Omoro sōshi, Ryūkyū seiten Omoro sōshi senshaku: Omoro ni arawaretaru ko-Ryūkyū no bunka* [Selected translations of the *Omoro sōshi*, sacred book of Ryūkyū: The culture of old Ryūkyū as revealed in the *omoro*] appeared. The 23-page introduction entitled "*Omoro sōshi* no rekishi" [History of the *Omoro sōshi*] is followed by a 238-page text containing 98 translations of *omoro* with copious annotations, and a supplement (pp. 239–283) of annotated translations of nine other Ryūkyūan songs including some from Miyako and Yaeyama.

In the following year, 1925, Iha published another major work, *Kōtei Omoro sōshi* [*Omoro sōshi*, revised], 3 volumes, 1,024 pages. There is a 28-page introduction, 4-page preface, and a 32-page postscript. Iha used his "Tajima copy" as the basic text, with the copy in the family of Marquis Shō and the copy in the possession of

Mr. Nakayoshi Chōjo as reference texts. The publication of these two books, *Omoro sōshi senshaku* and *Kōtei Omoro sōshi*, is indeed an epochal event which marks the beginning of Ryūkyūan studies in modern times. The former of these two works has shown the fruit of Iha's prodigious labors using the methodology of modern linguistics and ethnography, and the latter has at long last made the *Omoro sōshi* available for extensive perusal and study.

The publication of Iha's *Kōtei Omoro sōshi* in 1925 stirred public interest in the *Omoro sōshi* and led to the formation of a number of *Omoro* study groups. In the late 1920s there appeared in Okinawa a group called "Shin Omoro gaku-ha" (New Omoro Study Group) under such leaders as Shimabukuro Zenpatsu, Miyagi Shinji, Higa Seishō, Miyasato Eiki, and Serei Kunio. They were popularizers of *Omoro* study, emplified by Shimabukuro's outstanding contribution, in 1933, of a new method of reading comprehension of the *Omoro* poems called "Tendoku-hō."

Another member of this group, Higa Seishō, moved to Taihoku (Taipei) in 1940. With Professor Toshi'ichi Sudō of Taihoku Higher School, Higa organized the Nantō kenkyū no kai (Society for Southern Islands Study). Members included Taihoku University professors such as Kobata Atsushi, Kanaseki Takeo, Matsumura Kazuo, and Ryūkyūan residents of Taihoku such as Haebaru Chōho, Kabira Chōshin, Miyara Kentei, and others. The society published a journal called *Nantō* [Southern Islands] in August 1940. A second volume was published in March 1942 and a third, in September 1944. Volumes 1 and 2 contain translations of twenty-two of the songs in volume 1 of the *Omoro sōshi* with extensive annotation.

In 1940, using the pseudonym Hanagusuku Gushi, Ono Shigeo wrote "Birō no hana: Omoro to fūdo" [Betel palm flower: Omoro and nature] in *Okinawa kyōiku*. It dealt with such topics as the ambience of the *Omoro sōshi*, its animals, plants, topography, heavenly bodies, climate, and seasons.

In the same year, Serei Kunio published "Ryūkyū ongaku kayō shiron" [On the history of Ryūkyūan music and ballads] in 87 installments in the *Ryūkyū shimpō* newspaper. This work, together with his study "Kumejima Omoro ni tsuite" [On the omoro of Kume Island], published in *Nantō*, II, in 1942, did much to establish the *omoro* as music and ballad, rather than literature, within the context of the history of Ryūkyūan music and ballads.

In 1943, Nakahara Zenchū published a small but important study, *Kagari-ito* [Darning thread] in mimeograph. It is a detailed study of the Kume Island songs in volume 21 and elsewhere in the *Omoro sōshi*. This was the basic material for the study of the *Omoro sōshi* and marks his first important step towards a full-scale study of the *Omoro sōshi*. In the meanwhile, Iha Fuyū, who had started the study of the *Omoro sōshi* as a study in linguistics, found himself getting deeper and deeper into the fields of ethnography and history. This trend is clearly perceived in his "Shō Hashi no bokkō no Ryūkyū no sōseiki to saishi to ni oyoboseru eikyō: Omoro sōshi maki-ichi kenkyū josetsu" [The influence of Shō Hashi's rise upon the genesis and ritual of Ryūkyū: A preliminary study of volume 1 of the *Omoro sōshi*] in *Okinawa kyōiku*, in 1934. The two decades following publication of *Kōtei Omoro sōshi* in 1925 found him completely engrossed in the study of the *Omoro sōshi* and Ryūkyūan history and ethnography. He published the fruits of his labor rapidly one after another: in 1926, *Shinshū Okinawa kaikyō zenshi* [Prehistory of the propagation of Shinshū Buddhism in Okinawa], *Ryūkyū kokon ki* [Records of Ryūkyū, past and present], *Kotōku no Ryūkyū-shi* [History of the tribulations of isolated, insular Ryūkyū]; in 1928, *Okinawa yo, izuko e* [Whither, O Okinawa?]; in 1929, *Kōchū Ryūkyū gikyoku-shū* [Collection of Ryūkyūan plays, with annotations]; in 1931, *Nantō shi-kō* [Thoughts on the history of the Southern Islands]; in 1934, *Nantō hōgen shikō* [Historical study of the dialects of the Southern Islands]; in 1938, *Ryūkyū gikyoku jiten* [Dictionary of Ryūkyūan plays], *Onarigami no shima* [Islands of the sibling deities]; in 1939, *Nihon bunka no nanzen* [Southward diffusion of Japanese culture]; in 1942, *Okinawa kō* [Okinawan monographs], revised edition of *Ko Ryūkyū* [Ancient Ryūkyū]. In 1945, however, he was dealt a nearly fatal blow: in an American air raid, his home and his entire collection of research materials and manuscripts were reduced to ashes. He made one more desperate effort and published his last major manuscript, *Okinawa rekishi monogatari* [Historical tales of Okinawa] in 1946. Shortly after he finished the manuscript of a revised edition on July 9, 1947, he died suddenly on August 13, 1947.

After Iha's death, Nakahara Zenchū became the leading *omoro* scholar. In *Bunka Okinawa* (formerly *Okinawa bunka*), in 25 installments, from December 1948 to October 1952, Nakahara published "Omoro hyōshaku: Omoro no kenkyū" [Critical translations of *omoro: Omoro* study]. He presented translations of 94 *omoro* poems which had been left untouched by Iha Fuyū. As a historian, he was able to see these *omoro* poems from a more historical perspective, presenting fresh insights. In 1957, Nakahara published *Omoro shinshaku* [New translations of the *Omoro*], clarifying his own method of *omoro* study and translation as well as 140 translations of *omoro* poems. There are two other articles by Nakahara which deserve mention: "Omoro no kenkyū: Omoro kenkyū no hōkō to saishuppatsu" [*Omoro* study: *Omoro* study's direction and re-launch], in *Minzokugaku kenkyū*, 15:2 (November 1950), and "Nakagusuku dōran no omoro" [*Omoro* on the Nakagusuku disturbance] in *Okinawa bunka*, 1 (1961). These indicated a new direction in *omoro* study, with more emphasis on historical and economic-historical perspectives.

Having completed these preparatory steps, Nakahara embarked upon an endeavor to produce a complete revised text of the *Omoro sōshi*, dictionary, and index. However, he died suddenly in 1964 with his work unfinished. His unfinished manuscripts were entrusted to Hokama Shuzen, his student and junior partner in research. Hokama completed *Kōhon Omoro sōshi* [Emended text: *Omoro sōshi*] in 1965 and *Omoro sōshi jiten-sōsakuin* [Dictionary and index to the *Omoro sōshi*] in 1967.

Having inherited the implicit post of leadership, Hokama proceeded to stir Japanese academic interest in the *Omoro sōshi*, an effort in which he was eminently successful. The *Okinawa bunka* [Quarterly bulletin of Okinawan studies] was started by the Okinawa Bunka Kyōkai (Japanese Society for Okinawan Studies) in Tokyo in 1948 with such Okinawan leaders as Higa Shunchō, Nakahara Zenchū, Miyara Tōsō, Shimabukuro Genpachi, and Kinjō Chōei as the nucleus. Under Hokama's editorship, the *Okinawa bunka* became more vigorous as well as almost fully devoted to the study of Okinawan literature, especially the *Omoro sōshi*.

Hokama also assumed the directorship of the Okinawa Bunka Kenkyūjo (Institute of Okinawan Studies) at Hosei University in Tokyo, and started periodically publishing in full book length *Okinawa bunka kenkyū* [Studies in Okinawan culture]. *Okinawa bunka kenkyū*, now numbering volume 11 (as of the original publication of the current volume), appears to give priority to publishing articles on literary topics (though not exclusively) such as studies of the *Omoro sōshi*. This may be confirmed by a glance at Appendix B, Bibliography of the Study of the *Omoro sōshi*, later in this book.

Hokama has to his credit not only studies on the *Omoro sōshi* but other studies on the literature of Okinawa. He published *Nantō jōcho* [Sentiments of the Southern Islands] with Nakahodo Masanori, on the Okinawan short poem, in 1974; *Nantō bungaku* [Literature of the Southern Islands] in 1976, which covers the *Omoro sōshi*, *ryuka* short poems, and *kumiodori* operetta; and *Okinawa bungaku no sekai* [The world of Okinawan literature] in 1979.

In addition, there are other studies of the *Omoro sōshi* which are worthy of mention. To cite a few, there are Kinjō Chōei's "Omoro no sōsaku katei ni tsuite: Omoro kenkyū shiron" [On the process of composing *omoro:* An attempt on the study of *omoro*], in *Bunka Okinawa*, 27, 1953; Okusato Shōken's *Insei kizoku-go to bunka no nanten* [Southward development of the language and culture of the aristocrats of the cloistered government of Japan], 1954, on the phonology and grammar of the *Omoro sōshi;* Miyagi Shinji's *Kodai Okinawa no sugata* [Appearance of the Ancient Okinawa] in 1954; Saigō Nobutsuna's "Okinawa no koyō omoro ni tsuite" [On the ancient ballads of Okinawa, *omoro*] in the *Shin Nihon bungaku* in 1957, Yamanouchi Seihin's *Ryūkyū ōchō koyo hikyoku no kenkyū* [A study of the secret music of the ancient songs of the Ryūkyūan dynasty] in 1964, and Ono Shigeo's "Omoro no hassei: Jojika yori jojōka e" [On the genesis of the *'Omoro'*: Epics from *'kwena'* lyrics] in *Okinawa bunka*, 21 (July 1966). There is also Torigoe Kenzaburō's *Omoro sōshi zenshaku* [Complete translations of the *Omoro sōshi*] in 1968. This is certainly an ambitious attempt, being the first complete translation of the *Omoro sōshi*, consisting of more than 3,000 pages in five volumes. It has many excellent insights from the viewpoint of religion, according to Hokama Shuzen, but it also contains several still unanswered problems relating to the selection of the text, the phonology, and the grammar of the *Omoro sōshi*. Finally, in recent years, Higa Minoru of Hōsei University in Tokyo has successfully broken new ground in the study of the *Omoro sōshi* and ancient Okinawa with the publication of his *Kō Ryūkyū no sekai* [The world of ancient Ryūkyū] in 1982.

Bibliography of the Study of the *Omoro Sōshi*

A. Books

Higa, Minoru. 1982. *Kō Ryūkyū no sekai* [The world of ancient Ryūkyū].

Higa, Shunchō. *Higa Shunchō zenshū* [Complete works of Higa Shunchō]. 5 vols., 1971–1973.

Hokama, Shuzen. *Konkōkenshū: kōhon to kenkyū* [The Konkōkenshū (ancient Ryūkyūan dictionary): its text and study]. 1970.

——. *Nihon shomin seikatsushiryō shūsei: #19, Nantō kayō* [Collection of historical materials on the life of the common people of Japan, #19, old ballads of the Southern Islands]. 1971.

——. *Okinawa bungaku no sekai* [The world of Okinawan literature]. 1979.

——. *Okinawa bunka ronsō: #4, Bungaku geinō-hen* [On Okinawan culture, #4, literature and performing arts]. 1971.

——. *Okinawa no gengoshi* [History of the language of Okinawa]. 1971.

——. *Omoro-go jisho: Okinawa no kojishō Konkōkenshū* [Dictionary of *Omoro* terms: ancient dictionary of Okinawa, Konkōkenshū]. 1971.

——. *Urizun no shima* [Island of Urizun]. 1971.

——, and Saigō Nobutsuna. *Omoro sōshi* [Anthology of *omoro* poems]. 1972.

Hōsei daigaku Okinawa bunka kenkyūjo, comp. *Kimihae no hajimari aitsutauru no ki; Ōwan norokumoi kawariai no toki nikki; Kaku magiri norokumoi no omori* [Record of transmission of the beginnings of Priestess Kimihae; Daily records of the succesion of the Ōwan priestess; *Omori* poems of the priestesses of every district]. 1984.

Iha, Fuyū. *Iha Fuyū senshū* [Selected works of Iha Fuyū]. 3 vols., 1961–1962.

——. *Iha Fuyū zenshū* [Complete works of Iha Fuyū]. 11 vols., 1974–1976.

——. *Kō Ryūkyū* [Ancient Ryūkyū]. 1911.

——. *Kōtei Omoro sōshi* [*Omoro sōshi*, revised]. 3 vols., 1925.

——. *Okinawa joseishi* [History of women in Okinawa]. 1919.

——. *Okinawa kō* [Okinawan monographs]. 1942.

——. *Ryūkyū seiten: Omoro sōshi senshaku* [Selected translations of the *Omoro sōshi*, sacred book of Ryūkyū]. 1924.

——. *Onarigami no shima* [Islands of the sibling deities]. 1938.

——. *Ryūkyū kokon ki* [Records of Ryūkyū, past and present]. 1926.

Ikemiya, Masaharu. *Ryūkyū bungaku ron* [on Ryūkyūan literature]. 1976.

Inamura, Kenpu. *Okinawa no kodai buraku makyo no kenkyū* [A study of the *makyo*, the ancient village community in Okinawa]. 1968.

Kamida, Sōei. *Ryūkyū bungaku hassōron* [On conceptions in Ryūkyūan literature]. 1968.

——. *Ryūkyū bungaku josetsu* [Introduction to Ryūkyūan literature]. 1966.

Katō, Sango. *Ryūkyū no kenkyū* [Study of the Ryūkyūs]. (1906) Rev. 1941.

Kinjō, Chōei. *Kinjō Chōei zenshū* [Complete works of Kinjō Chōei]. 2 vols., 1974.

Makishi, Kōyū. *Omoro ni yoru Shuri no gogen to Okinawa no chimei ni tsuite* [On the derivation of the word Shuri, and of the place names of Okinawa according to the *Omoro sōshi*]. 1967.

Morioka, Kenji. *Okinawa no bungaku* [Literature of Okinawa]. 1967.

Nagazumi, Yasuaki. *Okinawa ritō* [Isolated island Okinawa]. 1970.

Nakahara, Zenchū. *Kagari-ito* [Darning thread]. 1943.

——. *Nakahara Zenchū senshū* [Selected works of Nakahara Zenchū]. 3 vols., 1969.

——. *Omoro no fushina shusshō sakuin: Omoro sōshi no kihonteki kenkyū, dai'ni-shū* [Index of the places in which the names of *omoro* tunes appear]. 1951.

——. *Omoro shinshaku* [New translations of the omoro]. 1957.

——, and Hokama Shuzen, eds. *Kōhon Omoro sōshi* [Emended text: *Omoro sōshi*]. 1965.

——, ed. *Omoro sōshi jiten-sōsakuin* [Dictionary and index to the *Omoro sōshi*]. 1967.

Nakamatsu, Yashū. *Kami to mura* [Kami and villages]. 1968.

——. *Kosō no mura: Okinawa minzoku bunka ron* [Villages of the ancient stratum: discourse on the folk culture of Okinawa]. 1977.

Noboru, Shomu. *Dai Amami-shi* [History of great Amami]. 1949.

Okinawa-shi kyōiku iinkai, comp. *Ōfu omoro* [Royal government *omoro*]. 1983.

Okuzato, Shōken. *Insei kizoku-go to bunka no nanten* [Southward development of the language and culture of the aristocrats of the cloistered government of Japan]. 1954.

Ono, Shigeo. *Ryūkyū bungaku* [Ryūkyūan literature]. 1943.

Torigoe, Kenzaburō. *Okinawa no shinwa to minzoku* [Mythology and folk customs of Okinawa]. 1970.

——. *Ryūkyū shūkyō-shi no kenkyū* [A study of the history of religion in Ryūkyū]. 1965.

——. *Omoro sōshi zenshaku* [Complete translation of the *Omoro sōshi*]. 5 vols., 1968.

Yamanouchi, Seihin. *Ryūkyū ōchō koyō hikyoku no kenkyū* [A study of the secret music of the ancient songs of the Ryūkyūan dynasty]. 1964.

B. Articles

Adaniya, Setsuko, "Omoro ni fuku kaze" [The winds in the *Omoro*], *Okinawa bunka*, no. 39, IX:4 (June 1972), 40–57.

Akiyama, Kenzō, "Omoro sōshi to Man'yōshū" [On the *Omoro sōshi* and *Man'yōshū*], *Nisshi kōshō shiwa* (4th edition, 1937), 204–217.

Asato, Hidemasa, "Jūfuku Omoro o chūsin ni mita *'Omoro sōshi'* dai-sankai ni tsuite—kannai no kozo to sono seiritsu" [Volume 3 of the *Omoro sōshi* with emphasis on duplicated *omoro*—internal structure and formation], *Okinawa bunka*, no. 62, XX:2 (March 1984), 36–54.

Hanagusuku, Gushi (pseud. Ono Shigeo), "Birō no hana: Omoro to fūdo" [Betel palm flower: *Omoro* and nature], *Okinawa kyōiku* (October 1940), 9–31.

Hateruma, Eikichi, "Sodetare shōkō" [An essay on the *Omoro* phrase 'sode tare'], *Okinawa bunka*, no. 61, XX:1 (September 1983), 66–76.

——, "Ono Shigeo 'Nantō ko-kayō no kakei no keifu' ni kansuru jakkan no gimon" [Some problems of 'A genealogy of the forms of old poems in the Southern Isles' by Ono Shigeo], *Okinawa bunka*, no. 55, XVII:2 (May 1981), 88–95.

Hattori, Shirō, "Ryūkyū-go oyobi ryūka ni tsuite" [On the Ryūkyūan language and *ryuka* poem], *Kokoro no hana*, nos. 60–68, 1956.

——, "Yama, Mori, Take" [Hills, woods, and groves], *Kokugogaku*, no. 69, 1967.

Higa, Kisei, "Kokugo-hōgengaku ni yoru 'Man'yō' 'Omoro' kaishaku" [*Omoro* and *Man'yō*], *Okinawa bunka*, nos. 26–27, VI:3–4 (March 1980), 52–57.

Higa, Minoru, "Chihō omoro seiritsu no shūhen" [Periphery of the formation of the local *omoro*], *Kō Ryūkyū no sekai*, 1982, 151–178. First appeared under the same title in *Okinawa bunka kenkyū*, Hōsei daigaku Okinawa bunka kenkyūjo, comp., IV (1977), 105–140.

——, "Omoro kajin no gunzō" [Group image of the *Omoro* poets], *Kō Ryūkyū no sekai*, 1982, pp. 233–246.

——, "Omoro ni miru kō Ryūkyū no shisō" [Thoughts on ancient Ryūkyū as seen in the *Omoro*], *Kō Ryūkyū no sekai*, 1982, pp. 55–78.

——, "Omoro no dokukaihō ni tsuite" [On the method of reading and comprehending the *Omoro], Kō Ryūkyū no sekai*, 1982, pp. 126–150.

——, "Omoro no kaidokuhō ni tsuite: Bunri kaidokuhō no mondaiten" [On the method of reading comprehension of the *Omoro:* problems in the separate reading method], *Bungaku*, by Iwanami shoten, no. 43, 7, 1975.

——, "Ryūka no genryū to sono seiritsu" [Origin of the *ryūka* poem and its formation], *Okinawa bunka kenkyū*, Hosei daigaku Okinawa bunka kenkyūjo, II (1975), 97–142.

——, "Ryūkyū bungaku gaisetsu" [Outline of Ryūkyūan literature], *Gengo*, XII:4 (August 1983), 99–109.

Higaonna, Kanjun, "Ryūkyū kogojiten Konkōkenshū o chūsin to shite" [With emphasis on the *Konkōkenshū*, the ancient Ryūkyūan language dictionary], *Takushoku daigaku ronshū*, no. 16 (1958).

Hirosaki, Junko, "Natsu o matsu Omoro-bito" [People of the *Omoro* era awaiting summer], *Okinawa bunka*, no. 45, XII:2 (August 1976), 37–44.

Hiyane, Teruo, "Omoro sōshi kenkyū no shisoteki danmen [The background of historical thoughts of the three *Omoro* investigators: Iha, Nakahara, and Hokama], *Okinawa bunka*, no. 24, VI:1 (August 1967), 16–30.

Hokama, Shuzen, "Aji ko" [On *aji* petty lords], *Okinawa bunka,* no. 3 (August 1961), 25–30.

———, "Aji no gogen" [Etymological origin of 'aji'], *Okinawa bunka,* no. 35, VIII:4 (April 1971), 18–30.

———, "Chūsei bunken ni arawareta Ryūkyū hōgen no dōshi" [Verbs in the Ryūkyūan dialect which appear in medieval documents], *Kokugogaku,* 41 (August 1960), 106–114.

———, "Iwanami-bon 'Omoro sōshi' no seigo" [Errata in the Iwanami edition *Omoro sōshi*], *Okinawa bunka,* no. 45, XII:2 (August 1976), 98–101.

———, "Ko jishō Konkōkenshū no kenkyū" [Study of the ancient dictionary *Konkōkenshū*], *Okinawa bunka,* no. 10 (February 1963), 6–9; no. 11 (April 1963), 8–11; no. 12 (September 1963), 7–14.

———, "Nantō kayō no genryū" [Origin of the ballads in the Southern Islands], *Bungaku,* no. 39, 7 (1971).

———, "Nantō kayō no keifu" [Genealogy of the Southern Island ballad], *Bungaku,* no. 40, 4–5 (1971).

———, "Okinawa bungaku no gaikan [An outline of Okinawan literature], *Okinawa bunka,* nos. 26–27, VI:3–4 (March 1968), 1–4.

———, "Okinawa bungaku no zentaizō" [The entirety of the Okinawan literature], *Okinawa bunka kenkyū,* VI (1979), 338–395.

———, "Okinawa bunka-ron—Bunka o chūshin to shite" [On Okinawan culture—with culture at its center], *Sekai,* February 1975.

———, "Okinawa no gengo-shi" [History of the Okinawan language], *Bungaku,* XXXVI:1 (1968).

———, "Okinawa no gengo-shi josetsu" [Introduction to the history of the Okinawan language], *Totritsu daigaku hōgengakkai kaihō,* no. 26 (1968).

———, "Okinawa no kodai to Esa-omoro" [Esa-omoro and antiquities of Okinawa], *Okinawa bunka,* no. 29, VII:2 (December 1970), 26–30.

———, "Okinawa no koten Omoro sōshi" [Classics of Okinawa, *Omoro sōshi*], *Bungaku,* 35:6 (1967).

———, "Omoro-go 'afu' ni tsuite" [On 'afu' in the *Omoro*], *Okinawa bunka,* no. 41, X:2 (March 1974), 37–41.

———, "Omoro-go 'i' no yōrei to bunpōteki seikaku" [Examples of the Omoro word 'i' and their grammatical characters], *Okinawa bunka,* no. 46, XIII:1 (December 1976), 42–53.

———, "Omoro-go kenkyū ni kansuru jakkan no mondai" [Some problems related to the study of Omoro terms], *Okinawa no gengo-shi,* 1969.

———, "Omoro-go 'urizun' to 'wakanatsu'" [On the Omoro terms 'urizun' and 'wakanatsu'], *Okinawa bunka kenkyū,* III (1976), 244–257.

———, "Omoro no gen'i" [Original meaning of *omoro*], *Okinawa no gengo-shi,* 1971.

———, "Omoro no onki ni taisuru gimon" [Questions on the transcription of *omoro*], *Ryūkyū bungaku,* no. 11 (1960).

———, "Omoro sōsei shinwa ni okeru joshi, 'na' no kaishaku" [Interpretation of the particle 'na' in the Omoro myth of creation], *Okinawa bunka,* no. 61, XX:1 (September 1983), 1–15.

——, "Omoro sōshi no jodōshi" [Adverbs in the *Omoro sōshi*], Okinawa bunka, no. 1 (April 1961), 39–43.
——, "Omoro sōshi no kanazukai to hyōkihō" [Use of the *kana* syllabary and transcription in the *Omoro sōshi*], *Okinawa bunka,* no. 19 (1965), 7–11.
——, "Omoro sōshi no shohon to keifu" [Various copies and genealogy of the *Omoro sōshi*], *Ryūkyū daigaku bunrigakubu kiyō,* no. 10 (1966).
——, "Ryūkyū bungaku no tenbō" [Overview of Ryūkyūan literature], *Bungaku,* 33:7 (1965).
——, "Ryūkyū hōgen no dōshi—chūsei bunken ni arawareta" [Verbs in the Ryūkyūan dialect—as appear in medieval literature], *Kokugo-gaku,* no. 41 (1960).
——, "Shohyō 'Torigoe Kenzaburō cho, Omoro sōshi zenshaku: Omoro bunpo no ayamari" [Book review of Torigoe Kenzaburō's *Omoro sōshi zenshaku:* errors in the *Omoro* grammar], *Bungaku,* XXXVII:3 (1969).
——, "Urasoe ni Okinawa bunka no rekishi o miru, 'Omoro sōshi' o chūsin ni shite" [Urasoe and Okinawan cultural history: evidence from the *Omoro sōshi*], *Okinawa bunka,* no. 62, XX:2 (March 1974), 71–87.
Iha, Fuyū, "Kwaina o megutte: Okinawa bungeishi kō" [On the *kwainya* songs: discussion on Okinawan literary history], *Kaizō* (January 1932), reprinted in *Okinawa rekishi monogatari,* 1946, pp. 185–210.
——, "Shō Hashi no bokkō no Ryūkyū no sōseiki to saishi to ni oyoboseru eikyo: Omoro sōshi maki-ichi kenkyū josetsu" [Influence of Shō Hashi's rise upon the genesis and ritual of Ryūkyū: preliminary study of volume one of the *Omoro sōshi*], *Okinawa kyōiku,* IX:1 (January 1934), 41–59; IX:2 (February 1934), 14–23.
——, "Man'yōgo to Ryūkyūgo" [Man'yō language and Ryūkyū language], *Man'yōshū* kōza, vol. 3 (1933), 429–449.
——, "Aibiki o utatta Omoro" [Omoro about lovers' dates], *Tabi to densetsu,* 5:4 (April 1932), 61–65, *Nantō danwa,* 4 (April 1932), 3–7.
——, "Omoro ni honomieta Ryūkyū shakaishi no akebono" [A glimpse of the Ryūkyūan society in the *Omoro*], *Gekkan mingei,* 2:11–12 (December 1940), 14–22.
——, "Omoro ni tsuite" [On the Omoro], *Okinawa kyōiku,* no. 151 (February 1926), 42–47.
——, "Omoro sōshi ni mieru tsuzumi ni tsuite" [On the drum in the *Omoro sōshi*], *Okinawa kyōiku,* no. 138 (July 1924), 24–32.
——, "Omoro shichishū" [Seven kinds of *omoro*], *Ko Ryūkyū,* 1942, 161–175.
——, "Onarigami" [Sibling deities], *Minzoku,* 1:2 (1926), 45–58; 2:2 (1927), 45–58.
——, "Ryūkyū no koshō bungei" [Oral literature of Ryūkyū], *Kokugo to kokubungaku,* 9:10 (October 1932), 72–90.
——, "Shinka ni arawareta 'Okinawa'" [The term 'Okinawa' which appears in the divine songs], *Okinawa kō,* 1942, 1–57.
——, "Onarigami wo utatta Ōshima no omori" [Ōshima Island *omori* songs which sing of the sibling deities], *Kō Ryūkyū,* 1942, 326–338.
——, "Kō Ryūkyū no ni-shijin" [Two poets of ancient Ryūkyū], *Kaizō,* VII:2, 1925.
——, "Kō Ryūkyū no kayō ni tsukite" [On the songs of ancient Ryūkyū], *Ryūkyū kokonki,* 1926, pp. 283–334.

——, "Saishiki buyo omori kwainya" [Ritual dance *omori-kwainya*], *Ryūkyū kokonki,* 1926, pp. 335–360.

Iihara, Ayako, "Kiyora no bi-ishiki: kiyora ni okeru dō to sei no megutte" [Aesthetic consciousness of *kiyora* centering around inactivity and activity in *kiyora*], *Okinawa bunka,* no. 48, XIV:1 (October 1977), 47–64.

Ikemiya, Masaharu, "Jojōshi to shiteno ryūka no hassei" [Emergence of *ryūka* poetry as lyrics], *Okinawa rekishi kenkyū,* IX (March 1971), 53–70.

——, "Miseseru ni tsuite; sono shintaku-takusen to iyu koto" [A study of *miseseru:* its being oracle], *Okinawa bunka,* no. 28, VII:1 (August 1969), 38–52.

——, "Okinawa no sōsei shinwa ni tsuite" [On the genesis of Okinawa in the *Omoro sōshi*], *Okinawa rekishi kenkyū,* no. 8 (September 1970), 45–62.

——, "Omoro mishōgo 'yomuikinokasu' ni tsuite" [On the unclarified Omoro term 'yomuikinokasu'), *Kenkyū yoteki,* nos. 98–99, 1970.

Ikuta, Shigeru, "Omoro sōshi ni mieru ōmei ni tsuite [On royal names in the *Omoro sōshi*], *Nantō shigaku,* no. 13 (February 1979), 1–29.

Kadekaru, Chizuko, "Omoro sōshi kakiaratame to Konkōkenshū hensan ni tsuite" [A study concerning *omoro* and the compilation of the *Konkōkenshū*], *Nantō shigaku,* XI (January 1978), 23–47.

Kamida, Soei, "Hōgen no sujō [On the origin of the dialect: *Omoro* terms], *Okinawa bunka,* no. 14, III:14 (January 1964), 11–22.

Kaneshiro, Atsumi, "Ōfu omoro tonaehō no genryū to chihō umui tonaehō" [The origin of methods of chanting *omoros* in the Ryūkyū dynasty and methods of chanting local *umuis*], *Okinawa bunka,* no. 59, XIX:1 (November 1982), 1–13.

Katō, Sango, "Okinawa no ogami narabini Omoro sōshi ni tsuite" [On the *Omoro sōshi* and worship in Okinawa], *Jinruigaku zasshi,* XVI (1900), 175.

Kinjō, Chōei, "Omoro kenkyū zenshi: Tajima Risaburō sensei hyōden" [On early studies of the *Omoro:* Professor Tajima Risaburō's resume], *Nantō ronsō* (1937), 363–375.

——, "Omoro no sōsaku katei ni tsuite: Omoro kenkyū shiron" [On the process of composing *omoro:* an attempt on the study of *omoro*], *Bunka Okinawa,* no. 27, 1953.

——, "Omoro sōshi yakuchū sakuin: Iha sensei no chosho ni keisai sareta omoro no kaisetsu" [Index to the footnotes on the *Omoro sōshi* translations: commentaries on the *omoro* printed in Mr. Iha's books], *Bunka Okinawa,* no. 10 (1949).

——, "Ryūkyū min'yō no kigen to hensen" [Origin and change in Ryūkyūan ballads], *Ryūkyū no min'yō,* ed. by Kanai Kikuko, 1954.

——, "Ryūka no kigen ni tsuite" [On the origin of *ryūka* poetry], *Okinawa,* no. 32, 1954.

Kobata, Atsushi, and nine others, "Omoro sōshi kenkyū, dai-ikkai" [Study of the *Omoro sōshi,* first meeting], *Nantō,* II (1942), 131–162.

Kobata, Atsushi, and others, "Omoro sōshi kenkyū, dai-nikai" [Study of the *Omoro sōshi,* second meeting], *Nantō,* III (1944), 199–228.

Koyama, Kazuyuki, "Omoro goi-kō, 'yo' ni tsuite" [Omoro vocabulary: a study of the concept 'yo'], *Okinawa bunka,* no. 61, XX:1 (September 1983), 26–37.

Kriner, Josef, "Nansei shotō ni okeru kami-kan'nen, takai-kan no ichi-kōsatsu" [Some remarks on conceptions of god and the other world in the religion of the Ryūkyūs], *Okinawa bunka,* no. 23, V:3–4 (March 1967), 11–24.

Kuratsuka, Yōko, "Kodai kenkyū to Okinawa-gaku" [Study of ancient history and Okinawan studies], *Waga Okinawa,* vol. 5, 1971.

Kuwabara, Masao, "Omoro kakei-ron ronsō eno ichishikaku" [A point of view on disputations of poetic structure of *omoro*], *Okinawa bunka,* no. 45, XII:2 (August 1976), 19–26.

Maeshiro, Naoko, "Omoro sōshi no seijisei" [The political ideas of the *Omoro sōshi*], *Okinawa bunka,* no. 63, XXI:1 (October 1984), 24–62.

Makishi, Kōyū, "Kojiki no kodai kayō no omoro ni yoru kaishaku" [Interpretation by the use of *omoro* of the ancient ballads in the *Kojiki*], *Kōnan kenkyū kiyō,* no. 7 (April 1981), 27–47.

Makishi, Yōko, "Niruya ōnushi no sujō [Birth of 'Niruya unishi'], *Okinawa bunka,* no, 45, XII:2 (August 1976), 27–36.

———, "Omoro sōshi ni okeru oya, ohya, nya ni tsuite" [*Oya* and *niya* in the *Omoro sōshi*], *Okinawa bunka,* no. 40, X:1 (January 1973), 27–46.

Mamiya, Atsushi, "Omoro sōshi ni okeru yondan katsuyō dōshi no saiko ren'yokei ni tsuite" [Conjugation of verbs in the *Omoro sōshi*], *Okinawa bunka,* no. 61, XX:1 (September 1983), 56–65.

———, "Omoro sōshi no kakari musubi ni tsuite" [Particles and verb conjugation in the *Omoro sōshi*], *Okinawa bunka,* no. 61, XX:1 (September 1983), 6–25.

Miyagi, Shinji, "Omoro sōshi no hatsuon ni tsuite" [On the pronunciation of the *Omoro sōshi*], *Kodai Okinawa no sugata,* 1954.

———, "Yanbaru no otake" [Holy groves in Northern Okinawa], *Nantō ronsō,* comp. by Shimabukuro Zenpatsu, 1937, pp. 95–109.

Miyara, Tōsō, "Omoro sōshi onki" [Transcription of the *Omoro sōshi*], *Ryūkyū bungaku,* nos. 1–12, 1960.

———, "Ryūkyū bungaku no gaikan" [Overview of Ryūkyūan literature], *Gekkan Ryūkyū bungaku,* 1960.

Murayama, Shichirō, "Shinateru-Terushino kō" [On Shinateru and Terushino], *Kokugogaku,* no. 82, 1970.

Nakahara, Zenchū, "Okinawa no minzoku: Kōshō bungei" [Okinawan folk customs: oral literature], *Nihon minzokugaku taikei,* vol. 12 (1962), 175–189.

———, "Okinawa no taiyō suhai to hi no kami" [Sun worship and fire deity in Okinawa], *Nihon minzokugaku taikei,* vol. 12 (1962), 161–174.

———, "Omoro hyōshaku: omoro no kenkyū" [Critical translations of *omoro: omoro* study], *Bunka Okinawa,* I:2 (December 1948) through IV:2 (October 1952), 25 installments.

Nakamoto, Masachie, "Omoro kanazukai no genryū" [Origin of the *kana* syllabary usage in the *Omoro sōshi*], *Ryūkyū no rekishi to bunka,* 1985, pp. 267–290.

Nakamura, Akira, "Taiyō no ki to tori" [Tree and bird in the sun], *Okinawa bunka kenkyū,* III (1976), 209–228.

Nakasone, Seizen, "Sanbon no yubi: Omoro sōshi kōhon, jiten, to sōsakuin" [Three fingers: revised edition of the *Omoro sōshi* dictionary, and index], *Bungaku,* XXXVI:1 (1968), 105–109.

Nakazawa, Shin'ichi, "Seji saikō" [Some considerations on *shiji*], *Okinawa bunka,* no. 40, X:1 (January 1973), 47–52.

Obata, Atsushi, and eight others, "Omoro sōshi kenkyū" [Study of the *Omoro sōshi*], *Nantō*, II (May 1932), 131–162.

Okayama, Iwao, "Ryūkyū bungaku no kachi" [On the literary merits of Ryūkyūan literature], *Gekkan mingei*, II, nos. 11–12 (December 1940), 10–13; *Ryūkyū no bunka* (1941), 141–158.

Okuzato, Shōken, "Kokugo-hō to Omoro-gohō" [Japanese grammar and *Omoro* grammar], *Bunka Okinawa*, no. 15, 1950.

Ono, Shigeo, "Asanagi yūnagi no omoro" [The calms of morning and evening recited in *omoro*], *Okinawa bunka*, no. 38, IX:3 (February 1972), 1–11.

——, "Jojōshi no hassei—Ryūkyū bungaku shiron yori [Emergence of lyrical poetry—in view of Ryūkyūan literary history], *Geirin*, I:1–4, 1954.

——, "Koneri omoro ni tsuite" [On the *koneri omoro*], *Okinawa bunka*, no. 44, 1975.

——, "Nantō kayō no hassei to tenkai [Emergence and development of the ballads of the Southern Islands], *Waga Okinawa*, vol. 5, 1972.

——, "Nantō ko-kayō no kakei no keifu" [A Genealogy of the forms of old ballads in the Southern Islands], *Okinawa bunka*, no. 41, X:2 (March 1974), 1–26.

——, "Omoro kajin no seikaku" [Personalities of the *omoro* poets], *Bungaku*, comp. by Iwanami shoten, no. 43, 4, 1974.

——, "Omoro ni miru kaiyō bungaku no tenkai" [Development of marine literature in the *Omoro sōshi*], *Bungaku*, comp. by Iwanami shoten, no. 42, 8, 1974.

——, "Omoro ni miru renka no hassei" [Appearance of love poems in the *Omoro*], *Bungaku*, comp. by Iwanami shoten, no. 41, 6, 1973.

——, "Omoro no jojōsei to sakusha—bunri kaidoku-hō hihan ni Kotaete" [Lyrics and poets in the *Omoro sōshi*—in answer to criticism of the separate-reading method], *Bungaku*, comp. by Iwanami shoten, no. 43, 11, 1975.

——, "Omoro no hassei: jojika yori jojōka e" [On the genesis of the *omoro:* epics from *kwena* lyrics], *Okinawa bunka*, no. 21, V:1 (July 1966), 1–12.

Otaki, Masami, "Jōdai ni okeru iro 'aka' to Omoro sōshi ni okeru 'aka' "[On 'red' in ancient times and in the *Omoro sōshi*], *Okinawa bunka*, no. 44, XII:1 (November 1975), 32–35.

Saigō, Nobutsuna, "Okinawa no koyō omoro ni tsuite" [On the ancient ballads of Okinawa, *omoro*], *Shin Nihon bungaku*, October 1957.

Serei, Kunio, "Kumejima omoro ni tsuite" [On the *omoro* of Kume Island], *Nantō*, II (1942), 41–86.

——, "Omoro to minzoku ishiki" [On *omoro* and racial consciousness], *Bunka Okinawa*, IV:5 (May 1943), 14–18.

——, "Ryūkyū ongaku kayō shiron" [On the history of Ryūkyūan music and ballads], in 87 installments beginning circa April 1940, *Ryūkyū shimpō*.

Shimabukuro, Genshichi, "Akoniwa no hitobito" [People in Akoniwa], *Okinawa bunka sōsetsu*, ed. Yanagita Kunio, 251–311, 1947.

Shimabukuro, Zenkō, "Shin Omoro-gakuha no koto" [On the new *Omoro* school], *Okinawa bunka*, no. 46, XIII:1 (December 1976), 1–9.

Shimabukuro, Zenpatsu, "Omoro sōshi no yomikata: tendoku-hō no kenkyū" [On the reading of the Omoro sōshi: study of the *tendoku* method of reading], *Okinawa kyōiku* (January 1933), pp. 43–53.

Shimamura, Kōichi, "Omoro sōshi no fushina ni tsuite" [On the names of *omoro* tunes], *Okinawa bunka kenkyū,* comp. by Hōsei daigaku Okinawa bunka kenkyūjo, X (1983), 304–345.

———, "Shohon ga shijisuru 'jūfuku Omoro' no chūshin ni" [Centering on the duplication indicated in the manuscripts of the *Omoro sōshi*], *Okinawa bunka,* no. 61, XX:1 (September 1983), 38–55.

Shimizu, Hirokazu, "Omoro dokukai eno zenshō" [An introduction to understandiing *omoro*], *Okinawa bunka,* no. 45, XII:2 (August 1976), 1–18.

Tabata, Chiaki, "Amami no jutō-teki kayō no ichi-kōsatsu—omori to tahabue o chūshin ni" [A study of songs of prayer in Amami, centering around *omori* and *tahabi*], *Okinawa bunka,* no. 47, XIII:2 (March 1977), 20–36.

Tajima, Risaburō, "Ryūkyū-go kenkyū shiryō" [Materials for the study of the Ryūkyūan language], *Kokko,* January 1898. Republished as *Ryūkyū bungaku kenkyū* [Studies of Ryūkyūan literature] in 1924.

Takahashi, Shunzō, "Omoro sōshi no joshi" [Adverbs in the *Omoro sōshi*], *Kokusai daigaku kokubungaku,* no. 1, 1970.

Takeuchi, Shigeo, "Chihō omoro no chiriteki bunpu" [The geographical distribution of local *omoro*], *Okinawa bunka,* no. 51, XV:2 (March 1979), 44–62.

———, "Okinawa kayōshi kenkyū no sokuseki—Serei Kunio o chūshin ni" [The course of study seen in the history of Okinawan ballads], *Okinawa bunka,* no. 47, XII:2 (March 1977), 10–19.

———, "Omoro ni utawareta chiiki to hito" [Areas and people sung (about) in the *Omoro sōshi*], *Okinawa bunka kenkyū,* comp. by Hōsei daigaku Okinawa bunka kenkyūjo, XIII (1981), 377–408.

Tamaki, Masami, "Omoro no kōzō" [Structure of *omoro*], *Okinawa bunka kenkyū,* comp. by Hōsei daigaku Okinawa bunka kenkyūjo, III (1976), 61–124.

———, "Omoro to ryūka" [*Omoro* and *ryūka*], *Gengo,* XII:4 (August 1983), 110–121.

Taniguchi, Kei, "Omoro to sono onritsu" [*Omoro* and its metrical scheme], *Okinawa bunka,* no. 44, XII:1 (November 1975), 20–24.

Tanoi, Toshiko, "Omoro sōshi ni mirareru seibutsu" [Animals in the *Omoro sōshi*], *Okinawa bunka,* no. 45, XII:2 (August 1976), 45–52.

Tawada, Shinjun, "Omoro shokubutsu" [Plants in *omoro*], *Okinawa bunka,* no. 55, XVII:2 (May 1981), 1–12.

Thompson, Robin, "Six *Omoro* from Volume One of the *Omoro sōshi.*" *Okinawa bunka,* no. 61, XX:1 (September 1983), 1–30. In English.

Toguchi, Seisai, "'Kiyorasa' to 'shiorashiya' no biteki naiyō: omoro to ryūka o chūshin ni" [Aesthetics of two adjectives, *kiyorasa* and *shiorashiya,* in *omoro* and *ryūka* poems], *Okinawa bunka,* no. 40, X:1 (January 1973), 1–12.

———, "Omoro-bi ni okeru 'mojiyoru' no keifu" [A genealogy of *mojiyoru* in *omoro*], *Okinawa bunka,* no. 41, X:2 (March 1974), 27–36.

———, "Omoro-bi no ichibetsu" [One glance at the *omoro* beauty], *Okinawa bunka,* I (1974), 245–275.

Torigoe, Kenzaburō, "Shika no juryokusei: Ryūkyū omoro no kenkyū" [On the magic of poetry: a study of the Ryūkyūan *omoro*], *Kobunka,* I:1 (November 1952), 41–48.

———, "Ryūkyū Omoro sōshi no bunpō—sonkei, shieki no jodōshi ni tsuite" [Grammar of the *Omoro sōshi* in Ryūkyū: on the adverbs of respect and causative], *Osaka gakugei daigaku kiyō,* A-15 (1967).

Uchima, Kan'yū, 'Minzokubungaku toshite no 'Omoro sōshi' no aramashi: sono rekishiteki shakaiteki haikei" [Outline of the *Omoro sōshi* as a folk literature: its historical and social background], *Okinawa,* no. 32 (October 1953), 21–32.

———, "Omoro to ryūka" [*Omoro* and *ryūka*], *Ryūkyū bungaku,* nos. 1–4 (1960).

Yamada, Minoru, "Konkōkenshū to Yorongo tono goi no kenkyū" [*Konkōkenshū* dictionary and the dialect of Yoron Island], *Okinawa bunka,* no. 40, X:1 (January 1973), 69–82.

———, "Omoro sōshi no 'eri', 'emu' ni tsuite" [On *weri* and *wemu* in the *Omoro sōshi*], *Okinawa bunka,* no. 45, XII:2 (August 1976), 53–67.

Yamashita, Kin'ichi, "Ryūkyū ōchō shinwa to minkan shinwa no mondai" [Ryūkyūan royal myth and myth of the common people], *Ryūdai shigaku,* no. 7 (June 1975), 65–105.

Yamanouchi, Seihin, "Ryūkyū kayō no shikei to sono hassei" [Pattern of the Ryūkyūan ballads and their emergence], *Ryūkyū ongaku geinō-shi,* 1959.

C. Special Issues of Periodicals

Chikuma Shobō, *Gengo seikatsu,* no. 251 (August 1972). Special issue on "Okinawa no kotoba to bunka" [Language and culture of Okinawa].

Iwanami Shoten, *Bungaku,* no. 33, 7 (1965). Special issue on "Okinawa no bungaku" [Okinawan literature].

———, *Bungaku,* no. 36, 1 (1968). Special issue on "Okinawa no gengo to kayō" [Language and ballads of Okinawa].

———, *Bungaku,* no. 40, 1 (1972). Special issue on "Okinawa no bungaku-bunka" [Literature and culture of Okinawa].

Okinawa Times, *Shin Okinawa bungaku,* no. 23 (1972). Special issue on Serei Kunio.

Taishukan Publishers, *Gengo,* no. 2, 8 (August 1973). Special issue on "Okinawa no gengo to bunka" [Language and culture of Okinawa].

———, *Gengo,* XII:4 (August 1983). Special issue on Okinawan studies.

Notes

Chapter 1: Introduction

1. *Ko Ryūkyū*, pp. 380–386.

2. *Ryūkyū shintōki*, ed. Yokoyama Shigeru, 1943, p. 108. The original work was written in 1605 by the Japanese Buddhist priest Taichū, who, waylaid on a journey to China, found himself in Okinawa from 1603 to 1606.

3. Editor's note: the modern Okinawan *mui*, corresponding etymologically to Japanese *mori* 'woods', means 'mountain' or 'hill'. In the *omoro* period, however, there are not a few examples of its use as a synonym for *(o)take*, although the original term refers to a raised area in which an *(o)take* might be found. The author addresses this issue later in the text.

4. *Kodai Okinawa no sugata*, pp. 393–426.

5. *Omoro shinshaku*, pp. 25–39. Referred to hereafter as *OS*.

6. Advanced by Miyagi (*Kodai Okinawa*, pp. 393–426) and supported by Nakahara (*OS*, pp. 25–39) and Kanai Kikuko, *Ryūkyū no min'yō*, p. 7.

7. Editor's note: More accurately, '[countries bordering on, and islands in,] the seas to south'; i.e., modern Indonesia, Malaysia, and the countries of Southeast Asia, etc.

8. Editor's note: While at the time of the original publication of *A Short History* no emerging scholars of *omoro* were said to "break completely new ground," in the intervening decades scholars as Shimamura Kōichi (*Omoro saushi*, 2012, among others) and Leon Serafim and Rumiko Shinzato (*The Language of the Old-Okinawan Omoro Sōshi*, 2020, for example) have made significant contributions to *omoro* studies.

9. James G. Frazer, *The Golden Bough: A Study in Magic and Religion* (1890) (New York: MacMillan, 1947), pp. 83-91.

10. The date traditionally cited for the unification of Okinawa is 1429. Cf. George Kerr, *Okinawa: The History of an Island People*, p. 86; Higa Shunchō, *Shinkō Okinawa no rekishi*, p. 99. However, in this book, 1422, the date proposed by Wada Hisanori is adopted. See Wada, "Ryūkyū-koku no sanzan tōitsu ni tsuite no shin-kōsatsu" (A new interpretation of the unification of San-shan 'three principalities' in fifteenth century Ryūkyū), *Ochanomizu University Studies in Arts and Culture*, XXVIII: Part 2 (March 1975), pp. 13–39.

11. Editor's note: As mentioned in the Preface to this reprint, this account is based on the traditional histories. The actual situation was considerably more complex.

12. *OS*, p. 13. Revised by present author.

Chapter 2: Creation Myths

1. Stith Thompson, *The Folktale*, p. 4.

2. *Omoro sōshi*, X:2 #512. The roman numeral refers to the volume number in the *Omoro sōshi.* The arabic numeral immediately following the colon refers to the *omoro* poem in the volume. The last arabic numeral, preceded by #, indicates the poem's serial number within the entire twenty-two volumes of the *Omoro sōshi.* These numberings are in accordance with those given in the *Kohon: Omoro sōshi*, ed. Nakahara Zenchū and Hokama Shuzen, 1965; *OS*, pp. 328–334; Iha, *Okinawa kō*, pp. 192–204; and *Kō Ryūkyū*, pp. 162–166. There is a separate index of *omoro* poems mentioned in the text in the aftermatter.

In the *omoro* poems cited, there are some lines which are in parentheses. These lines, while reiterated from the preceding stanza, are omitted when written. Hence, these lines are not actually written down in the *Omoro sōshi.* I am following Professor Nakahara Zenchū's practice, in his *Omoro shinshaku*, of repeating these lines precisely because that was the way in which the ancients sang these *omoro* poems.

3. Miyara Tōsō, *Nantō sōkō*, pp. 398–400; Iha, *Okinawa kō*, pp. 201–203.

4. Iha, *Okinawa kō*, pp. 197–200.

5. Shō Jōken, *Chūzan sekan* (1650), reprinted in *Ryūkyū shiryō sōsho*, ed. Iha et al., V:13. Hereinafter *Ryūkyū shiryō sōsho* will be referred to as *RSS*.

6. "Ryūkyū shinwa to shūi shominzoku shinwa tono hikaku" in *Okinawa no minzokugakuteki kenkyū*, comp. by Nihon minzokugakkai, 1972, p. 313.

For the reading of the title of the book which is usually known as *Chūzan seikan*, throughout my work I have adopted the reading *Chūzan sekan* in accordance with personal instructions from the late Professor Higa Shunchō in the spring of 1962.

7. Araki Moriaki, *Shin Okinawa shiron* (1980), pp. 23–24.

8. Kanaseki Takeo reports the existence of hermaphroditic sorcerers in ancient as well as present day Okinawa and some areas of the South Seas. *Hakkutsu kara suiri suru* (1975), pp. 97–99.

9. *Konkōkenshū* (1711), reprinted in *Kō Ryūkyū*, by Iha Fuyū, 1942 edition, p. 435. Hokama Shuzen, ed., *Konkōkenshū*, pp. 118–119.

10. *Konkōkenshū*, in *Kō Ryūkyū*, 1942 edition, p. 416. Hokama, ed., *Konkōkenshū*, p. 88.

11. Torigoe Kenzaburō, *Ryūkyū kodai shakai no kenkyū*, pp. 177–178.

12. Amamiku and Shineriku are merely variant spellings of Amamikyo and Shinerikyo.

13. Yokoyama Shigeru, ed., *Ryūkyū shintōki* by Taichū (1605), p. 108.

14. Shō Jō-ken, *Chūzan sekan*, in *RSS*, V:13–14.

15. Vol. 1, p. 299.

16. Higaonna Kanjun, "Chūzan sekan, Chūzan seifu oyobi Kyūyō," in *RSS*, V:55–57.

17. Sakaguchi Tokutarō, *Amami-Ōshima shi*, p. 25.

18. Iha, *Okinawa kō*, pp. 201–203.

19. Katō Sango, *Ryūkyū no kenkyū*, p. 22.

20. On the identification of *amami* with *amabe*, Iha quotes the statement by Arai Hakuseki that *tami* 'people' is *tabe*, the occupational group of farmers. Therefore, it does not seem unreasonable to deduce that *amami* is identical to *amabe* also. Iha, *Okinawa kō*, p. 202.

21. Iha, *Okinawa kō*, p. 203.

22. Editor's note: The term *arp* is of unknown provenance.

23. Iha, *Kotōku no Ryūkyū shi*, pp. 5–6.

24. Richard Pearson, "The Contribution of Archaeology to Japanese Studies," *Journal of Japanese Studies*, II:2 (April 1976), 318–319.

25. Kamida Sōei, *Ryūkyū bungaku josetsu*, pp. 199–201.

26. Ikemiya Masaharu, *Ryūkyū bungaku ron*, pp. 105–106.

27. Iha, *Okinawa kō*, p. 200.

28. Nakahara, "Seji no shinkō ni tsuite," in *Okinawa bunka sōsetsu*, p. 149.

29. Hokama Shuzen, "Omoro sōsei shinwa ni okeru joshi, 'na' no kaishaku," *Okinawa bunka*, No. 61, XX:1 (September 1983), 1–15.

30. W. A. Fairservis, *Origins of Oriental Civilization*, p. 161.

31. For a comprehensive treatment of Ryūkyūan mythology, see Ōbayashi Tairyō, "Ryūkyū shinwa to shūi shominzoku shinwa," *Nihon minzoku to kuroshio bunka*, pp. 102–128; Itō Kanji, "Nihon shinwa to Ryūkyū shinwa," and Kojima Yoshiyuki, "Ryūkyū kaibyaku shinwa no bunpu to hikaku," *Nihon shinwa to Ryūkyū*, pp. 1–25 and pp. 26–51, respectively.

Chapter 3: Life in and about the Village

1. Miyagi Shinji, "Yanbaru no otake" in *Nantō ronsō*, ed. Shimabukuro Zenpatsu, pp. 95–96. Also for chapter 3, I owe much to Torigoe Kenzaburō, *Ryūkyū kodai shakai no kenkyu*, chapter 2.

According to W. P. Lebra, "... the *utaki*, or sacred grove, constitutes the most sacrosanct site for community rites. It usually consists of little more than a heavy clump of trees and underbrush with a small clearing at its center; here, a large rock and small censer will be found. The stone is said to represent *ibi* or *ibi ganashii mee*, which is the *kami* name (*kaminaa*) for the founding *kami* or ancestor of the village, suggesting the Japanese *ujigami* or *ubusunna gami* (village tutelary deity). Sometimes a three-stone hearth, symbolizing the *fii no kang*, may be found here, but this *kami* is not the object of worship here as many have assumed. When present, it serves as an intermediary between the supplicants and the *kami* of the *utaki*." *Okinawan Religion*, pp. 139–140.

After a survey of many *otake* sites, Nakamatsu Yashū concludes that the *otake* originated as a grave for the village founder and thus was considered as a place of awe and sanctity, taboo to the ordinary lay person. After many generations, the function of the *otake* has undergone change. The *otake* has finally come to be considered a sacred grove for the worship of the *kami*. *Kosō no mura: Okinawa minzoku bunka ron*, 1977, pp. 203–210.

2. Though *omoro* and *umui* are synonyms meaning 'to think' or 'thought' and both refer to the same kind of poem, for the sake of convenience and according to general academic practice, a distinction is often made in that *omoro* is used to designate those poems which are in the *Omoro sōshi*, and *umui*, those which are not, the term often pertaining to poems actually sung by *noro* priestesses.

According to Nakahara, the *kwenya* (variantly, *koina, koenya, kuinya, kwainya*) is a type of *umui*. It is an epic poem consisting of a series of couplets, typically accompanying a circling group dance. *OS*, p. 70.

3. *Utaki* and *umui* or *otake* and *omori* are used synonymously to refer to the same object—the sacred grove. This *umui* consists of *u*, honorific, and *mui*, grove, and should not be confused with a frequently used homonym, *umui*, poem.

4. Miyagi, "Yanbaru no otake," p. 102.

5. In Japan as well as in Okinawa, before the appearance of the *mura*, there was a consanguineous group called *maki* which formed a one clan village. For Japanese *maki*, see Yanagita Kunio, *Tōno monogatari*, p. 180.

6. Significantly, the creation myth in the *Chūzan sekan* cited earlier relates that the female deity Amamikyu, in creating Okinawa, first started out with the creation of the seven holiest groves and then all the other holy groves. Only after these came the creation of the

human being. If the mythology is not merely a product of fantasy or imagination but a reflection of the actual life lived by the ancients, this creation myth must also mean that the founding of the village community began with the holy grove.

7. On the origin of the *makyo* village community, here I follow the traditional views of Iha Fuyū, Nakahara Zenchū, Inamura Kenpu, and Higa Shunchō that the *makyo* village community was a consanguineous group and that it preceded the *mura* village community, but Nakamatsu Yashū's new theory, which does not wholly negate the traditional view, is noted as follows: the *makyo* is better defined as "a village community, not necessarily consanguineous, which shares a common *otake* sacred grove." The term *makyo* began to be used during the fifteenth century. Nakamatsu Yashū, *Kosō no mura: Okinawa minzoku bunka ron*, 1977, pp. 139–161, and "Makyo" in *Okinawa daihyakka*, 1983, III:507–508

8. Elizabeth K Nottingham, *Religion and Society*, 1954, p. 20.

9. Torigoe, pp. 31–42.

10. Torigoe, pp. 46–54.

11. W. P. Lebra, "The Yaa n Naa (House Name) System in the Ryūkyū Islands," *Ryūkyūan Names*, ed. Shunzo Sakamaki, 1964, pp. 51–61.

12. *Omoro sōshi*, XXI:1 #1394. *OS*, pp. 189–191.

13. *Omoro sōshi*, XI:72 #627. *OS*, pp. 189–191.

14. Shidehara Hiroshi, *Nantō enkaku shiron*, 1899, pp. 53–63. Sakamaki Shunzo, "The Heike: from Defeat at Dannoura to a Golden Age in Ryūkyū?" *JAS*, XXVII:1 (November 1967), 115–122.

15. Shinzato Keiji, Taminato T., and Kinjo S. *Okinawa-ken no rekishi*, 1972, p. 12. Kokubu Naoichi and Sasaki Kōmei, *Nantō no kodai bunka*, 1973, pp. 38–41. Kokubu Naoichi, "The Prehistoric Southern Islands and East China Sea Areas," *Asian Perspectives: The Bulletin of the Far Eastern Prehistory Association*, VII: Summer–Winter 1963, 233.

16. *Omoro sōshi*, V:31 #242. *OS*, pp. 179–180.

17. *Ryūkyū-koku yuraiki* (1713), in *RSS*, Vol. 1:25. The following description is given: *Abushi barai.* In the fourth month, an auspicious day is chosen by the government. In each village, a man believed to be of good fortune for the day, facing the lucky direction, clears grasses away from the rice paddy dykes. This is done to get rid of destructive insects such as locusts. All men and women take two days off for pleasure.

It is also stated in the *Ryūkyū-koku yuraiki* that *yamadome* (mountain closed) and *umidome* (sea closed) were observed for two months from the first day of the fourth month to the last day of the fifth month of the lunar calendar. However, it seems not to have been uniformly observed. On Tarama Island it was observed twice a year in the second and eighth months, for ten days starting from the day of Mizunoe (Water Senior in the Sexagenary Cycle), in Ohama Village on Ishigaki Island it lasted for two months from the fifteenth of the third month to the fifteenth of the fifth month, in Itarashiki Village in Yonabaru on Okinawa it was from the twentieth of the fourth month to the fourth of the fifth month. See "Yamadome" and "Umidome" in *Okinawa daihyakka jiten*, III:53 and I:315. See also W. P. Lebra, *Okinawan Religion*, pp. 51–52.

18. Iha, *Onarigami no shima*, pp. 72–143.

19. Iha, *Onarigami no shima*, p. 85.

20. *Omoro sōshi*, II:16 #57. *OS*, pp. 147–152.

21. *Omoro sōshi*, II:34 #75. *OS*, pp. 124–128.

22. *OS*, p. 127. It is also often written as *kami-asobi*, literally, 'god's playing or pleasure'.

23. *OS*, pp. 126–127.

24. Iha, *Kotōku no Ryūkyū shi*, p. 19. The *shinugu* dance seems to be a magical dance to assure an abundant harvest. Cf. J. G. Frazer, chapter XI, "The Influence of the Ses on Vegetation," in Part I, The Mgic Art and the Evolution of Kings, *Golden Bough*, 1932, pp. 97–119.

25. *Omoro sōshi*, XX:20 #1350, XII:68 #719. *OS*, pp. 281–283.

26. In 1385, Ming Tai-tzu, founder of the Ming dynasty, granted one ocean-going ship to each of three kingdoms in Okinawa, and this seems to have started the custom of granting tribute ships from China to Okinawa. Since it is said that one of these ships carried 120 horses and 12,000 *kin* (one *kin* = 1.323 lbs.) of sulphur the following year, 1386, the ship must have been quite large. Higa, *Okinawa no rekishi*, p. 64.

27. Iha, *Onarigami no shima*, pp. 72–143.

28. One of the creation myths tells that Amamikyu, the creator deity, sent an eagle to *Nirai-kanai* beyond the ocean to fetch some rice seeds. Iha, *Kotōku no Ryūkyū shi*, p. 15. For a fuller discussion of *Nirai-kanai*, see Tanigawa Ken'ichi, "Nirai-kanai to tokoyo no shisō," *Nantō no kodai bunka*, pp. 119–147.

29. The following *otakabe* (prayer) chanted by the priestess at the *shinugu* festival on Takahanari Island in the sixth and seventh months indicates that food—products of the seas or the hills—was thought to come from *Nirai-kinai*: "Shinugu of the age of Aman (age of Amami, i.e., in the time of the ancient gods), field rice having sprouted up, we, commoners, farmers, present this celebration in your honor. Please grant us a full harvest. Please help us to be blessed with the blessings that come from and drift from *Nirai-kanai*. Please let this country, this era, and all your subjects prosper and multiply." Iha, *Kotōku no Ryūkyū shi*, p. 18.

30. *Omoro sōshi*, XIII:78 #823. *OS*, pp. 100–102.

31. *Omoro sōshi*, XIII:89 #834. *OS*, pp. 99–100.

32. *Omoro sōshi*, XXI:11 #1404. *OS*, pp. 120–122.

33. *Omoro sōshi*, XIII:47 #792. *OS*, pp. 155–159.

34. *Omoro sōshi*, XIII:50 #795. *OS*, pp. 159–162.

35. Iha Nantetsu, *Ryūkyū fudoki*, pp. 60–77. In 1473, Korean castaways on Yonaguni Island observed that islanders did not share the catch with their father on the ground that it would also give away their luck.

36. *Omoro sōshi*, IX:30 #505. *OS*, pp. 139–144.

37. Higa Shunchō, *Okinawa no rekishi*, pp. 12–13.

38. *Omoro sōshi*, XI:95 #650. *OS*, pp. 144–147.

39. William W. Burd, *Karimata*, p. 43.

40. On the etymology of *okinamasusese* and *hetanamasusese*, Shimabukuro interprets *oki* to be the *omoro* style transcription of *uchi*, inside or inner, and *heta* to be its opposite, outside or outer. This is in direct contradiction to Nakahara who takes *oki at* its face value to mean 'the offing' and therefore its antonym *heta* 'to be near the shore'. Shimabukuro does not take *namasu* to mean the *namasu* fish salad but dissects it into *na*, fish, and *masu*, Japanese square box measure, which together then describes the form of the weir. Also he believes *sese* is merely the *omoro* transcription of *shiji*, the tribe. Shimabukuro Genshichi, "Akoniwa no hitobito," *Okinawa bunka sōsetsu*, ed, Yanagita Kunio, pp. 251–311.

41. Shimabukuro Genshichi, p. 302.

42. *Omoro sōshi*, XIII:93 #838. *OS*, pp. 112–115.

43. *Omoro sōshi*, XIII:94 #839. *OS*, pp. 115–116.

44. On this granary, Kerr states as follows; "We have today a very clear idea of the warehouse system which may have been used in Eiso's day. In Okinawan villages untouched by

World War II—that is to say, principally in the off-lying islands—there are thatched community storehouses of an ancient type. They are usually associated with village shrines or community common land. In all respects they could have served as models for the line drawings which we find on bronze bells *(dōtaku)* unearthed in prehistoric sites in Japan; they are virtually indistinguishable (to the layman's eye) from the thatched and elevated structures of the primitive Yami tribesmen who dwell on an island three hundred miles south of Okinawa, or from the storehouses built in aboriginal Tayal villages of Formosa." *Okinawa: The History of an Island People*, p. 53. Also see Yanagita Kunio, ed., *Nihon minzoku zuroku*, p. 15.

45. *Omoro sōshi*, XIX:45 #1326. *OS*, pp. 186–188.
46. *Omoro sōshi*, XV:53 #1104. *OS*, pp. 236–238.
47. *Chūzan seifu*, IV under Shō Hashi, *RSS* IV:54, V:32.
48. Higa, *Okinawa no rekishi*, p. 49.
49. Iha, *Kotōku no Ryūkyū shi*, pp. 56–57. Also cited on the same page is an apt observation on this matter made by Prof. K. Higaonna that the southern and northern branches of the imperial dynasty were involved in a prolonged war of succession (Yoshino period, 1336–1392) at the time. This long civil war in Japan disrupted trade between Okinawa and Japan. This is the reason, Higaonna says, for Okinawa's not wanting the expensive fine silk goods from China which were in times of peace to be exported to Japan, and instead wanted pottery and iron goods for home needs. In any case, it is certain that around this time, iron agricultural implements began to be used on a larger scale than before. Furthermore, the elite class wealthy enough to afford these expensive silk goods must have been quite small in Okinawa at the time.
50. *Chūzan sekan*, II, in *RSS*, V:29.
51. *Omoro sōshi*, XIV:1 #982. *OS*, pp. 267–270. Iha, *Kotōku no Ryūkyū shi*, p. 53.
52. *Omoro sōshi*, XI:88 #643. *OS*, pp. 369–373.
53. *Omoro sōshi*, XII:80 #731. *OS*, pp. 117–120.

Chapter 4: Life of the Ruling Class

1. *Chūzan seifu* (1701), in *RSS*, IV:3–62; *Chūzan sekan* (1650), in *RSS*, V:3–50.
2. Pp. 37–38.
3. Higa, pp. 42–43. Iha, *Kō Ryūkyū*, pp. 83–84.
4. *Omoro sōshi*, XV:15 #1066. Iha, *Kotōku no Ryūkyū shi*, p. 45.
5. *Omoro sōshi*, XV:17 #1068. Iha, *Kotōku no Ryūkyū shi*, p. 46.
6. *Omoro sōshi*, XV:16 #1067. Iha, *Kotōku no Ryūkyū shi*, p. 47.
7. *Omoro sōshi*, XV:18 #1069. Iha, *Kotōku no Ryūkyū shi*, p. 47.
8. *Chūzan sekan*, in *RSS*, V:15.
9. Iha, *Kotōku no Ryūkyū shi*, pp. 77, 85–86. Higaonna, *Nantō fudoki*, p. 79.
10. Views of Majikina and Shimabuku are treated in "Okinawa rekishi sankō shiryō" by Shimabuku Zenpatsu, in Kinjō Yuikyō, ed. *Shin Okinawa bunka shi*, p. 3.
11. Okuzato Shōken, "Shuri sento no jidai," *Okinawa Times*, March 6–10, 1958.
12. *OS*, p. 207.
13. *Omoro sōshi*, XV:26 #1077. Iha, *Kotōku no Ryūkyū shi*, pp. 49–50.
14. *Omoro sōshi*, XV:21 #1072. *OS*, pp. 206–208.
15. *Omoro sōshi*, II:18 #59. *OS*, pp. 241–242.
16. *Omoro sōshi*, II:19 #60. *OS*, p. 242.
17. *Omoro sōshi*, X:28 36–37. #538. Iha, *Kotōku no Ryūkyū shi*, pp. 36–37.

18. *OS*, p. 240.

19. *Omoro sōshi*, IX:24 #499. *OS*, pp. 239–241.

20. Tei Hei-tetsu, *Kyūyō* (1745), ed. Kuwae Kokuei, 1969. The seventh year of King Eiso.

21. *Omoro sōshi*, XIII:183 #928. *OS*, pp. 137–139.

22. *Omoro sōshi*, XIII:24 #769. *OS*, pp. 132–135.

23. *Chūzan seifu*, in *RSS*, IV:21. Rice cultivation seems to have started in Japan during the Yayoi period about the beginning of the Christian era. On Okinawa, however, rice cultivation seems to have begun about the third or fourth century AD. Nakahara Zenchū, *Ryūkyū no rekishi*, p. 11.

24. *Omoro sōshi*, XVII:54 #1228, XVIII:10 #1258. *OS*, pp. 106–108.

25. *Omoro sōshi*, XIII:100 #845. *OS*, pp. 108–110.

26. *Omoro sōshi*, XIII:102 #847. *OS*, pp. 110–112.

27. Samejima Kunizō, 1958. "Kinsei Okinawa bunka no rekishiteki haikei," *Okinawa Times*, February 18. With respect to navigational terminology, Samejima points out the following vocabulary items of Chinese origin: *hui ten* (captain), *tai hung* (helmsman), *tao ting* (mooring chief), *ya pan* (chief of sails and watching), *tsai fu* (ship's accountant), *tsung kuan* (business manager), *shang ha kung* (ship's carpenter), *kung sha* (chief sailor), and *hiyon kung* (chief of rituals).

28. Higaonna, *Nantō fudoki*, p. 172.

29. Dugout canoes continued to serve as fishing boats until as late as 1881 when superior cedar boards became available. Morita Shinko, "Gyogyo no enkaku," Kinjō Yuikyō, ed. *Shin Okinawa bunka shi*, p. 87. No evidence is available to show whether these ancient canoes were equipped with outriggers or whether they were built as double canoes.

30. Mozai Torao, "Kuroshio-ken no kaikyō to kōkai," *Nihon minzoku to kuroshio bunka*, 1977, pp. 129–141.

31. Kerr, p. 22.

32. Ibid., p. 23.

33. Ibid.

34. Yanagita Kunio, the father of Japanese folklore studies, briefly mentions this suspicion regarding the sudden flowering of Okinawan culture during the fourteenth century and suggests the possible importance of the research on the Pacific Coast. Preface to *Okinawa no rekishi* by Higa Shunchō, p. 6.

Sakamaki Shunzo has hypothesized that the first king of Ryūkyū, Shunten, who ascended the throne in 1187, might have been the young Emperor Antoku of Japan who allegedly perished with the defeated Heike clan in 1185, and that the Heike refugees established themselves as the ruling elite of Okinawa. "The Heike: From Defeat at Dannoura to a Golden Age in Ryūkyū?" *JAS*, XXVII: 1 (November 1967), 115–122.

The first part of this hypothesis may be a little too imaginative; the second part may be possible, but may never be proved. The Heike clan's power was largely due to their control of trade with Sung China. If a number of Heike warriors arrived on Okinawa in 1185, they must have brought with them not only wealth and military power but also a knowledge of overseas trade, shipbuilding, and navigational technology. Then it would be natural for them to ally with local rulers to embark upon overseas trade. This hypothesis would explain the apparent sudden transformation of Okinawa from scattered, isolated village society with subsistence agricultural economy to a unified state capable of transoceanic trade with China and the South Seas during the late fourteenth century.

35. *Chūzan sekan*, in *RSS*, V:15.

36. For a summary of the tale of Amawari, Lord of Katsuren, in English, see Kerr, *Okinawa*, pp. 98–99.

37. *Omoro sōshi*, XVI:18 #1144. *OS*, pp. 310–311. Iha. *Kotōku no Ryūkyū shi*, pp. 94–95.

38. *OS*, p. 311.

39. *Omoro sōshi*, XVI:7 #1133. *OS*, pp. 311–313. Iha. *Kotōku no Ryūkyū shi*, p. 93.

40. *Omoro sōshi*, XVI:8 #1134. *OS*, pp. 313–316. For a study of Lord Amawari as a hero rather than traitor-villain, see Iha, "Amawari kō," in *Kō Ryūkyū*, pp. 82–98.

41. *Omoro sōshi*, V:8 #289. *OS*, pp. 199–203.

42. *Omoro sōshi*, XV:36 #1087. *OS*, pp. 208–210.

43. In 1941, shards of a Korean roof tile were found at the site of Urasoe Castle. On a piece were written eight characters meaning "made by a Korean tile master in the year of Mizunoto-tori." The tile piece was later determined to have been made during the Kamakura period (1192–1333). During the Kamakura period there were three years of Mizunoto-tori: 1213, 1273, and 1333. Regardless of the year it was made, it is remarkable that such tiles were imported from Korea or that a Korean tile maker produced them in Okinawa—an almost ostentatious show of wealth and power. Iha, *Kō Ryūkyū*, pp. 62–63.

44. The jeweled ladle is also mentioned in the *omoro* "Amawari, Lord of Katsuren."

45. *Omoro sōshi*, XV:22 #1073, *OS*, pp. 203–204.

46. Trade with China is supposed to have begun in 1372, during the reign of King Satto. However, judging from the items of tribute, largely of foreign origin long before Satto's time sent by Satto to China, Okinawa was already engaged in foreign trade through which some Chinese knowledge came to Okinawa.

47. *Omoro sōshi*, XV:10 #1061. *OS*, pp. 265–266.

48. *OS*, p. 271.

49. *Omoro sōshi*, XV:49 #1100. *OS*, pp. 270–272.

50. It is interesting to note that in the third century AD when Japan was still in the process of forming a nation, Queen Pimiku, head of a small but leading state among several in northern Kyūshū, sent an envoy with ten slaves and some cloth materials as gifts to the king of Wei in China. They started out in the sixth month and reached Loyang in the twelfth month in AD 238 Wei had conquered the neighboring state of Kungsung Shih and had begun to be known as a rising power in East Asia. Queen Pimiku's mission seems to have been a political move as a result of this change in international relations. The king of Wei gratefully acknowledged the tribute and in return gave 100 copper mirrors, 50 *kins* of pearls, 50 *kins* of cosmetics, some wool and silk materials, some gold coins, and swords. With these generous gifts he sent a message to Queen Pimiku to show these gifts to her countrymen and to tell them how affectionately he regarded them. This must have greatly boosted Queen Pimiku's prestige among her rivals in northern Kyūshū at the time. Tōma Seita, *Nihon minzoku no keisei*, p. 174. King Satto's action seems to closely parallel that of Queen Pimiku nearly a thousand years before.

51. *Omoro sōshi*, XV:66 #1117. *OS*, pp. 274–275.

52. Iha, *Kotōku no Ryūkyū shi*, p. 56.

53. *Omoro sōshi*, XV:68 #1119. *OS*, pp. 276–279.

54. *Omoro sōshi*, XXXI:12 #1405. *OS*, pp. 249–251. The word *mashikesu* in the next to last line of the *omoro* also appears in variant forms such as *mamakesu*, noted in the *Kōhon Omoro sōshi*, ed. Nakahara and Hokama, p. 737.

55. *Omoro sōshi*, XIX:10 #1290. *OS*, pp. 291–293. For *tomoyagaru* in the third line, the *Kōhon Omoro sōshi* lists a variation, *toriyakaru*, p. 688.

56. Wada Hisanori, "Ryūkyū-koku no sanzan tōitsu ni tsuite no shin-sosatsu" [A New Interpretation of the unification of San-shan 'three principalities' in fifteenth century Ryūkyū], *Ochanomizu University Studies in Arts and Culture*, XXVIII, Part 2 (March 1975), p. 32.

57. *Omoro sōshi*, XIX:19 #1299. *OS*, pp. 295–297.

58. *Omoro sōshi*, I:5 #5. Iha, *Kotōku no Ryūkyū shi*, pp. 78–79.

59. *Omoro sōshi*, XIV:37 #1018. Iha, ibid., p. 89.

60. *Omoro sōshi*, XIX:30 #1310. *OS*, pp. 298–300.

61. *Omoro sōshi*, XIV:5 #986. *OS*, pp. 214–218.

62. *Omoro sōshi*, X:9 #519. *OS*, pp. 254–257.

63. Iha, *Okinawa kō*, pp. 177–178. Majikina, *Okinawa issen'nenshi*, p. 237.

64. Sakamaki, "Ryūkyū and Southeast Asia," *Journal of Asian Studies*, XXIII:3 (May 1964), 383–389.

65. Akiyama Kenzō, *Nisshi kōshō shi no kenkyū*, pp. 77–78.

66. Ibid., p. 102. Also Sakamaki, op. cit.

67. Akiyama, p. 101. Sakamaki, op. cit.

68. Akiyama, p. 95. Sakamaki, op. cit. Majikina, op. cit, p. 234.

69. Sin Suk-ju, *Haedong Choguk Ki* (*Kaitō shokoku ki* in Japanese). Preface is dated 1471. Reprinted in the *Chōsen shiryō sōkan*, II, 1933.

70. *Omoro sōshi*, XIII:8 #753. Iha, *Kotōku no Ryūkyū shi*, pp. 103–104.

71. *Chūzan sekan*, in *RSS*, V:158.

72. *Omoro sōshi*, V:2 #213. *OS*, pp. 302–303.

73. Since Shō En's son, Shō Shin, was only twelve years old at the time, he was too young to reign, so Shō En's younger brother, Shō Sen'i ascended the throne. However, the royal priestess received a divine message favoring Shō Shin (seemingly a court intrigue plotted by his mother, Queen Yosoidon), and accordingly Shō Sen'i abdicated after reigning only about six months. This episode indicates how powerful the influence of the priestesses was at this time.

74. Kerr, *Okinawa*, p. 115.

75. *Omoro sōshi*, V:3 #214. *OS*, pp. 303–305.

76. Translated from the original as appears in the *Ryūkyū-koku-chū himonki* [Monument inscriptions in the country of Ryūkyū], 1479. Most achievements are self-explanatory, but Article 4 needs some comment. In 1926 Iha Fuyū misread the passage therein to mean "this country used the armor for utensils," and assumed that the king had confiscated all arms which were then made into practical tools such as farm implements. Thus originated the fallacy of a disarmed, peace-loving Ryūkyū, which by chance fitted very well with another famous episode of a disarmed Ryūkyū reported by Captain Basil Hall to Napoleon Bonaparte in 1816, which together erted much influence upon many later historians and writers. King Shō Shin, far from abolishing arms, accumulated them and was proud of his superior weapons. The truth is that Ryūkyū has never in her history been officially disarmed.

77. *Omoro sōshi*, V:5 #216. *OS*, pp. 305–307.

78. *Omoro sōshi*, XIII:44 #436. *OS*, pp. 384–385.

79. *Omoro sōshi*, VIII:7 #399. *OS*, pp. 385–387.

80. *Omoro sōshi*, V:6 #217, *OS*, pp. 393–395.

81. One *tsubo* equals about four square yards, and one *koku* equals about five bushels.

82. Cited by Higa Shunchō et al., *Okinawa*, p. 70.

83. *Omoro sōshi*, V:72 #283. *OS*, pp. 408–412.

84. On the role of the priestesses and the state, see W. P. Lebra, *Okinawan Religion: Belief, Ritual, and Social Structure*, pp. 110–115.

85. Kerr comments on this era as follows: "Okinawa was entering upon a century of creative activity. The elaborate new court ceremonies, borrowed from China and modified, required construction of a large new palace in Chinese style. The stone 'Dragon Pillars' set before the entrance to the main audience hall reflect cosmopolitan experience. The prototype is not found in Japan or China, but in the temples and palace compounds of Cambodia and Siam. Enkakuji Temple constructed in 1492 under the supervision of immigrant Japanese priests, was patterned after the great Enkakuji which stands in the seaside groves of Kamakura in Japan." *Okinawa*, p. 109.

86. Iha, *Onarigami no shima*, p. 129; *Songjong Taewang Sillock*, No. 104, pp. 11a–12b (1479); No. 105, pp. 13–20a (1479); Kobata Atsushi, "Richō jitsuroku, Chūsei Ryūkyū shiryō, *Nantō*, II (1942), 26–38.

87. *Omoro sōshi*, XVIII:12 #1260; XVII:56 #1230. *OS*, pp. 309–310.

88. *Omoro sōshi*, V:40 #251. *OS*, pp. 320–323.

89. In contrast with the Tokugawa system of alternate attendance under which the daimyos and their retinues served as unwitting conveyers of the urban culture of Kyoto, Osaka, and Edo to the daimyos' home domains throughout Japan, Shō Shin's system, which did not require the petty rulers' coming and going between the urban center and their home territories, tended to widen the disparity between the urban center and the rural areas. This disparity was often noted by Chinese envoys and European visitors in later centuries. Thus in the long run the Okinawan system proved unfavorable to the peasantry who were gradually reduced to near serfdom.

90. *Nantō shi*, Edo, 1719, pp. 3–4.

91. Akiyama, *Nisshi kōshō shi no kenkyū*, pp. 81–82.

92. *Songjong Taewang Sillock*, No. 104, pp. 112–112b; Kobata, "Richō jitsuroku," *Nantō*, II, 26–28.

93. Sakamaki, "Ryūkyū and Southeast Asia," *JAS*, XXIII (May 1964), p. 387.

94. Ibid., p. 388.

95. *Omoro sōshi*, VII:12 #356. Iha, *Kotōku no Ryūkyū shi*, pp. 108–109.

96. *Omoro sōshi*, XIII:17 #762. Iha, op. cit., pp. 109–112.

97. *Omoro sōshi*, XIII:180 #925. *OS*, pp. 336–337.

98. For the concept of sister deity, see Lebra, *Okinawan Religion*, under *uminai-gami*, pp. 24, 101, 104. Also Iha, *Onarigami no shima*.

99. *Omoro sōshi*, XIII:35 #780. *OS*, pp. 334–336.

100. Kerr, op. cit., pp. 93–94.

101. Akiyama, op. cit., pp. 123–125.

102. *Omoro sōshi*, V:1 #212. *OS*, pp. 300–302.

103. *Chūzan seifu*, in *RSS*, IV:88–89.

104. Iha, *Okinawa rekishi monogatari*, pp. 113–114.

105. *Chūzan seifu*, in *RSS*, IV:98.

106. *Omoro sōshi*, I:36 #36. *OS*, pp. 226–233. Lines 23–34 in the *Kōhon Omoro sōshi* (ed. Nakahara and Hokama) are missing in the *Omoro shinshaku* (Nakahara). The text given is according to the *Kōhon Omoro sōshi*.

107. Higa, *Okinawa no rekishi*, pp. 127–128.

108. Akiyama, op. cit., pp. 436–437.
109. Iha, Kotōku no Ryūkyū shi, p. 158.
110. Higa, op. cit., pp. 123–126.
111. *Omoro sōshi*, IV:58 #209; VI:5 #295; XII:93 #744; XX:48 #1378. *OS*, pp. 422–423.
112. Higa, op. cit., pp. 145–146.
113. *Ryūkyū shintōki*, p. 112.
114. *Omoro sōshi*, IX:35 #510. *OS*, pp. 469–471.

Chapter 5: Conclusion

1. G. H. Kerr, *Okinawa*, p. 187.

Bibliography

Akiyama, Kenzō. *Nisshi kōshō-shi no kenkyū* [A study of the history of Sino-Japanese intercourse]. Tokyo: Iwanami, 1939.

Arai, Hakuseiki. *Nantōshi* [Gazetteer of the Southern Islands]. Edo: private, woodblock print, 1719.

Araki, Moriaki. *Shin Okinawa shiron* [New historical treatise on Okinawa]. Naha: Okinawa Times, 1980.

Burd, William W. *Karimata*. Washington, D.C.: Pacific Science Research Council, 1952. Mimeograph.

Fairservice, W. A. *Origins of Oriental Civilization*. New York: New American Library, 1959.

Frazer, Sir James G. *The Golden Bough: A Study in Magic and Religion* (1890). New York: Macmillan, 1947. Vols. 1–2.

General Headquarters, SCAP. Report No. 121. *Systematic List of Economic Plants in Japan*. Tokyo: 1949.

Higa, Shunchō. *Okinawa no rekishi* [History of Okinawa]. Naha: Okinawa Times, 1959.

———. *Shinkō Okinawa no rekishi* [New edition, History of Okinawa], Naha: Okinawa Times, 1970.

———, Shimota Seiji, and Shinzato Keiji. *Okinawa*. Tokyo: Iwanami, 1963.

Higaonna, Kanjun. *Gaisetsu Okinawa shi* [Outline of Okinawan history]. Tokyo: Shinsei sangyo, 1950.

———. *Nantō fudoki* [Account of the natural resources of the Southern Islands]. Tokyo: Okinawa Bunka Kyokai and Okinawa Zaidan, 1950.

———. *Nantō ronkō* [Discourses on the Southern Islands]. Tokyo: Jitsugyo no Nihon, 1941.

———. *Reimeiki no kaigai kōtsū shi* [History of overseas contacts at the dawn of a new age]. Tokyo: Teikoku Kyōikukai, 1941.

Hokama, Shuzen. *Konkōkenshū: kōhon to kenkyū* [The *Konkōkenshū* (ancient Ryūkyūan dictionary): its text and study]. Tokyo: Kodokawa, 1970.

———. "Omoro sōsei shinwa ni okeru joshi, 'na' no kaishaku" [Interpretation of the particle 'na' in the Omoro myth of creation]. *Okinawa bunka*, no. 61, XX:1 (September 1983), 1–15.

———, and Saigō Nobutsuna. Omoro sōshi [Anthology of *omoro* poems]. Tokyo: Iwanami, 1972.

Iha, Fuyū. *Iha Fuyū senshū* [Selected works of Iha Fuyū]. 3 vols. Naha: Okinawa Times, 1961–1962.

——. *Kotōku no Ryūkyū shi* [Ryūkyūan history of the sufferings of isolated islands]. Tokyo: Shun'yōdō, 1926.

——. *Kō Ryūkyū* [Ancient Ryūkyū]. Tokyo: Seijisha, 1942 edition.

——. *Nantō hōgenshi kō* [Discourses on the history of the dialects in the Southern Islands]. Tokyo: Gakurō shoin, 1934.

——. *Okinawa kō* [Discourses on Okinawa]. Tokyo: Sōgensha, 1942.

——. *Okinawa rekishi monogatari* [Okinawa as it was and is—an epitome of Japan]. Tokyo: Okinawa Seinen Dōmei, 1947.

——. *Onarigami no shima* [Islands of the sibling deities]. Tokyo: Rakuro shoin, 1942.

——, Higaonna Kanjun, and Yokoyama Shigeru, eds. *Ryūkyū sōsho* [Collection of historical sources on the Ryūkyūs]. 5 vols. Tokyo: Natori, 1940.

Vol. 1. *Ryūkyū-koku yuraiki* [Accounts of the Ryūkyūs]. Vols. 1–11, compiled by the Kyūki-za, 1713.

Vol. 2.——, vols. 12–21.

Vol. 3. *Ryūkyū-doku kyūki* [Old records of the Ryūkyūs]. 11 vols. compiled by Tei Heitetsu, 1731.

Vol. 4. *Chūzan seifu* [Chronology of the Chūzan dynasty]. Vols. 1–13, compiled by Sai On and others, 1701–1874.

Vol. 5. *Chūzan sekan* [Mirror of the Chūzan dynasty]. 5 vols. Shō Jo-ken [Haneji Chōshu], 1650; *Chūzan seifu* (continued), vols. 14–20.

Iha, Nantetsu. *Ryūkyū fudoki* [Gazetteer of Ryūkyū]. Tokyo: Taikodō,1944.

Ikemiya, Masaharu. *Ryūkyū bungaku ron* [Discourse on Ryūkyūan literature]. Naha: Okinawa Times, 1976.

Inamura, Kenpu. *Miyako-tō shomin shi* [History of the common people of Miyako Island]. Naha: Kyodo Insatsu, 1954.

——. *Okinawa no kodai buraku makyo no kenkyū* [A study of the *makyo*, the ancient village community in Okinawa]. Naha: Ryūkyū bunkyo, 1968.

Itō, Kanji. "Nihon shinwa to Ryūkyū shinwa," *Nihon shinwa to Ryūkyū* [Japanese mythologies and Ryūkyū], comp. Koza Nihon no shinwa henshubu. Tokyo: Yuseido, 1977.

Kamida, Sōei. *Ryūkyū bungaku josetsu* [Introduction to Ryūkyūan literature]. Naha: Okinawa kyoiku tosho, 1966.

Kanai, Kikuko. *Ryūkyū no min'yō* [Folksongs of the Ryūkyūs]. Tokyo: Ongaku no tomo, 1954.

Kanaseki, Takeo. *Hakkutsu kara suiri suru* [Deducing from the excavations]. Tokyo: Asahi shinbunsha, 1975.

Katō, Sango. *Ryūkyū no kenkyū* [Study of the Ryūkyūs]. Tokyo: private (1906), rev. 1941.

Kawamura, Tadao. *Nanpō bunka no tankyū* [Searches into the culture of the Southern Islands]. Tokyo: Sogensha, 1939.

——. *Zoku nanpō bunka no tankyū* [Searches into the culture of the Southern Islands, continued]. Tokyo: Sogensha, 1942.

Kerr, George H. *Okinawa: The History of an Island People*. Rutland and Tokyo: Charles Tuttle, 1958.

Kinjō, Yuikyō, ed. *Shin Okinawa bunka shi* [New history of Okinawan culture]. Osaka: Kyodo-shi kenkyūkai, 1956.

Kojima, Yoshiyuki. "Ryūkyū kaibyaku shinwa no bunpu to hikaku," *Nihon shinwa to Ryūkyū* [Japanese mythologies and Ryūkyū], comp. Koza Nihon no shinwa henshūbu. Tokyo: Yuseido, 1977.

Kokubu, Naoichi. "The Prehistoric Southern Islands and East China Sea Areas," *Asian Perspectives: The Bulletin of the Far-Eastern Prehistory Association,* VII: Summer–Winter 1963.

———, and Sasaki Kōmei, eds. *Nantō no kodai bunka* [Ancient culture of the Southern Islands]. Tokyo: Asahi shinbun, 1973.

Koza Nihon no shinwa henshūbu, comp. *Nihon shinwa to Ryūkyū* [Japanese mythologies and Ryūkyū]. Tokyo: Yuseido, 1977.

Kuroshio bunka no kai, comp. *Nihon minzoku to kuroshio bunka* [Japanese race and the Black Current culture]. Tokyo: Kadokawa, 1977.

Kuwae, Kokuei, ed. *Kyūyō* (Tei Heitetsu, 1745). Naha: private, 1969.

Lebra, William P. *Okinawan Religion: Belief, Ritual, and Social Structure.* Honolulu: University of Hawai'i Press, 1966.

Majikina, Ankō, and Shimakura Ryūji. *Okinawa issennen-shi* [One thousand year history of Okinawa]. Fukuoka: Okinawa shinminpō, 1952.

Miyagi, Shinji. *Kodai Okinawa no sugata* [Appearance of the ancient Okinawa]. Naha: Okinawa insatsu, 1954.

———. "Yanbaru no otake" [Holy groves in Northern Okinawa], *Nantō ronsō,* Shimabukuro Zenpatsu, ed. Naha: Okinawa nippo, 1937.

Miyara, Tōsō. *Nantō sōkō* [Discourses on the Southern Islands]. Tokyo: I'sseisha, 1934.

Morishima, Chūryō. *Ryūkyū dan* [Stories of the Ryūkyūs]. Edo: woodblock print, 1790.

Morita, Shinkō. "Gyogyo no enkaku" [Origin of the fishing industry], *Shin Okinawa bunka shi.* Osaka: Kyodo-shi kenkyūkai, 1956.

Mozai, Torao. "Kuroshio-ken no kaikyō to kōkai" [Condition of the ocean and voyage in the Black Current area], *Nihon minzoku to kuroshio bunka.* Tokyo: Kadokawa, 1977.

Nakahara, Zenchū. *Omoro shinshaku* [New translations of *omoro*]. Naha: Ryūkyū bunkyo, 1957.

———. *Nakahara Zenchū senshū* [Selected works of Nakahara Zenchū]. 3 vols. Naha: Okinawa Times, 1969.

———, and Hokama Shuzen, eds. *Kōhon Omoro sōshi* [Emended text: *Omoro sōshi*]. Tokyo: Kadokawa, 1965.

———, ed. *Omoro sōshi jiten-sōsakuin* [Dictionary and index to the *Omoro sōshi*]. Tokyo: Kadokawa, 1967.

———. *Ryūkyū no rekishi* [History of Ryūkyū]. Naha: Okinawa bunka kyokai, 1978.

Nakamatsu, Yashū. *Kosō no mura: Okinawa minzoku bunka ron* [Villages of the ancient stratum: discourse on the folk culture of Okinawa]. Naha: Okinawa Times, 1977.

Nantō [Southern Islands], no. 2 (May 1932).

Nottingham, Elizabeth. *Religion and Society.* New York: Doubleday, 1954.

Ōbayashi Tairyō. "Ryūkyū shinwa to shūi shominzoku shinwa," [Mythologies of Ryūkyū and of various adjacent races], *Nihon minzoku to kuroshio bunka,* Kuroshio bunka no kai, comp. Tokyo: Kadokawa, 1977.

Okinawa Times, comp. *Okinawa daihyakka jiten* [Encyclopedia of Okinawa]. 3 vols. Naha: Okinawa Times, 1983.

Okuzato, Shōken. *Insei kizokugo to bunka no nanten* [Southward development of the language and culture of the aristocrats of the cloistered government of Japan]. Osaka: Sankyōsha, 1954.

———. *Okinawa ni kunrinshita heike* [The Taira clan who ruled over Okinawa]. Naha: Okinawa fudokisha, 1969.

———. "Shuri sento no jidai" [Era when the capital was transferred to Shuri]. *Okinawa Times,* March 6–10, 1958.

OS. See Nakahara, Zenchū, and Hokama Shuzen, eds. *Kōhon Omoro sōshi* [Emended text: *Omoro sōshi*]. Tokyo: Kadokawa, 1965.

Pearson, Richard. "The Contribution of Archaeology to Japanese Studies," *Journal of Japanese Studies,* II:2 (April 1976), 305–327.

Ryūkyū-koku-chū himonki [Monument inscriptions in the Ryūkyū country]. MS., 1479.

Sakaguchi, Tokutarō. *Amami-Ōshima shi* [History of the Amami-Ōshima Islands]. Kagoshima: Sanshudo, 1921.

Sakamaki, Shunzo, ed. *Ryūkyūan Names.* Honolulu: East-West Center, 1964.

———. "The Heike: From Defeat at Dannoura to a Golden Age in Ryūkyū?" *Journal of Asian Studies,* XXVII:1 (November 1967), 115–122.

Samejima, Kunizō. "Kinsei Okinawa bunka no rekishiteki haikai" [Historical background of the recent history of Okinawa]. *Okinawa Times,* February 18, 1958.

Sansom, George. *A History of Japan to 1334.* Stanford, 1958.

Shidehara, Hiroshi. *Nantō enkaku shiron* [History of the origin of the Southern Islands]. Tokyo: Fuzanbo, 1899.

Shimabukuro, Genshichi, "Akoniwa no hitobito" [People in Akoniwa], *Okinawa bunka sōsetsu,* ed. Yanagita Kunio, 251–311, 1947.

Shimabukuro, Zenpatsu, ed. *Nantō ronsō* [Essays on the Southern Islands]. Naha: Okinawa nippo, 1937.

Shō, Jo-ken. *Chūzan sekan* (1650), reprinted in Iha et al., eds. *Ryūkyū hiryō sōsho.* Tokyo: Natori, 1940.

Sin, Suk-ju. *Haedong choguk ki* [Account of countries east of the sea] (1471). In the *Chosen shiryo sokan* [Korean Historical Materials Series]. Keijo: Chosen sotokufu, 1933.

Tawada, Shinjun. *Okinawa yakuyō shokubutsu yakkōzen* [Complete list of the medicinal plants of Okinawa]. Naha: Kyuyodo, 1951.

Thompson, Stith. *The Folktale.* New York: The Dryden Press, 1951.

Tōma, Seita. *Nihon minzoku no keisei* [Formation of the Japanese Race]. Tokyo: Iwanami, 1958.

Torigoe, Kenzaburō. *Ryūkyū kodai shakai no kenkyū* [Study of ancient Ryūkyūan society], Tokyo: Mikasa shobo, 1944,

Tylor, E. B. *Primitive Culture.* New York: Holt, 1899.

Wada, Hisanori. "Ryūkyū-koku no sanzan tōitsu ni tsuite no shin-kosatsu" [A new interpretation of the unification of San-shan 'three principalities' in fifteenth century Ryūkyū], *Ochanomizu University Studies in Arts and Culture,* XXVIII: Part 2 (March 1975), 13–39.

Wakamori, Taro. *Nihon mizoku-shi* [History of the Japanese race]. Tokyo: Chikuma shobo, 1963.

Yanagi, Muneyoshi. *Ryūkyū no toki* [Ceramics of the Ryūkyūs]. Tokyo: Showa shobo, 1942.

Yanagita, Kunio, ed. *Nihon minzoku zuroku* [Pictorial book of the folkways of Japan]. Tokyo: Asahi shinbunsha, 1955.

———, ed. *Okinawa bunka sōsetsu* [Collections of essays on Okinawan culture]. Tokyo: Chuo koronsha, 1947.

———. *Tōno monogatari* [Stories of Tōno]. Tokyo: Kadokawa, 1955.

Yokoyama, Shigeru, ed. *Ryūkyū shintōki* [Records of Shintō in Ryūkyū], by Priest Taichū, 1605. Tokyo: Ookayama shoten, 1943.

Index

A special mention regarding "Okinawa(n)" and "Ryūkyū(an)": there are over 1,000 mentions of these terms in the text, not unexpected in a work that is primarily concerned with these very subjects. (The reader can turn to any page and some version of these terms is likely to appear.) They will not appear in the following, selective, index, which lists historical figures, place names, and certain technical and cultural terms. In addition, mentions of the authors in the Bibliographies will not be repeated here.

Index of *Omoro*

Chapter 2

1. "In the Beginning," from *Omoro sōshi*, X:2 #512. The roman numeral refers to the volume number in the *Omoro sōshi*. The arabic numeral immediately following the colon refers to the *omoro* poem in the volume. The last arabic numeral, preceded by #, indicates the poem's serial number within the entire twenty-two volumes of the *Omoro sōshi*. These numberings are in accordance with those given in the *Kōhon: Omoro sōshi*, ed. Nakahara Zenchū and Hokama Shuzen, 1965 (hereafter, *OS*); *OS*, pp. 328–334; Iha, *Okinawa kō*, pp. 192–204; and *Kō Ryūkyū*, pp. 162–166.

Chapter 3

1. "Building a Village," not an *omoro* proper, as contained in the *Omoro sōshi*, but rather a *kwenya umui*, a song sung by *noro* priestesses. See Note 2 (*OS*, p. 70).
2. "Immigration of the Miruya People," from Endnote 12, *Omoro sōshi*, XXI:1 #1394. *OS*, pp. 189–191.
3. "Man of Miruya Is a Worldly God," from Endnote 13, *Omoro sōshi*, XI:72 #627. *OS*, pp. 189–191.
4. "Rice Ear Ceremony," from Endnote 16, *Omoro sōshi*, V:31 #242. *OS*, pp. 179–180.
5. "Village Festival," from Endnote 20, *Omoro sōshi*, II:16 #57. *OS*, pp. 147–152.
6. "Dancing Priestess," from Endnote 21, *Omoro sōshi*, II:34 #75. *OS*, pp. 124–128.
7. "Divine Parade," from Endnote 25, *Omoro sōshi*, XX:20 #1350, XII:68 #719. *OS*, pp. 281–283.
8. "Worship of the Sunrise," from Endnote 30, *Omoro sōshi*, XIII:78 #823. *OS*, pp. 100–102.

9. "In Praise of the Sunrise," from Endnote 31, *Omoro sōshi*, XIII:89 #834. *OS*, pp. 99–100.
10. "Prayer for Driftwood," from Endnote 32, *Omoro sōshi*, XXI:11 #1404. *OS*, pp. 120–122.
11. "The Launching Ceremony," from Endnote 33, *Omoro sōshi*, XIII:47 #792. *OS*, pp. 155–159.
12. "The Launching Ceremony," from Endnote 34, *Omoro sōshi*, XIII:50 #795. *OS*, pp. 159–162.
13 "The First Fishing in the Spring," from Endnote 36, *Omoro sōshi*, IX:30 #505. *OS*, pp. 139–144.
14. "The Village Goes to the Shore," from Endnote 38, *Omoro sōshi*, XI:95 #650. *OS*, pp. 144–147.
15. "Sailing of the Priestess Akeshino," from Endnote 42, *Omoro sōshi*, XIII:93 #838. *OS*, pp. 112–115.
16. "Sailing of Priestess Akeshino," from Endnote 43, *Omoro sōshi*, XIII:94 #839. *OS*, pp. 115–116.
17. "Building Granaries," from Endnote 45, *Omoro sōshi*, XIX:45 #1326. *OS*, pp. 186–188.
18. "Drumming Priestesses," from Endnote 46, *Omoro sōshi*, XV:53 #1104. *OS*, pp. 236–238.
19. "In Praise of King Satto," from Endnote 51, *Omoro sōshi*, XIV:1 #982. *OS*, pp. 267–270. Iha, *Kotōku no Ryūkyū shi*, p. 53.
20. "Banquet at the Castle Town," from Endnote 52, *Omoro sōshi*, XI:88 #643. *OS*, pp. 369–373.
21. "Evening When the *Ankwena* Was Crying," from Endnote 53, *Omoro sōshi*, XII:80 #731. *OS*, pp. 117–120.

Chapter 4

1. "Castle of Ezo," from Endnote 4, *Omoro sōshi*, XV:15 #1066. Iha, *Kotōku no Ryūkyū shi*, p. 45.
2. "Castle of Ezo," from Endnote 5, *Omoro sōshi*, XV:17 #1068. Iha, *Kotōku no Ryūkyū shi*, p. 46.
3. "Castle of Ezo," from Endnote 6, *Omoro sōshi*, XV:16 #1067. Iha, *Kotōku no Ryūkyū shi*, p. 47.
4. "Young Lord of Ezo," from Endnote 7, *Omoro sōshi*, XV:18 #1069. Iha, *Kotōku no Ryūkyū shi*, p. 47.
5. "To the Renowned Urasoe," from Endnote 13, *Omoro sōshi*, XV:26 #1077. Iha, *Kotōku no Ryūkyū shi*, pp. 49–50.

6. "For the Renowned Urasoe," from Endnote 14, *Omoro sōshi*, XV:21 #1072. *OS*, pp. 206–208.
7. "Imported Folding Screen," from Endnote 15, *Omoro sōshi*, II:18 #59. *OS*, pp. 241–242.
8. "Armor and Shoulderpiece," from Endnote 16, *Omoro sōshi*, II:19 #60. *OS*, p. 242.
9. "Trade at Lower Ishiki," from Endnote 17, *Omoro sōshi*, X:28 36–37. #538. Iha, *Kotōku no Ryūkyū shi*, pp. 36–37.
10. "Shipbuilding," from Endnote 19, *Omoro sōshi*, IX:24 #499. *OS*, pp. 239–241.
11. "Ship from Yoron Island," from Endnote 21, *Omoro sōshi*, XIII:183 #928. *OS*, pp. 137–139.
12. "Voyage of the Priestess of Erabu Island," from Endnote 22, *Omoro sōshi*, XIII:24 #769. *OS*, pp. 132–135.
13. "Springtime on the Coast of Hyakuna," from Endnote 24, *Omoro sōshi*, XVII:54 #1228, XVIII:10 #1258. *OS*, pp. 106–108.
14. "Springtime on the Coast of Hyakuna," from Endnote 25, *Omoro sōshi*, XIII:100 #845. *OS*, pp. 108–110.
15. "Springtime on the Coast of Hyakuna," from Endnote 26, *Omoro sōshi*, XIII:102 #847. *OS*, pp. 110–112.
16. "Katsuren and Kamakura," from Endnote 37, *Omoro sōshi*, XVI:18 #1144. *OS*, pp. 310–311. Iha. *Kotōku no Ryūkyū shi*, pp. 94–95.
17. "In Praise of Katsuren," from Endnote 39, *Omoro sōshi*, XVI:7 #1133. *OS*, pp. 311–313. Iha. *Kotōku no Ryūkyū shi*, p. 93.
18. "Amawari, Lord of Katsuren," from Endnote 40, *Omoro sōshi*, XVI:8 #1134. *OS*, pp. 313–316. For a study of Lord Amawari as a hero rather than traitor-villain, see Iha, "Amawari kō," in *Kō Ryūkyū*, pp. 82–98.
19. "Ezo's Housewarming," from Endnote 41, *Omoro sōshi*, V:8 #289. *OS*, pp. 199–203.
20. "They Have Wine in Urasoe," from Endnote 42, *Omoro sōshi*, XV:36 #1087. *OS*, pp. 208–210.
21. "Jeweled Ladle," from Endnote 45, *Omoro sōshi*, XV:22 #1073, *OS*, pp. 203–204.
22. "Rejoicing over the Payment of Taxes," from Endnote 47, *Omoro sōshi*, XV:10 #1061. *OS*, pp. 265–266.
23. "Tribute Tax from the Sea," from Endnote 49, *Omoro sōshi*, XV:49 #1100. *OS*, pp. 270–272.
24. "First Trade Ship," from Endnote 51, *Omoro sōshi*, XV:66 #1117. *OS*, pp. 274–275.

25. "To Welcome the Returning Trade Ship," from Endnote 53, *Omoro sōshi*, XV:68 #1119. *OS*, pp. 276–279.
26. "Lord and Priestess," from Endnote 54, *Omoro sōshi*, XXXI:12 #1405. *OS*, pp. 249–251.
27. "The Birth of King Shō Hashi," from Endnote 55, *Omoro sōshi*, XIX:10 #1290. *OS*, pp. 291–293.
28. "Shō Hashi's Attack," from Endnote 57, *Omoro sōshi*, XIX:19 #1299. *OS*, pp. 295–297.
29. "The Priestess Leads the Army," from Endnote 58, *Omoro sōshi*, I:5 #5. Iha, *Kotōku no Ryūkyū shi*, pp. 78–79.
30. "First Envoy to China," from Endnote 59, *Omoro sōshi*, XIV:37 #1018. Iha, ibid., p. 89.
31. "Chinen-mori Castle," from Endnote 60, *Omoro sōshi*, XIX:30 #1310. *OS*, pp. 298–300.
32. "Mounted Young Lord," from Endnote 61, *Omoro sōshi*, XIV:5 #986. *OS*, pp. 214–218.
33. "Lord Aorikumo at War," from Endnote 62, *Omoro sōshi*, X:9 #519. *OS*, pp. 254–257.
34. "Port of Naha," from Endnote 70, *Omoro sōshi*, XIII:8 #753. Iha, *Kotōku no Ryūkyū shi*, pp. 103–104.
35. "Coronation of the King," from Endnote 72, *Omoro sōshi*, V:2 #213. *OS*, pp. 302–303.
36. "In Praise of Shuri," from Endnote 75, *Omoro sōshi*, V:3 #214. *OS*, pp. 303–305.
37. "Building Shuri Castle," from Endnote 77, *Omoro sōshi*, V:5 #216. *OS*, pp. 305–307.
38. "In Celebration of the August Fountain," from Endnote 78, *Omoro sōshi*, XIII:44 #436. *OS*, pp. 384–385.
39. "August Fountain," from Endnote 79, *Omoro sōshi*, VIII:7 #399. *OS*, pp. 385–387.
40. "Walls of Shuri Castle," from Endnote 80, *Omoro sōshi*, V:6 #217, *OS*, pp. 393–395.
41. "Enkakuji Temple," from Endnote 83, *Omoro sōshi*, V:72 #283. *OS*, pp. 408–412.
42. "Hyakuna Villagers' Attendance at Shuri Castle," from Endnote 87, *Omoro sōshi*, XVIII:12 #1260; XVII:56 #1230. *OS*, pp. 309–310.
43. "Carrying in the Tribute Tax," from Endnote 88, *Omoro sōshi*, V:40 #251. *OS*, pp. 320–323.

44. "Let Them All Serve Our King," from Endnote 95, *Omoro sōshi*, VII:12 #356. Iha, *Kotōku no Ryūkyū shi*, pp. 108–109.
45. "Departure of the *Sejiaratomi*," from Endnote 96, *Omoro sōshi*, XIII:17 #762. Iha, op. cit., pp. 109–112.
46. "Monsoon Wind in Spring," from Endnote 97, *Omoro sōshi*, XIII:180 #925. *OS*, pp. 336–337.
47. "When the Southern Wind Whispers," from Endnote 99, *Omoro sōshi*, XIII:35 #780. *OS*, pp. 334–336.
48. "The King and the Sun," from Endnote 102, *Omoro sōshi*, V:1 #212. *OS*, pp. 300–302.
49. "Chastisement of Yaeyama," from Endnote 106, *Omoro sōshi*, I:36 #36. *OS*, pp. 226–233. Lines 23–34 in the *Kōhon Omoro sōshi* (ed. Nakahara and Hokama) are missing in the *Omoro shinshaku* (Nakahara). The text given is according to the *Kōhon Omoro sōshi*.
50. "In Congratulation on the Coronation of King Shō Nei," from Endnote 111, *Omoro sōshi*, IV:58 #209; VI:5 #295; XII:93 #744; XX:48 #1378. *OS*, pp. 422–423.
51. "Sorrow of the Queen," from Endnote 114, *Omoro sōshi*, IX:35 #510. *OS*, pp. 469–471.

About the Author and Editor

Mitsugu Sakihara (1928–2001) was a native of Okinawa who earned his bachelor's and master's degrees at the University of Oregon. He possessed the rare quality of being trilingual in Japanese, Okinawan, and English. He first came to Hawai'i in 1962 for a training program on the microfilming of rare, old documents so that he could microfilm the Hawley Collection before it came to the University of Hawai'i. He returned to UH to pursue a doctorate in history under Shunzō Sakamaki, completing his dissertation, "The Significance of Ryukyu in Satsuma Finances during the Tokugawa Period," in 1971. He taught for some years at UH and produced a number of scholarly works on the history of Okinawa. When he passed away he left unpublished what he considered to be his most important life's work—an Okinawan language dictionary. A portion of his manuscript was edited by scholars from UH and the University of the Ryukyus and was published in 2006 as the *Okinawan-English Wordbook*.

Stewart Curry has studied and worked at the University of Hawai'i at Mānoa since 1989. He earned his PhD in 2004 with a dissertation on a northern Okinawan language, and currently is an instructor in the Department of East Asian Languages and Literatures, teaching Japanese language and linguistics, and Okinawan language, culture, and literature. He served as an editor and book designer of the first of two works derived from Professor Sakihara's Okinawan-English dictionary, the *Okinawan-English Wordbook* (University of Hawai'i Press, 2006), and is laboring on a larger-scale dictionary.